-emails

W9-AAC-476

Shimmering Literacies

def. of literacy - 18

A discuss Fan Forums related 2 BB, makes students feel more comfortable (41)

Colin Lankshear, Michele Knobel,
and Michael Peters
General Editors

Vol. 35

PETER LANG
New York • Washington, D.C./Baltimore • Bern
Frankfurt am Main • Berlin • Brussels • Vienna • Oxford

Bronwyn T. Williams

Shimmering Literacies

Popular Culture & Reading
& Writing Online

PETER LANG
New York • Washington, D.C./Baltimore • Bern
Frankfurt am Main • Berlin • Brussels • Vienna • Oxford

Library of Congress Cataloging-in-Publication Data

Williams, Bronwyn T.
Shimmering literacies: popular culture and reading and writing online /
Bronwyn T. Williams.
p. cm. — (New literacies and digital epistemologies; v. 35)
Includes bibliographical references and index.
1. English language—Rhetoric—Study and teaching.
2. Computers and literacy. 3. Popular culture. 4. College students—
Effect of technological innovations on. I. Title.
PE1404.W5337   808.042'0711—dc22   2009005539
ISBN 978-1-4331-0333-9 (hardcover)
ISBN 978-1-4331-0334-6 (paperback)
ISSN 1523-9543

Bibliographic information published by **Die Deutsche Bibliothek**.
Die Deutsche Bibliothek lists this publication in the "Deutsche
Nationalbibliografie"; detailed bibliographic data is available
on the Internet at http://dnb.ddb.de/.

The paper in this book meets the guidelines for permanence and durability
of the Committee on Production Guidelines for Book Longevity
of the Council of Library Resources.

© 2009 Peter Lang Publishing, Inc., New York
29 Broadway, 18th floor, New York, NY 10006
www.peterlang.com

All rights reserved.
Reprint or reproduction, even partially, in all forms such as microfilm,
xerography, microfiche, microcard, and offset strictly prohibited.

Printed in the United States of America

For Griffith and Rhys, their amazing friends, and my students, all of whom teach me so much about the world in which we live.

Contents

ACKNOWLEDGMENTS

As with any book, there are many people who offered me crucial support, advice, and inspiration. First, I thank Michele Knobel and Colin Lankshear for their support for this work and their willingness to include the project in their series on new literacies and digital epistemologies. I am honored to be part of one of the most dynamic and innovative scholarly projects currently taking place in literacy studies. I also want to thank Chris Myers at Peter Lang Publishing Group for approving the project and Sophie Appel and Valerie Best for their work in the production of the book.

Many people have helped shape my thinking on the issues I address in this book. Dan Keller has kept me from slipping into simplistic conclusions; his thoughtful comments have been indispensable. I also thank Myrrh Domingo, Julie Faulkner, Alanna Frost, Alec Hudson, Julie Myatt, Annette Powell, and Amy Zenger for their advice and feedback.

Parts of chapter 4 originally appeared in the article: "Which *South Park* Character Are You?": Popular Culture, Literacy, and Online Performances of Identity," published in *Computers and Composition* 25 (1) 2008, 24–39. I thank Jonathan Alexander, the editor of the special issue of *Computers and Composition,* for his useful comments on that article.

I am grateful to Elizabeth Corbett for transcribing some of the participant interviews and Christine Romesburg for compiling the Index. I thank Linda Baldwin, who saves my professional life on a regular basis, for doing so this time by carefully proofreading my drafts.

Finally, I thank my family for their unending support. My sons, Griffith and Rhys, provided me with insights, feedback, and a never-ending stream of new examples of participatory popular culture. Their thinking on this subject is as adept as most scholars and they are invaluable intellectual resources—and they make me laugh. My only remaining question is, "Why is the rum gone?"

This book exists only as a result of the constant emotional and intellectual support of my wife, Mary. I cannot calculate, nor adequately express, all the ways I am grateful to you, in this as in everything. You are my best friend, my intellectual soulmate, and my dearest love.

CHAPTER 1

Introduction

There is a parable about an old fish who, on passing two energetic younger fish frolicking in the stream, asks them, "How's the water?" After the old fish passes, one of the young fish turns to the other and asks, "What's water?"

Sometimes it's not easy to get past the obvious.

There is nothing particularly insightful in noticing that adolescents spend a great deal of time reading and writing online. We can all conjure images of young people sitting at computers, sometimes for hours at a time, typing away and reading intently. Similarly, observing that the Internet is filled with popular culture content that attracts high school and college students is not a controversial position.

Consider Ashley. She is a first-year university student who has personal webpages on four different social networking sites such as *MySpace*, all filled with images, songs, and video from *Charmed* to *Pirates of the Caribbean*. She contributes to several fan forums on the *Harry Potter* and *Lord of the Rings* series of books and films and is writing two ongoing fan fictions about Harry Potter on *FanFiction.Net*, each of which are more than 20,000 words long. And that does not touch on the instant messaging conversations she carries on around the world that often, again, focus on popular culture. Or listen to Brianna describe her literacy practices at the computer:

> Average…I might spend five-and-a-half, like six hours on there. I multitask so I might be on there listening (to music); I do this all the time 'cause I just got to doing it. I was doing a paper for class; I started typing the paper for class; I was on *Facebook*; I was on *MySpace*; I had my AIM going and I was listening to music; all of the time I was texting somebody too at the same time, so I was doing like three or four different things at once. And I study mainly at nighttime, so I'm always on the computer then.

To be sure, not all young people are as immersed in reading and writing about popular culture as Ashley or Brianna, though they are hardly exceptional. So consider Tony, who says he does little reading or writing online, but in fact checks sports websites and reads sports fan forums daily. Or there is Amy, who does not read fan fiction or visit fan forums or check popular culture websites, but who defines her identity on her *Facebook* page to a great degree by listing more than a hundred movies, bands, television programs, and books that she likes. Talk to students about their lives outside the classroom and the extent to which they are involved with popular culture becomes quickly apparent. Like young people from their parents' generation, they watch movies and television programs, listen to music, and play computer games. What makes these students different is that they also go online and read about, comment on, sample, combine, and rewrite the popular culture material they find. Their hours are filled with popular culture and the interpretation and composing of words, images, and sound. In short, popular culture is the water in which they swim.

There are times when what is obvious, almost unworthy of comment, is what needs to draw our attention. Popular culture may be ubiquitous, as are young people reading and writing online, but taking time to pause and explore the way popular culture intersects with these daily literacy practices is essential in our consideration of making meaning in an age of multiliteracies. If we, as teachers and scholars, spend so much time thinking about online reading and writing, and so much time thinking about popular culture and its influence on young people—and we do—then we need to give more thought to the implications raised by the reality that many of the online literacy practices students engage in are focused on and shaped by popular culture content and rhetorical frameworks. This key focus and form of writing and reading happens outside of school yet touches on how students engage with issues of authorship, genre, audience, emotion, evidence, and other key rhetorical concepts. What's more, such literacy practices, like new media popular culture, are happening across media and genres. The question is, what do students such as Ashley, Brianna, Tony, and Amy learn and think about reading and writing after their time online with popular culture?

It is not difficult to find evidence that popular culture is a central part of many of the ways that reading and writing happen online. On personal webspaces, such as *MySpace* and *Facebook*, people use popular culture images, catchphrases, and music as ways of performing identities, rather than expository, written personal statements. Online

sites about movies and television and computer games are filled with pages and pages of written reviews, analysis, and discussion, sometimes connected to images as well. On fan fiction and fan film sites, people draw on existing characters and icons to create new narratives. Not only is popular culture changing how people are reading and writing, such shifts in reading and writing online are changing popular culture. Creators of television programs, movies, computer games, and popular music use the interactive and multimedia potential of new technologies, often reading and reacting to the comments and critiques that appear online, as well as creating interactive spaces that extend their narratives.

In this book I examine the powerful role popular culture plays in the online literacy practices that young people around the world engage in every day. Whether as subject matter, discourse, or rhetorical patterns, popular culture often shapes the content and form of current online reading and writing. It is important that we understand not just how online technologies have changed literacy and popular culture practices but why popular culture has dominated the online literacy practices of our students. I focus on the ways in which young people use popular culture in their online literacy practices, altering their attitudes toward both literacy and popular culture. It is important in a time when popular culture has spread across media and when students such as Brianna are multitasking on the computer, to study how their literacy practices and rhetorical skills develop across media and genres. Consequently, this book does not focus on one form of online writing and popular culture—such as fan fiction—but instead explores what skills and practices students are developing with multiple popular culture forms that move fluidly online and off.

I explore how the discourses and rhetorical forms of popular culture are significant in a culture of multiliteracies in shaping students' perceptions of reading and writing and their conceptions of audience, authorship, text, and identity. I approach these questions through a combination of textual analysis of online content through the lens of cultural studies and rhetorical theory, and through interviews, both face-to-face and online with secondary and university students from several countries.

Although there has been strong and creative research and theorizing about the changes new media technologies have brought about in both popular culture and in reading and writing, less has been written about the ways in which these changes influence each other and what implications these connections hold for our studies of young people and literacy. In this chapter, I will outline how new media and online technologies have changed popular culture and literacy practices in recent years, sometimes by creating new practices and opportunities and other times by allowing individuals and groups to expand and extend existing practices. I will then discuss how this book connects and develops such research, as well as how I conducted my research. Finally, I will describe the structure of the book.

Participatory Popular Culture

I have argued in previous work (Williams 2001; 2002; 2003; 2004) that students' experiences with popular culture should not be dismissed or disdained when we think about their literacy practices. I think student ideas about literacy and their approaches to important rhetorical concepts such as audience, genre, and authorship are shaped in no small part by the popular culture in which they have such long and varied experiences. Talking with students about the intersections of popular culture and literacy practices and taking them seriously is not a matter of "bringing" popular culture into the classroom. Popular culture arrives with students every time they walk through the door and cannot be hung up outside like winter coats (Williams 2002). I have been struck, however, by the changes in popular culture that have happened in the last decade. Just ten years ago, I was conducting research for a book about how students' experiences with television influenced their reading and writing. In my interviews and focus groups for that book, we talked of many things concerning television, but the subject of online popular culture practices rarely emerged. Even when I asked students directly about whether they read or wrote on online fan groups for television programs, all but two said they did not and many did not even know such groups existed.

The changes brought by new online media technologies in the past ten years are impossible to ignore and are second nature to all of the students involved in the research for this book. Indeed, the question this time around was not about whether the students engaged in online discussions about television but whether they watched television regularly at all. Although I am wary of falling into the kinds of hyperbole that often surround discussions of new technologies, it is clear that young people swim in a popular culture world far different from that of their parents, teachers, and perhaps even older siblings.

If the twentieth century transformed popular culture from a local, participatory phenomenon to a mass-produced and consumed product, the start of the twenty-first century has seen online technology create a more widespread interactive popular culture. Not only do individuals use discussion forums and webpages to comment publicly on or rewrite mass popular culture such as television, films, music, and computer games, but increasingly the creators of these forms of mass popular culture are reading and reacting to these comments and critiques that appear online, as well as creating interactive spaces that extend their narratives (Storey 2003; Deery 2003; Brooker 2001; Jenkins 2006a).

As one example, the U.S. television series *Heroes,* which is about a group of people with miraculous super powers, has an official website with a wiki, message boards, previews, and episodes to watch online, as well as a graphic novel that complements the televised narrative and an interactive game for audience members. The series' producers also have websites for fictional organizations featured in the program, such the *Petrelli for Congress* campaign site, for one of the characters who is running for office, and *Primatech Paper*, the front company for the ominous organization hunting down the heroes. These fictional sites, which look authentic, often provide clues to the characters and plot not found in the broadcast episodes. Meanwhile, audience members have created hundreds of websites dedicated to the series and its characters. Sites such as *Television Without Pity* post detailed recaps of each episode as well as extensive fan forums; on the site *FanFiction.Net*, there are more than 2,300 stories and novels posted drawing on the characters from the series which is, as of this writing, only in its second season.

To reflect the changes in popular culture that have been created by changes in society and technology I draw on the terms defined by Michael Kammen (1999) and Henry Jenkins (2006a). Kammen draws a distinction between traditional popular culture of the pre-industrial world and mass popular culture of the nineteenth and twentieth centuries. Traditional popular culture would be the activities that people took part in with their communities, such as playing music or dancing or quilting bees. Mass popular culture defines the era of mass production, distribution, and consumption of popular culture begun with printing and continued with electronic media such as radio, television, and movies. Mass popular culture is defined by the industrial model of production, where large amounts of capital are necessary for producing and distributing the content and it is consumed by large audiences unable to alter the material. Labor, with specifically defined jobs such as sound engineers or camera operators, produce the work rather than individual artists.

Jenkins (2006a) argues that computers and online technologies have transformed the era of mass popular culture into one of participatory popular culture where the boundaries have been blurred between media and between producer and audience. Jenkins defines this as "the convergence culture." For Jenkins, the elements that mark convergence culture include the opportunities for participation by the audience and the flow of information across multiple media platforms. These elements combine to encourage an interactive and "migratory behavior of media audiences who will go almost anywhere in search of the kinds of entertainment experiences they want" (2). Jenkins conceives of convergence culture as more than the technological ability to move information across media platforms. Instead, "convergence occurs within the brains of individual consumers and through their social interactions with others" (3). The social aspect of convergence culture is crucial to our understanding of young people and their motivations and practices involving popular culture online. The still-prevalent image of popular culture as isolating individuals in front of their computer or television screens is one we should quickly move beyond. Instead, we should focus on how the convergence of media and the interactive nature of online communications are changing the roles of both producer and audience member to those of participants in a social phenomenon where popular culture is a central organizing force.

The participatory opportunities of convergence culture reminds us more than ever that we should approach popular culture content as texts that people read and write about and with. If, for example, we continue to refer to a television broadcast as a *program* or *show*, it reinforces connotations of spectacles being presented to passive audience members. Regarding what is broadcast on television as one text that we read in relation to other texts on the same or similar subjects on webpages, fan forums, and other media brings us more closely to the experiences of convergence culture. In this book, then, I consider a popular culture *text* as any work produced and distributed broadly, including books, magazines, newspapers, television, movies, and computer games, music, and online content of media producers. (For the sake of simplicity, I use the term *computer games* for both computer and video games.) For students involved with participatory popular culture, these texts are available for interpretation but also critique, appropriation, response, and reuse. It is important to emphasize that while this definition of *texts* includes print, both for media producers and for individuals, it also includes other semiotic resources that can be interpreted or produced, including images, sound, and video.

Language and print literacy cannot provide the full meaning of the multimodal content that is obvious to anyone within moments of connecting to the Internet (Kress 2003). The concept of multiliteracies instead "focuses on modes of representation much broader than language alone" (Cope and Kalantzis 2000, 5) and includes communication through multiple modes such as images, sound, and video. These new capabilities have raised increasingly complex and exciting questions about the rhetorically most effective ways to communicate. Not only do new media technologies offer different affordances for each choice made in composing a text, the ability to compose with images, graphics, and video have challenged the traditional print literacy emphasis on linearity in communication. Now it is possible to compose a text on a computer that emphasizes the juxtaposition of elements in space and works associatively, rather than linearly (Kress 2003). New media technologies have also increased the speed at which texts can be composed, distributed, and read, which in turn influences the ways texts are created.

All of these changes in technology demand that we attend to the texts we encounter in popular culture and online with a more flexible and multimodal approach to how they are constituted, produced, and interpreted. Kress, drawing on the work of Michael Halliday, argues that a "fully functioning human semiotic resource"—what in this book I will label a *text*—has three central qualities:

> To represent states of affairs or events in the world—the ideational function; to represent the social relations between the participants in the process of communication—the interpersonal function; and to represent all that as message-entity, a "text" which is internally coherent and which coheres with its environment—the textual function (66).

Though arguments can be made about internal coherence and representation in online texts, this definition does serve to highlight the discursive, social, and rhetorical qualities that popular culture and online multimodal texts fulfill in contemporary culture. And it requires us to consider how students are, on a daily basis, reading and "writing" texts with print, images, video, and sound. They are learning about multimodal literacy through working with it day after day and popular culture is a central part of this work.

A growing emphasis on speed, visuals, and combining multiple modes of communication on any given text means that individuals now have the same concerns and capabilities that have been available to popular culture producers for decades. Television, film, comics, magazines, and newspapers have emphasized multimodal communication for years and generations have become adept at decoding and interpreting these popular culture texts. Just as earlier generations learned through experience to read television and other popular culture quickly and critically (Williams 2002; Lembo 2000) younger generations are learning to read both these texts and new popular culture forms such as websites and computer games. It is difficult to imagine that students, in composing their own multimodal texts, do not draw at least in part from the most pervasive multimodal texts they encounter—those from popular culture

New multimodal media technologies have allowed individuals to easily appropriate, reproduce, mix, and reconstruct any kind of popular culture material that is either online or that can be changed to digital form. Such abilities have changed both the reading and composing practices of young people. Not only do they read popular culture texts with the possibility of appropriation and remix always nearby, but they compose using practices closer to bricolage and collage than to traditional linear constructions of texts. As Lankshear and Knobel (2007) point out, "Almost anything available online becomes a resource for diverse kinds of meaning making" (5).

It is important, then, to consider what a student must be able to do to read and write in convergence culture. Individuals are faced with multiple complex rhetorical decisions when reading and writing online when they must recognize and negotiate audience assumptions, sample and reuse popular culture content, create new texts with collages of that content, and compose online identities that others will find engaging. On top of that, when people compose new texts on blogs, fan fictions, fan forums, or personal webpages, they are faced with the possibility that the audience will not only read the content but very likely respond.

For example, Mitchell has a blog that is primarily focused on science fiction and fantasy movies. There is a photo of the Creature from the Black Lagoon at the top of the page and each entry is illustrated with images from the films that he has sought out, copied, and pasted on his page. Several readers of his page—who use popular culture images rather than personal photos as their icons—make regular comments, to which he also responds, carrying on a lively dialogue on the subject. Or consider Amy, who has posted to her *MySpace* page the results of a quiz from the *Quizilla* website on "Which Disney Princess Are You? (A True Psychological Test)" with an image of the animated character of Belle from *Beauty and the Beast* and a caption that describes her, among other things, as an "intelligent, just, dreamer with a rational base."

Amy's image, comparing herself to a Disney princess as the result of a "True Psychological Test," is in contrast to other content on the page, such as her listing her favorite television program as *South Park*—the antithesis of Disney—and her favorite movie as the vampire film *Underworld Evolution*. Certainly we read Disney images on Amy's page with an irony we would not bring to that of a younger girl. Although Disney as a corporate entity works hard to protect the use of its images, we see in this example how students' literacy practices with popular culture work to parody or subvert dominant cultural meanings and ideologies.

Such ironic and subversive uses of popular culture demonstrate how young people are not simply passive cultural dupes helpless before the onslaught of popular culture. For a number of years, scholars (Buckingham 1993; Morley 1992; Fiske 1996; Morse 1998) have challenged in both theory and research the conception of uncritical audience reception of mass popular culture. While acknowledging that popular culture reflects and reproduces dominant cultural ideologies, it is not accepted without question by individuals in the audience who interpret such texts in the contexts of their own experiences, adapting them to ideas that may or may not conform to dominant cultural values. Rather than argue about whether television, movie, and computer screens are lenses that project ideology or mirrors that reflect our own experiences, it is more useful to consider Margaret Morse's (1998) metaphor of the screen as "membrane" whose "function is to link the symbolic and immaterial world on the monitor with an actual and material situation of reception" (18). Far from being passive dupes, individuals have always engaged in interactions with mass popular culture, whether by discussing television programs with friends or seeking out more information about celebrities in fan magazines. As people have read and adopted popular culture texts to their social contexts, popular culture has long served functions of both identity construction and community building.

At the same time, the changes in popular culture emerging from participation and convergence of media have also not necessarily ushered in a utopian, democratic world of online popular culture. As Jenkins (2006a) points out, some "participants" in convergence culture are more powerful than others. Certainly it would be foolish to argue that students are always resistant to the dominant ideologies reproduced in popular culture or that every image displayed with a hint of irony is actually conscious resistance rather than just a good joke. Dominant cultural conceptions of social class, race, gender, sexual orientation, and other components of ideology are reproduced by students in participatory popular culture just as often as parody and irony—and often exist side by side. Although media industries are alarmed at many of the activities people now engage in through the appropriation and reconstruction of popular culture content, they are simultaneously embracing convergence culture "because convergence-based strategies exploit the advantage of selling content to consumers; because convergence cements consumer loyalty at a time when the fragmentation of the marketplace and the rise of file sharing threatens old ways of doing business" (Jenkins 2006a, 243). Rather than regarding the emergence of convergence culture as either oppressive or liberating, it is important to examine the emerging relationships enabled by new media and trace both the tensions and opportunities for creativity they provide.

The rapid emergence of new media technology has, of course, drawn the attention of many media and communication scholars with a variety of focuses including, for example, popular culture consumption (Jenkins 2006a; Ito 2008; Gee 2003), identity (Buckingham 2008; boyd 2008; Everett and Watkins 2008; Scodari 2003; Willet 2008), education (Goldman, Booker, and McDermott 2008; Frechette 2006; Burn and Durran 2006), community (Smith 1999; Johnson-Eilola 2005; Davies 2006), and fan studies (Black 2007; Thomas 2007; Gray 2005). All of this research is valuable for the insights it provides us into the practices of young people with participatory popular culture. Even so, literacy and rhetoric, how students approach interpreting and composing texts in this evolving environment, is usually not explicitly addressed in such work.

At the same time that media scholars have focused on the changes in how young people experience and use participatory popular culture, a growing body of research has focused on the connections between literacy practices and popular culture. As this research has demonstrated (Alvermann, Moon and Hagood 1999; Dyson 1997; Williams 2002; 2003; Gee 2003; Lankshear and Knobel 2003; Knobel and Lankshear 2007), individuals read popular culture texts more critically than conventional wisdom assumes and adapt the genres and discourses of popular culture into their literacy practices both in and out of school. Such research has also indicated that, when motivated by their own interests, students are willing to struggle to understand and create challenging texts (Gee 2003; Williams 2002), belying the common cultural image of lazy young people unwilling to work to make meaning from complex texts. This is not to say that the study of popular culture is always accepted in the context of literacy research and pedagogy. As I find every time I write an article or give a presentation or workshop, to be a literacy researcher interested in how popular culture plays in contemporary literacy practices is to continue to encounter considerable resistance from others in research and teaching.

Yet even as these and other literacy researchers have demonstrated the necessity of paying attention to popular culture, much of the research into popular culture and literacy has remained focused on well-established popular culture forms such as film, television, popular music, and advertising. Only recently have scholars such as Gee (2003), Bury (2005), Black (2008), and Thomas (2007) begun to explore literacy practices in youth interactive popular culture. These studies have focused more on the ways in which online technologies have shaped literacy practices and not looked in depth at the influence of the discourses and rhetorics of popular culture itself. By and large, however, there has been limited attention to how the convergence of technology and participatory popular culture shapes the reading and writing practices of young people across media and genres.

Research into popular culture and literacy still struggles to make an impact in the ways reading and writing are taught in schools. Too often, when popular culture is addressed in the classroom, it is still addressed as a hazard against which students need to be protected (Tobin 2000; Williams 2002). This inoculation model of teaching popular culture reflects many teachers' wariness of the subversive pleasures students find in popular culture. David Buckingham (2003) says such attitudes among teachers:

Are often based on a paternalistic contempt for the children's tastes and pleasures and are bound to be rejected (by the students). The notion that students might somehow be weaned off of what they perceive as their own popular culture in favor of the teacher's cultural or political values would seem to be increasingly impossible. Even where teachers have sought more positive engagements with students' media culture, they have often sought to colonize students for their own purposes. In the process they frequently end up re-inscribing traditional notions of what counts as valid knowledge (314).

Instead of approaching students' literacy practices with participatory popular culture as a problem to be solved, we need to be listening carefully to them and paying attention to how and why they read and write outside of school. We need to recognize that most of the reading and writing they do in a day is taking place online and with popular culture. This is not necessarily a call to teach our courses solely through popular culture, but to ignore its complex influence on students' perceptions and practices is to ignore our responsibility to draw on their experiences to create the most effective pedagogies possible.

Adapting Popular Culture Online

If we want to understand how young people engage in daily literacy practices online, it is worth taking a moment to consider why popular culture adapted so quickly to online technologies that allowed both interactive and inter-media participation by individuals. Jenkins (2006a) writes that popular culture dominates much of convergence culture "on the one hand because the stakes are so low; and on the other because playing with popular culture is a lot more fun than playing with more serious matters" (246). Yet that statement by itself does not explain the easy symbiosis of popular culture and online technologies. Instead, it is important to understand that the development of interactive online technologies allowed people to continue and expand the interpretive and social uses to which they were already putting their readings of movies, television, and music.

Participatory popular culture activities and texts existed before online technologies. "New literacies like fan fiction, manga-anime fan practices, scenario planning, popular music remixing, and zine publishing among others, pre-date their digital electronic internetworked forms—sometimes by decades and, in the case of fan practices, arguably for centuries" (Lankshear and Knobel 2007, 21). Certainly Jenkins' (1992) work on fan fiction illustrates this point. What online technologies have done is made such activities easier and more accessible, and enabled their rapid spread. Though online technologies have allowed for the creation of some new forms of popular culture, the larger impact of online technologies in terms of extending and expanding participatory popular culture practices has been in three areas.

First, new technologies have, through the ease with which they allow interaction and the appropriation and combination of multiple media, vastly increased the number of people engaging in interactive popular culture activities. Fan fiction, fan forums, webpages, appropriating texts in multiple ways—all activities that used to take a substantial commitment of time and energy—are now accomplished with little effort and little time invested, making available the kinds of activities only undertaken by the most dedicated fans that Jenkins described in the early 1990s.

Also, the ease and speed of movement of popular culture content across media now enables both faster shifts in meaning as well as juxtapositions of popular culture words, images, and video that create new meanings. Online technologies, like other electronic popular culture media on screens that preceded them, often privilege images, speed, and sound (Selfe and Hawisher 2004). The capabilities of online technologies to reproduce and distribute multiple media simultaneously have allowed the producers of mass popular culture from television to music to computer games to make all or part of their content easily available online. The equivalent of old print fan magazines or tours of studios, for example, are now available to us as we sit in our homes at our computers. At the same time, many of these new combinations of texts happen at the hands of individuals, not just corporate organizations with vast material resources. Of course, cross-media content existed before online technologies, as anyone with a *Star Wars* novelization or soundtrack can confirm. The difference now is that the ability to engage with and combine content across media is quick, easy, and shared by traditional producers and individual members of the audience, with each drawing the interest of fans. Individuals can combine and publish these texts with technologies that make posting photos of movie stars on a website far faster and easier than cutting up photos and pasting them inside a locker. Fan forum discussions of television programs often begin as the final credits begin to roll. Of course, such increases in speed and online publication can create new tensions for people whose texts are misread or communities of fans who resent newcomers entering their discussions.

Finally, online technologies have changed the relationship of audience members not just to popular culture producers but also to each other. The kinds of performances of identity and community building, such as wearing concert T-shirts or talking about a television program around the watercooler, were confined to face-to-face interactions for most people. If someone asked if I liked a television program, not only would I probably already have another context for knowing the person, when I answered I could tell the effect of my response by watching the other person's reactions. Now, however, the use of popular culture images to create a personal webpage may have a global audience who knows nothing else about the creator of the page. As Jenkins (2006b) notes, "Where fans might have raced to the phone to talk to a close friend (about a television program) they can now access a much broader range of perspectives by going online" (141). Not only have online technologies increased the range of perspectives about a given program but the variety of popular culture from around the world that can be accessed and discussed and appropriated has grown with astonishing speed.

Just as important as the creation of a more interactive relationship between popular culture producers and audience members have been the ways in which online technologies have created opportunities for establishing and sustaining social networks or relationships. Convergence culture is also a networked culture "both in the sense of communication networks and concepts, objects, and subjects being constructed by interconnected social and technical forces" (Johnson-Eilola 2005, 9). Young people engage in online popular culture to maintain both local social relationships, for example, through social networking sites, and to connect to others on a global scale with whom they share interests in common, through fan forums and blogs, for example. Some students engage in both these practices, for both these reasons, within the same day. Jenkins (2006b) also points out that participants in online networks connected to a particular popular culture genre or text develop a kind of "collective intelligence" in which knowledge about a mutual interest is shared and its value increases with social interaction.

New Media and New Literacy Studies

At the same time that media scholars have been studying the explosion of interactive practices available in popular media, literacy and composition scholars have been addressing the effect of online technology on literacy practices. As Cynthia Selfe (1999) notes, "[W]e have seen the twin strands of literacy and technology become woven into the fabric of our lives" (160). Indeed, it is impossible to think about literacy in contemporary society without connecting it to computer and online technologies. Increasingly in public policy debates and in the culture at large, computer technology is regarded as an essential gateway to sophisticated literacy practices, as we can see in everything from government legislation to corporate advertising. Research on writing with computers or composing email and webpages now stretches back ten to twenty years (Slatin 1990; Eldred 1991). Few are unaware that print literacy has often moved from pen and paper to computer and that new media technologies have allowed new ways of composing and writing that bring together word, image, sound, and video. What's more, computer technologies have emphasized the collaborative and unstable nature of composing texts (Cooper 1998; Anson 1999; Yancey 2004) and offered suggestions for how to use such technology in the classroom. In addition, a number of journals, such as *Computers & Composition*, *Kairos*, and *E-Learning*, are dedicated to the study of how students interpret texts and compose with computer and online technologies, particularly in connection with issues of literacy pedagogy. Not least, scholars in rhetoric and composition have opened, for the first time in centuries, fundamental questions of composing and distributing texts (Welch 1999).

Just as important has been the argument that computers are "not simply tools (of literacy); they are indeed, complex technological artifacts that embody and shape—and are shaped by—the ideological assumptions of an entire culture" (Hawisher and Selfe 2000, 2). Such rapid changes in the cultural conceptions of texts, of the creation and communication of knowledge, and of the performance of identity in print and image have been the subject of a growing body of scholarship (Selfe and Selfe 1994; Selfe 1999; Lankshear and Knobel 2003; Kress 2003; Selfe and Hawisher 2004; Johnson-Eilola 2005; Alexander 2006). Such research has increasingly included all the new media literacy practices of young people, not just those that happen in school. Yet in a moment when technology is changing so quickly that articles about computers and writing that are a mere ten years old seem to be dealing with archaic technology, our research often still seems to often be a step behind students' newest practices. This understanding of the shifting nature of technology makes it important that we ground our research in theoretical reflection that allows it to be useful in light of whatever may be the newest technological innovation.

As the advent of online technologies has facilitated and foregrounded the social nature of participatory popular culture, literacy studies have increasingly emphasized the role of social contexts in shaping literacy practices. The central shift in literacy studies in recent years has been from the conception of literacy as a set of stand-alone skills to the idea of literacy as a social practice. Such a shift requires an awareness that though literacy learning and activities are specific to individual behaviors, literacy practices are shaped through social relationships and "embedded in socially constructed epistemological principles. It is about knowledge: the ways in which people address reading and writing are themselves rooted in conceptions of knowledge, identity, being" (Street 2001, 7). Though the socially constructed nature of literacy is present even when writing in a private journal, the interactive capabilities of online technologies have highlighted and intensified the ways in which relations within discursive communities determine how reading and writing happen and who is able to participate in literacy practices. Participating in an online forum, for example, requires much more than simply being able to read and write. Without the crucial understanding of the social customs and power dynamics of the forum, which can vary widely from one online group to the next, it becomes difficult to negotiate the rhetorical situation and participate in a way that is meaningful and even comprehensible to others.

Participatory popular culture complicates such literacy practices even further as the social contexts for online users are shaped by the power relations between corporate producers of popular culture and the members of the audience. Although individuals may now have increasingly powerful ways to respond to and appropriate the texts created and distributed by corporate producers, differences of power and capital help determine the scope and nature of such responses. The most striking influence, of course, is that audience members by and large are responding to and appropriating texts that are created by popular culture producers, rather than producing such texts solely by themselves. As Barton and Hamilton (1998) point out:

[Literacy] practices are shaped by social rules which regulate the use and distribution of texts, prescribing who may produce and have access to them. They straddle the distinction between individual and social worlds, and literacy practices are more usefully understood as existing in the relations between people, within groups and communities, rather than as a set of properties residing in individuals (7).

As convergence culture evolves, popular culture producers and audience members are struggling with the tensions created by its effects on such social rules and power relationships. Such tensions can be seen, for example, in the debates about intellectual property and file sharing, in concerns about the effect of online media on young people, in changes in the connections between television programs and online content. The tensions, both creative and debilitating, offered by participatory popular culture are also evident in students' literacy practices as they negotiate and contemplate issues of audience, authorship, authority, and identity.

Reading and writing in any context, then, is always inextricable from cultural forces in the context in which the act takes place. Both popular culture scholarship and new literacy studies have been marked in recent years by their shared concerns with the social contexts in which texts are produced and consumed and the responses of individuals to the demands of multiliteracies in a world of new media technologies. Indeed, what Lankshear and Knobel (2003) write about the concerns underlying concepts of multiliteracies could apply equally to those underlying concepts of participatory popular culture:

The cultural and critical facets of knowledge integral to being literate are considerable. Indeed, much of what the proponents of multiliteracies have explicated are the new and changing knowledge components of literacies under contemporary social, economic, cultural, political, and civic conditions. In other words, being literate in any of the myriad forms literacies take presupposes complex amalgams of propositional, procedural, and "performative" forms of knowledge (12).

Approaching literacy as situated by historical and cultural forces makes clear that our conceptions of and attitudes toward how we read and write have a direct influence on our ideas of what constitutes popular culture, as well as what constitutes concepts of traditional print literacy such as literary and academic texts.

With the exploration of multiliteracies and multimodal forms of communication have come questions about how, in fact, can we define a term such as *literacy*. Although I agree with multiliteracy scholars that to define literacy as only a matter of reading and writing print is too narrow, I also am wary of the recent trend in both scholarship and the culture at large to use *literacy* as a synonym for advanced competency or knowledge. I grant the importance of having a sophisticated and critical knowledge in fields such as environmental studies or finance or medicine. Yet I am uncomfortable with referring to such knowledge as environmental, or financial, or medical "literacy." To define every advanced knowledge as "literacy" robs the term of its power to describe a specific and important form of human endeavor. For me, literacy is connected to the way humans communicate ideas, concepts, and emotions to one another. Humans are meaning-making creatures and we have learned to do so by creating representations of our ideas that can be interpreted by others when we are not present. I see it as important, then, to keep literacy connected to the communication of ideas through representation, whether of words, images, graphics, and so on. In this way, literacy can apply to writing print on a page, arranging images and words on a webpage, or arranging images and words on film or video. Each example illustrates the arrangement of signs or symbols or images to represent ideas. For this book, my working definition of literacy, at its most basic and yet most varied, is the ability to use sign systems to compose and interpret texts that communicate ideas from one person to another.

Everything Is Rhetorical

Along with theories of literacy and popular culture, rhetorical theory plays an essential role in how I approach this project. Thinking of students' online literacy practices in rhetorical terms, as situated acts of expression that exist in comprehensible and ideological combinations of appeals, allows the exploration of issues such as audience, ethos, genre, evidence, and style across media and across texts. Although it is clear that online texts are complex rhetorical objects that employ rhetorics of words, images, sound, and movement to create narratives, identities, and arguments, it is also clear that producers of popular culture and students alike draw from existing genres to create texts that have desired effects on specific audiences. What's more, where online technologies have created spaces for new kinds of texts—such as blogs or personal webpages—people have quickly created genres and conventions to go with those genres, even as they adapt elements from existing rhetorical forms.

The speed of change in popular culture and on the Internet, as well as the cross-media ideas of convergence culture, made it impossible to think about approaching this project or organizing this book by popular culture genre, media technology, or specific online literacy practice. Instead, I have approached this research from the rhetorical practices and skills I see students employing across genres and technologies when they read and write about and with popular culture online. The use of rhetoric as an organizing and thematic concept reveals how young people move as readers and writers across genres and technologies, mixing and matching different practices and skills to the variety of rhetorical contexts they encounter online. Even as literacy increasingly means the ability to choose between print, image, video, sound, and all the potential combinations they could create to make a particular point with a specific audience, what will not change are the rhetorical abilities of an individual to find a purpose, correctly analyze an audience, and communicate to that audience in a tone that audience will find persuasive, engaging, and intelligent.

In this book I bring together these strands of theory and research, from media and popular culture studies, computers and composition, new literacy studies, and rhetoric to address questions of how individuals in convergence culture compose, read, and write online and the powerful role popular culture plays in the online literacy practices that are central to media convergence.

In conducting research on young people, popular culture, and literacy practices, there are always several cautions to keep in mind. First, it is important not to overstate the causal relationships between any given popular culture text and a specific reading or writing act by a student. It may not be possible to demonstrate direct, irrefutable connections between any specific online popular culture practice and a specific way in which students read and write in the classroom. On the other hand, like fish in the water, we are surrounded by popular culture that influences our daily lives, including our perceptions and attitudes toward politics, economics, issues of identity, and ideas of community. We are not powerless dupes before this ubiquitous, multimedia flow of popular culture, yet escaping popular culture, even for those without televisions, computer games, or computers, is as impossible an idea as a fish swimming without water. As I have argued in previous work (Williams 2002; 2003), though it is impossible to measure precisely where the influence of popular culture on literacy practices begins and ends, it is foolish to imagine that the most pervasive and popular rhetorical and discursive forms in our culture do not have important articulations with how we read and write. My goal for this book is to explore these articulations and the possibilities they offer for a more nuanced understanding of how young people read and write.

It is also important to be judicious in the construction of student identities in conducting research about popular culture. What had, at one point, been a rush to see students as passive dupes of popular culture producers has now sometimes been replaced by an equally ill-advised rush to celebrate the ways in which young people in partici-patory popular culture resist the texts they encounter. Seen through the eyes of adults, it is often deceptively easy to see the activities of young people with popular culture as either sadly submissive or radically subversive, perceptions that may say more about our re-sponses to popular culture than they do about the struggles of young people to balance the programs, films, games, and websites they en-counter with the experiences of their daily lives and relationships. "Young people are not best served either by the superficial celebra-tion or the exaggerated moral panics" that often polarize discussion of their uses of popular culture (Buckingham 2008, 19). Instead, our interpretations of their words and actions should be "clear sighted, unsentimental, and constructively critical" (19), reminding us to keep in mind that, like all individual responses to culture and ideology, the responses of young people to popular culture are complex and often contradictory. Such considerations underscore the importance of tak-ing the time to listen carefully to students when they discuss and demonstrate their literacy practices online so that we can see them as "significant social actors in their own right, as 'beings,' and not sim-ply 'becomings' who should be judged in terms of their projected fu-tures" (19).

The enthusiasm that has greeted online technologies has also led to claims about the revolutionary nature of the activities allowed by new media. As this book will illustrate, the activities people engage in online may not be radically new as much as extensions of previous practices. Certainly new media and online technologies are changing much about how we read and write, but it is always necessary to ask the question of whether the current practices are revolutionary or evolutionary. Is there a substantial, transformational change occur-ring in how students read and write, or are new technologies simply putting new covers on old content (Willett 2008)? As with student identities, the reality may be both in the middle and often shifting and contradictory. In a similar way, in discussions of online technologies, reductive binaries are often constructed between young people, who are assumed to be "digital natives" (Prensky 2001), and their parents and teachers. However, the uses and perceptions of online technologies are not so easily defined by age and are always complicated by other facets of identity such as gender, race, and social class (Herring 2008).

Finally, though research concerned with online practices and research on popular culture poses challenges that I will discuss over the course of the book, the other concerns to highlight at this point are the problems raised by the size of popular culture, both on and offline, and the speed at which it changes. Popular culture has always been somewhat frustrating to write about because the content shifts so much more quickly than any scholarly work can make it into publication. Consequently, examples and illustrations quickly take on a somewhat faded and nostalgic aspect even when they are only a few years old. Once-popular television series such as *Seinfeld* or *Buffy the Vampire Slayer*—shows that were watched regularly and were the topic of much conversation—now seem old news and exist only in syndicated reruns, leaving viewers asking, "When was that show on anyway?" The "hot" television programs of the moment—*Heroes, Lost, The Wire*—may, by the time people read this book, also seem dated references.

Online technologies seem to change even faster and the popular website or application of the moment may disappear even more thoroughly than television programs in reruns. Anyone remember *Friendster*? *MySpace, Facebook,* and *SecondLife* all have, in recent years, reigned as the definition of hipness. Again, however, by the time this book is published, they may all have been replaced by new programs and websites or, at the very least, have lost their pop culture luster. The pace of change in popular culture is particularly rapid among young people, for whom determining their status based on whether they are in on the latest cultural obsession may determine their social status with their peers. Because popular culture is often a key element of identity construction and performance for young people, it is important to have the "right" popular culture elements for a desired social group. Many students report signing up for *MySpace* because their friends had (boyd 2008) and then leaving it for *Facebook* for the same reasons.

I don't pretend to offer a comprehensive examination of online popular culture and literacy practices for such an attempt would be doomed from the outset. As it is, I am continually finding new places online where convergence culture meets young people reading and writing. To try to stay on top of all these places is impossible. Instead, my project is exploring the qualities emphasized in the intersections of online literacy practices and popular culture. It is, of course, only a slice of what is going on at a particular moment in time. Yet, even as the specific practices may change, there will continue to be influences of popular culture in terms of issues such as audience, authorship, and identity on how and why students are reading and writing.

How This Material Was Gathered

The information for this book was gathered in three ways. The most obvious source was reading and analyzing a wide range of online material. This material included content published by popular culture producers—television and movie studios, bands, computer game companies, for example—and student-produced texts published online—such as personal webpages on social networking sites, blogs, fan forums, and fan fictions.

Just as important was the information that came from students themselves. If we are going to understand what students know and think, we need to talk with them in depth, let them show us what they can do, and be ready to be quiet and listen carefully to what they say. I chose a research approach that I believed would offer me enough breadth to begin to identify patterns of literacy practices and yet be small enough to be able to spend significant time interviewing and observing each student. First, I conducted a series of lengthy face-to-face interviews and observations with twenty-one first-year university students in the United States about their online literacy practices and their engagement with popular culture. I spent at least two hours with each student. For fifteen of the students, I spent at least eight hours in observations and interviews over several appointments. I began with an initial interview about their popular culture interests and online literacy practices. A list of the standard interview questions is available in the appendix. Next, I conducted observations of the students involved in their online literacy practices.

Of the twenty-one students I spoke with and observed in person, thirteen were women and eight were men. Eight of the students were first-generation university students from less affluent backgrounds. Of the remaining students, most were what would be considered middle class economically, with five who considered themselves affluent. The university the students attended is a state research institution with an undergraduate enrollment of approximately 15,000. It is located in a medium-sized metropolitan area (population of about 800,000) in the middle of the United States. Four of the students interviewed were African American, one was Chinese American, and one was Latina. All the students owned their own computers and had online access, which they all reported having had in some form for at least four years before coming to the university. In addition, all the students reported spending time online each day. Only two students said they spent less than two hours online each day. The majority of students said they spent three to four hours online each day—though that included time engaged in other activities while still online, such as studying—while twelve of the students said they spent more than six hours online each day. A list of the students and their demographic information is available in the appendix.

Obviously, the demographics of any research limit in some way the claims that can be made from the information gathered. For example, one of the important developments in participatory popular culture is the ability of students to be in contact with people in other countries, connected by common interests in popular culture. This book does not address that important development, though it is my goal to explore such connections in future research. What is most significant to me in terms of this book is that every student reported engaging in some form of online reading and writing that used popular culture either as content or as rhetorical form—every student. My attempts to find students who did not use popular culture online, in some form, proved fruitless. This book explores how their different activities and attitudes demonstrate both the patterns and diversity of such literacy practices.

There are clearly limitations to what can be learned from any kind of research, including concerns specific to research with online content and popular culture. Any group of interview participants, whether in person or online, offers only a limited set of perspectives and generalizations based on the information gathered must always be made carefully. In addition, when participating in a research project, students inevitably shape their responses to questions with the identity and presence of the researcher in mind. However, a series of interviews and observations that covers longer periods of time both help to build a sense of trust between the researcher and participant and allow for answers that are more frank and less guarded. In general, however, students both in person and online were eager to talk about these issues. For many students, these conversations were the first time that a teacher or an adult had taken seriously their expertise and skill with new media literacies as well as their passion for and knowledge of popular culture.

The Organization of the Book

As I mentioned before, the chapters of the book are organized not by genre or media but by rhetorical concepts that students employ across the convergence culture.

Chapter 2—Everyone Gets a Say: Changes in Audience and Community

The popular culture of the twentieth century presumed a mass audience that perceived popular culture texts and references as common cultural ground. Contemporary participatory popular culture, with its fragmented audiences and blurred lines between producer and audience, has challenged the traditional role of the popular culture audience member, as well as the concept of popular culture as a broadly common discursive terrain. This chapter will illustrate students' flexible, and often conflicted, conceptions of audience that emerge from their online reading and writing. In addition, it will describe the way that students negotiate participatory popular culture communities and the emergence of what Henry Jenkins (2006b) calls "collective intelligence." These changes have had a significant impact on how students regard the relationship between writer and reader.

Chapter 3—Looking for the Right Pieces: Composing Texts in a Culture of Collage

Participatory popular culture is altering the conception of texts for students. Rather than experiencing texts as autonomous written products, participatory popular culture texts are flexible and impermanent collages that are only one link in a larger network. Students' writing and reading practices in the much-discussed "sampling culture" of contemporary life have changed their ideas of composing. In addition, the multimedia capabilities of new technologies and popular culture have given students tools for composing that are changing their ideas about genre, reading, and response. This chapter will focus in particular on how ideas such as mosaic and collage, with their juxtapositions of disparate words, images, and video, are appealing to students when they read and write online with popular culture.

Chapter 4—"Which *South Park* Character Are You?": Popular Culture and Online Performances of Identity

Students engage in multiple performances of identity through popular culture references and content. This chapter focuses in particular on social networking sites such as *MySpace* and *Facebook*. In contrast to expository descriptions of identity in print text, students use popular culture icons, catchphrases, music, text, and film clips in postmodern, fragmented collages that present selves that seem simultaneously sentimental and ironic. However, the intertextual nature of popular culture texts creates opportunities for multiple readings of pages in ways that destabilize the identity students believe they have created. These multiple readings create ambivalence for students who realize that their practices in composing pages may be in conflict with how they read other pages, and how their own pages are read.

Chapter 5—A Story of One's Own: Social Constructions of Genre Online

Genre and narrative have been central and powerful elements of popular culture for more than a century. Participatory popular culture has allowed individuals both to borrow from and remake the genres and narratives that they enjoy. Fan fiction and other literacy practices are hugely popular with young people and demonstrate how they learn to read and write in the genres they learn.

Chapter 6—The Pleasure of Irony: Emotion and Popular Culture Online

Although the emotional appeal of popular culture has been the subject of much scholarly discussion, the advent of online technologies has changed the way individuals read and respond to such emotions. The online literacy practices of students highlight the dual-sided and mercurial nature of emotion in contemporary popular culture as they read and create texts that switch rapidly between irony and sentimentality. This chapter examines how emotion plays out in students' online reading and writing with popular culture, both as popular culture texts and references deployed in the performance of identity and as the perception of pleasure in the manipulation of popular culture texts motivates students' literacy practices.

Chapter 7—What's on Next? Conclusion and Implications

The final chapter of the book considers the implications of these changes in online technologies and popular culture in terms of how we consider the literacy practices of young people.

Conclusion

If we can move both literacy and media education in terms of popular culture away from a model of inoculating students against harm to a more honest and thoughtful discussion with students of their literacy practices, we can overcome student resistance and create critical and creative ways of reading and writing. In addition, it is important that we begin to think about how online technology has not only increased the contact people have with popular culture from around the world, it has also put them in contact with other audience members in other countries. Consequently, the literacy practices that are being shaped by popular culture online are also often simultaneously influenced by the ways that images, ideas, and references from popular culture texts are read across borders. Finally, we must think about how convergence culture is reshaping the way students engage with concepts of rhetoric and literacy.

The online literacy practices that students engage in with popular culture influence everything from audience to text to emotion, attention, motivation, and identity. What's more, these literacy practices cross media, genres, and cultural borders with a speed and fluidity that are also shaping students' ideas about technology and culture. In our teaching of writing and reading, both in and out of school, we need to increase students' understanding of the transformations in the symbiotic and exploding realm of popular culture and literacy practices. It is essential, then, that we pay attention to these popular culture literacy practices if we are to understand how students are making meaning and performing identity every day as they read and write online.

CHAPTER 2

Everyone Gets a Say

Changes in Audience and Community

For years, one of the standard frustrations for writing teachers was students' lack of experience in negotiating the demands of a "real" audience. Students were accustomed to writing for a teacher in the classroom but not to figuring out how different audiences with different assumptions and values would influence what and how they wrote. Many teachers spent a great deal of time figuring out assignments, such as letters to the editor of a newspaper, that would make students have to consider an audience outside the classroom. Today, however, it would be foolish to assume that a secondary or university student would lack experience in writing for varied audiences. Whether on a fan forum or fan fiction or *MySpace* page, young people know that what they post online could be read by a wide variety of people. Not only are they writing for "real" audiences, but when students write online, they also know they are writing for an audience that may very well write back. According to Catherine:

> Anything that you write online, well, you're having a conversation of sorts with people you might not otherwise call and talk to or even meet, and so you're going to get feedback from people you might not otherwise talk to. Like, I posted a blog one time, "This week has been just hellacious," and someone responded and said, "Like, me too" and told about hers and we went back and forth about it for a while and felt better. And it was like that social interaction never would have happened had I not put up that blog and she responded.

Though what is written online does not always provoke a response or such a positive response, students are aware that their writing will reach real people with real opinions. Amy said about her blog that "I'm not really looking for what people have to say or looking for anyone's advice or anything, but I always know that stuff could come back at me at any time. And, I mean, it is cool to know that people are reading it when I'm putting myself out there, but I don't always take people's comments that seriously."

There can be little doubt, then, that changing technologies have had a substantial effect on how students think about audience when they write online. At the same time, it's difficult to imagine any aspect of popular culture changing more because of the online technologies than the role of the audience. The growth of mass popular culture in the twentieth century was grounded in the ability of electronically amplified images and sound to reach large groups of people. The "mass" of popular culture of this period can be conceived of both as the production and distribution of popular culture material through the concentration of economic capital, as well as in the size of the audiences who could consume the material at the same time.

Just as electronic technology combined with particular economic and cultural forces to create the consumer-defined audiences of mass popular culture, contemporary online technologies have changed the relationship of audience and popular culture producer to something more interactive and participatory. That the interactive popular culture activities of audience members, particularly young people, are largely conducted through reading and writing has important implications for our study of current literacy practices. In this chapter, I explore how this shift in the definition of audience to a more interactive model affects the intersection of popular culture and literacy practices by focusing on three specific phenomena. First, the ability of individuals to share knowledge and ideas about popular culture with others online through what Levy (1997) and Jenkins (2006b) call "collective intelligence" has created new opportunities for people to interpret and analyze popular culture. The proliferation of "fan forums" where people discuss and argue over television, music, film, and computer games provide spaces where meaning making becomes a collaborative enterprise among audience members. These audience members may vary in age or sex or background but are drawn together by the popular culture text to help each other, through print, to make meaning.

People involved in fan forums, including students, are also faced with negotiating in writing the rhetorical demands of audience, evidence, and tone. Understanding audience expectations of a given discourse community and the subsequent influences on what evidence is persuasive shapes ideas of credibility and authority. The second focus of the chapter then is how interactive audiences for contemporary popular culture are shifting student concepts of credibility and authority in terms of texts and the producers of texts. Authority and credibility are increasingly not created only by the producers of popular culture, but by the responses of audience members on fan forums and on sites such as *Amazon.com* and the *Internet Movie Database*.

Finally, much has been made of the concept of "affinity spaces" online (Gee 2004; Knobel and Lankshear 2007; Black 2008) as virtual places where people connect by their interests first rather than identity characteristics such as age, race, gender, or social class. Certainly, there are fan forums and other online sites that draw people who would rarely meet otherwise into conversations about popular culture texts. At the same time, however, it is important to consider how popular culture itself shapes such interests in terms of identity. I finish the chapter with a discussion of how popular culture and identity shape the choices of audience members before they enter affinity spaces.

From Local Participant to Mass Audience

Before the industrial revolution, popular culture is perhaps best defined as the cultural production of people on the local community level. The playing of music, dances, local theater, and folk art such as quilting and carving were the popular culture activities available to the majority of people. With the exception of books and newspapers, which were often rare, these popular culture activities were marked by the necessity of proximity and the opportunity, and often expectation, of broad participation. A community dance or local fair or parade was open to people to take part in any number of different roles. The old small town joke is that the townspeople would take turns watching each other in the town's parade. Popular culture was in general low-tech, not-electronic, and each event was confined to those who could physically attend.

By the middle of the twentieth century, the changes brought by the development of an industrial, modernist culture had substantially altered the production and consumption of popular culture. Although no change happens at once, the effects of industrial culture in terms of the concentration of populations in cities, technological innovation, increased material capital that allowed leisure time and discretionary spending, transportation, and social organization had influenced conceptions and habits of popular culture. Specifically, the growth of mass-scale production and distribution in economic life moved deci-sively into popular culture activities, creating what is now often called the *popular culture industry.* Rather than learn to play a mu-sical instrument and participate in a square dance, people became just as likely to listen to a band on the radio or to a recording of the music. Rather than make a quilt, people were more likely to buy a blanket at Sears. Rather than perform in a community play, people would go to a movie. Like many activities in industrial, modernist society, popular culture became an industry of commodified, standardized, repro-ducible content created and distributed by professionals with highly specialized jobs. The employment of such professionals and the dis-tribution of their product required concentrations of economic capital not available to most people. A handful of people with a couple of musical instruments could hold a square dance, but the same few people could never hope to make a movie. At the same time, audi-ences became less content with the variable, and often inadequate, quality of locally produced popular culture. "Mass culture, then, must be nonregional, highly standardized, and completely commer-cial" (Kammen 1999, 18). Rather than settle for amateur, local, partici-patory popular culture, people wanted professional spectacles of a quality they could predict that were available for their immediate gratification.

At the same time that production and distribution of popular cul-ture changed, new electronic technologies allowed for the size of au-diences to increase. The ability to amplify sound and images created the opportunity for audiences to grow in size as the concentration of population in cities provided large numbers of people eager for enter-tainment and spectacle. The ability of electronic technologies to re-produce and broadcast popular culture content created a situation where audiences in cities across a nation could watch and listen to identical material simultaneously. The concept of audience changed from a group of people in the same physical location to the people in a society who might encounter and attend to the same program, con-cert, or film. Audience changed from the people you could see around you at a play or concert to the estimated 580 million people who watched Neil Armstrong take his first steps on the moon in 1969. To be a member of an audience was now a matter of whether you had encountered a particular text—film, television program, record—regardless of the context in which you encountered it.

The reliance on the reproduction and distribution of professional popular culture content also changed audience members' relationship to the texts they encountered. Watching or listening to an electronic popular culture text that had been produced thousands of miles away and reproduced or broadcast did not allow for the audience to interact with or alter the text. Movies could be watched, records listened to, but there was no dance to join nor even the heckling or audience–performer interplay that marked nineteenth century melodrama or Renaissance theater. Even popular culture that included audience interaction, such as rock concerts, was built on the audience experience of listening to the reproduced music first on records or the radio or even MTV. The experience of the audience with mass popular culture in the twentieth century was, for the most part, observational and directed outward. People understood that they were watching movies or television as part of a mass audience, but most did not have the opportunity to interact with other members of that audience, except for the people they knew, face to face, in their own lives.

The shift from a local, participatory popular culture to a mass-produced and -consumed popular culture raised questions almost from the beginning about the creation of a passive, unthinking audience. Even early silent films were criticized for creating a more passive audience (Kammen 1999). Kammen argues that the development of mass popular culture precipitates a shift from a seeking of experience to a seeking of information and, by extension, a "relative shift that I perceive from participatory to more passive" (23). The perception of a passive audience lapping up any popular culture contents placed in front of them is evident in popular nomenclature such as *couch potatoes* or *cultural dupes*. The assumption behind such terms is that mass popular culture is consumed uncritically by an undiscerning audience and that the result is a less intellectual, less inquisitive populace. Bemoaning the supposed passivity of the popular culture audience has been a popular pastime of popular commentators (Postman 1985; Birkerts 1994) as well as critics from both ends of the political spectrum. Though the goal of the indoctrination is perceived differently, critics from across the political landscape have agreed in their condemnation of mass popular culture as a vehicle for inculcating an unsuspecting populace that is unwilling and unable to withstand the messages of a potentially dangerous ideology.

Such condemnations inevitably provoked counter-arguments and reconsiderations of the relationship between audience and mass popular culture. These critics (Fiske 1996; Morley 1992; Grossberg 1997; Lembo 2000; Williams 2002) have argued that people watching movies or television or listening to music are more involved, creative, and critical interpreters of the texts than had been generally argued. Though the level of agency granted to audience members varies among these critics, there is agreement that audience members, including children, are more active readers of mass popular culture than generally assumed. The questions raised by the relationship of audiences to mass popular culture in terms of whether popular culture shapes or reproduces ideology and how individuals and communities respond to such texts continue in media studies and the culture at large. Yet, throughout these debates, it has been assumed that even if audience members did interpret popular culture texts more critically, it was still essentially an individual act as part of a mass audience. Even if audience members knew millions were seeing movies and television programs, most conversations about popular culture were confined to local communities. What's more, except for the most fervent fans, there was little sense that audience members regarded popular culture as in any way interactive. Instead, conceptions of mass popular culture reflected modernist ideas, from the role of culture to the influence of mass economic and political structures.

Devoted Fans and Participants

The exceptions to the prevalent producer-audience dynamic of mass popular culture were indeed the fervent fans. As many scholars (Jenkins 1992; 2006a; Scodari 2007; Crawford and Rutter 2007; Thomas 2007) have recognized over the past twenty years, some of the most devoted fans of particular popular culture films, programs, or music found ways to interact both with the texts they were watching, as well as with fellow fans. Rather than confine their interest in popular culture to watching and casual conversations with friends and co-workers, devoted fans instead found ways to make explicit their interpretations, appropriations, and re-imaginings of what they watched. While the interpretive and analytical moves of most members of the mass popular culture audience could only be perceived through interviews or observations that revealed their moves as readers, fans' activities challenged the divide between producer and consumer, between reader and writer. As Jenkins (1992) noted in his pivotal work *Textual Poachers*, "Fans do not simply consume preproduced stories; they manufacture their own fanzine stories and novels, art prints, songs, videos, performances, etc." (45). Fans responded to and reconfigured popular culture through self-produced fan fiction magazines, other forms of fan art, and fan conventions. Yet, in the world before online technologies, to engage in activities such as producing and distributing fan fiction or attending a convention required a dedication of time and money that made the activities appealing only to a small segment of the audience. One consequence of the devotion required to interact with texts and other audience members was that "fans" were perceived as odd, obsessed outsiders whose activities were to be pitied and dismissed, even as they engaged in interpretive and creative moves that, in a more conventional context such as reading literary texts, might be applauded (Jenkins 1992).

What online technologies have allowed is for the activities of "fans"—the ability to communicate with others of like interest and interact with popular culture texts—to become easily available for the majority of audience members. An increasing number of people, particularly young people, take advantage of these opportunities. "Certainly, there are still people who only watch the show, but more and more of them are sneaking a peek at what they are saying about the show on *Television Without Pity*, and once you are there, why not post a few comments? It's a slippery slope from there" (Jenkins 2007, 361). As more and more people chose to interact with popular culture texts through websites, fan forums, fan fictions, and other online technologies, they are changing the definition of a popular culture audience. The more people that engage in interactive activities once confined to ardent fans the more the perception of these activities moves from marginalized cult status to become part of mainstream popular culture (Jenkins 2006b).

For young people posting to a fan forum or writing fan fictions, thinking about audience goes beyond the concept of imagined communities. Unlike writers of the past, who had little sense if their work might be read, students online know that the audience is a very real community with the ability and interest in responding to their work. When students are part of the audience, they expect to be able to respond to the ideas and writing of others, whether producers of popular culture content or fellow audience members. Participation is the name of the game.

Although the interactive relationship between writer and audience is available in many contexts online, it is through popular culture that many students experience, and expect, such participation. It is also in the realm of popular culture where the relationships between producer and audience have particularly been shaken by participatory online technologies. As the interactive capabilities of online technologies became obvious, popular culture producers have created content in an effort to create and control audience loyalty. Almost all television programs, computer games, and movies have producer-sponsored websites that offer a combination of additional content and interactive activities and forums. Like fan clubs of previous eras, the goals of these sites are not to empower audience members or create truly interactive media as much as they are to intensify and broaden fan loyalty to a particular film, show, or game (Deery 2003). Indeed, many producer-created websites lack imagination and seem no better than extended commercials or trailers. Where the quality of producer-created sites is changing, it is creating changes in concepts of narrative and genre. I discuss this latter development more fully in chapter 5.

Other producers of popular culture are still working out how they will take part in the participatory game. For example, many musicians now maintain blogs or *MySpace* pages (as do many authors, actors, and other artists). This works to their benefit by keeping them in contact and in the minds of their fans. This is particularly attractive, and inexpensive, publicity for musicians who are less well known but have a growing fan following. For members of the audience, the access to musicians through their blogs and social networking sites offers a kind of contact with artists that was only a fantasy for most fans in the past. Such online spaces reconfigure the relationship of producer and reader. The musician or author no longer has to guess what fans think while the fans get a glimpse beyond the work to the person, and perhaps even a dialogue with the artist. And fans themselves participate with their own blogs about musicians. Yet, as some musicians have found, such a level of contact with fans can raise thorny issues of representation and the performance of self. Revealing information on their blogs that seems inconsistent with their onstage personas can result in resentment from fans or lead to information that is misinterpreted and spread across the web (Thompson 2007). As one musician said about learning to be more careful with what he posted in his blog, "You start acting like a pro athlete, saying all these banal things after you get off the field" (Thompson 2007, 46). While participation online has changed much about popular culture, it has not altered many fans' belief in the mythology of their favorite celebrities or interest in scandals that undermine it.

Fan Forums and Sharing the Conversations

The more significant development in terms of audience and student reading and writing, however, has been the growth and evolution of fan-created and fan-run sites and forums. Often more popular than producer-created sites, the online spaces created and dominated by audience members challenge the sanctioned corporate sites, "decentralizing the flow of information and providing a space for speculation, rumor, and even subversion of network control" (Deery 2003, 164). On such sites. audience members not only can take control of the meanings of popular culture texts, but through doing so create communities of shared interests and knowledge.

A person sitting alone watching television in the age of mass popular culture could assume others across the country were watching the same show but could not engage immediately with them to discuss the program. Online technologies make at least part of that assumed audience present and available for conversation. As Deery (2003) points out, this changes both the experience of watching the show and the act of making meaning from the show afterwards. "Knowing that one is watching a show with identifiable others and will discuss its details with them will undoubtedly affect the viewing experience, both in an anticipatory manner while watching the show, and subsequently if one is influenced by online discussion" (174). It is the production of new content from popular culture, specifically in fan forums, fan fiction, blogs, and popular culture groups on social networking sites, that both the role of audience and the rhetorical acts of reading and writing are altered in particularly intriguing ways. For the moment, for the sake of brevity, I wish to focus on fan forums.

Fan forums are online spaces where individuals can discuss a program, film, band, computer game, or any other element of popular culture such as a particular celebrity. Discussions are organized by specific threads, such as a discussion of a particular episode or actor, for example. Individuals post messages that can be read in the order in which they are posted, sometimes quoting pieces of earlier posts in their messages. While most fan forums are public and can be read by any person browsing the web, some forums do require some kind of registration before allowing a person to post messages. Fan forums exist for most movies, television programs, popular bands, sports teams, computer games, and celebrities, as well as often for genres, such as zombie films. Some fan forums exist on sites dedicated to a particular movie or show or game; others can be found on sites such as *Television Without Pity*. For the most popular texts, there are multiple forums, often serving a variety of audiences. (Though slightly different in configuration, similar discussions go on in groups dedicated to popular culture topics on blogs such as *Vox*, *LiveJournal*, and *Xanga*, through email lists, and on social networking sites such as *MySpace* and *Facebook*.)

The allure of fan forums draws on audience behavior that predates online technologies. Discussing and debating a movie or television show has been a common practice for years from watercooler to dorm room. Such conversations, whether focused on replaying the plot of a film or program to enjoy it again with friends or trying out competing interpretations of the text, are common activities often used to reinforce social bonds. The myth that mass popular culture is isolating and alienating has been challenged time and again by research (Buckingham 2000; Morley 1992; Meyrowitz 1985) that illustrates the social function talk about popular culture plays in our society. Online technologies have expanded the scope and speed of such conversations. Now, instead of only being able to discuss the show or movie with friends or others in the room, it is possible to connect immediately to a group of people with the same interest, to have one's ideas supported, one's interpretations responded to, and one's questions answered.

Take, for example, Ashley, who contributes to fan forums for the *Harry Potter* and *Lord of the Rings* novels and films. She says the conversations on the forums influence how she interprets the texts:

> I like the *Harry Potter.com* website. And then there is stuff for *Lord of the Rings* and then, of course, on *Facebook* or *MySpace* or *ShoutLife*, they have these different groups that you can create for things and then you read, discuss and stuff. The groups have names like "Orlando Bloom should always have long blonde hair and pointy ears" and you get to talk about the different actors and what your favorite part of the movie is. You get to thinking that since you never saw that you have to go back and watch that. It makes you watch movies more carefully, like "I want to see if I can find something that nobody else sees" or we discuss "what would have happened if this hadn't happened?" or "what's going to happen next?" It kind of helps you kind of figure out before the book or movie comes out what's going to happen and then you're not as surprised when you see the movie. It's like, "I knew that was going to happen, I knew it!"

Ashley points out one of the principal activities, as well as great pleasures, of popular culture fan forums: the communal making of meaning. We have all walked out of a movie or turned from a television show to others with us with questions or opinions about what we had just seen. For dedicated fans, Jenkins (1992) points out that meaning production has long been a social and communal enterprise. In fact, what Jenkins notes in the phrases fans used to begin posts on early fan forums of the 1990s sound familiarly like the kinds of conversations that might take place in a living room or coffee shop, "Entries often began with 'Did anyone else see...' or 'Am I the only one who thought...' indicating a felt need to confirm one's own produced meanings through conversations with a larger community of readers" (79). A great deal of the content on fan forums about film or television focuses on interpretive questions about the texts. In this way, fan forum members operate differently than academic critics. While critics focus on analyzing a text to determine its quality, and often to reveal its flaws, fan forum "criticism is playful, speculative, subjective. Fans are concerned with the particularity of textual detail.... Fan critics work to resolve gaps, to explore excess details and undeveloped potentials" (278). People post summaries, questions, ideas, suppositions, as well as predictions or spoilers for upcoming episodes, covering the smallest detail to the most sweeping theories and ranging in tone from humor to sober reflection. Here is an excerpt from one of Ashley's posts on a *Harry Potter* fan forum for a thread speculating about the ending of the series before the final book had been published.

> I'm hoping that Voldemort dies, of course. Because he's the evil one. They say one of the main characters dies. They've already killed off Sirius. That made me so mad that when I found that in the book I threw my book across the room and didn't read it for another three months because I was so mad I cried. But when they killed Professor Dumbledore I was happy. Which is kind of twisted because a lot of people are like "What?" But Dumbledore is in everybody's business. You know, mind your own business. He wants to know everything and tries to trick people. He wants to spin it his own way.

> So, in the seventh one, you've got to think "Well, Snape killed Dumbledore. Harry's mad that Snape killed Dumbledore. And he's always had a thing where he hated Snape anyways. So now is it going to be Draco or Snape that dies or is it going to be one of the best friends? I keep wondering if Harry is going to be one of the only ones left alive. Maybe Harry and maybe Draco. Because Draco's the main person in Slytherin and Harry's the main one in Gryffindor that are the two main houses. So you have to think that maybe those two will be the only ones left standing.

What is significant in terms of literacy practices is the way in which individuals, by writing about the text and reading and responding to the ideas of others, take ownership for the meaning of the text.

The tone of posts to fan forums, as well as recaps of films or television episodes on blogs, is often glib, ironic, and even aggressive toward the producers of popular culture. Take, for example, this quote from a fan forum comment about the television series *Grey's Anatomy* about a plot twist where a character tries to win the affection of another by outlining the floor plan of a house in candles. "The ending is the only thing I have a problem with. I am constantly being told by my family that when I watch television, I must suspend my belief in logic and reason so when I saw the Casa del candles, I didn't let it distract me. I just figured Mer had 1000 candles kickin' around in the trunk of her car just in case she might want to outline a floor plan someday" (*Television Without Pity*). As Ashley puts it, "Because it's (the movie) something that fans are really obsessed with, we get mad when we think things have been done wrong. We don't like it when they don't portray it right. We're like, "Your fans don't want this!" So forums allow you to talk and kind of vent on it."

Collaborative Interpretation and Collective Intelligence

Not only is the interpretive work not happening in isolation, but the degree to which those involved in fan forums assert their claims to their interpretations belies the image of passive consumers of popular culture. The confidence of forum participants in their ability to read, question, and make meaning from what they see stands in stark contrast to the often much more tentative interpretive moves the same students may make in the classroom. What is most strikingly different in the way students talk about their reading and writing on fan forums is the authority students feel as readers and as members of interpretive communities. The expertise many students report feeling in such forums is reflected in Ashley's comment on how the forums help her both predict and interpret popular culture texts such as the movie series she is dedicated to:

> You can piece together what everybody says and you're like, "OK, this is how the story is probably going to go." Everyone gets a say and you expect everyone to get a say. Then when you see them you're like "I knew it."

You're not as surprised when something goes wrong. Or like, "I knew that was going to happen. I'm not upset about that." But then when something happens that you don't expect because you're all completely wrong, you're like, "Oh no! What am I going to do? This is not what I was expecting!"

She is willing both to value her expertise and to be willing to admit to misreadings and then work toward new and more nuanced interpretations. Contrast this with her comment about reading for her classes: "I'm just lost sometimes with what we have to read. I know I'm supposed to get it, but I don't. So I just wait for someone in class or the teacher to explain it in class." Ashley's comments are consistent with what researchers examining the connections between literacy and more traditional forms of mass popular culture have found. Students act with more authority in discussing popular culture texts because they have varied and deep experience in interpreting and evaluating movies, television, music, and so on. In addition, because popular culture is generally dismissed as trivial and unimportant from the adult authority figures in their lives such as parents and teachers, students are left to play with and explore their interpretations of popular culture texts without worrying about being evaluated or sanctioned by the adult world.

From the pleasure that comes with control of a text and interpretive play grows the confidence to explore and express more evaluative and analytic ideas. Consequently, research with students at different age levels (Williams 2002; Buckingham 1993; Smith and Wilhelm 2002; Alvermann, Moon, and Hagood 1999) demonstrates that students are much more confident in their interpretations of popular culture and their willingness to engage in conversations with their peers than they are with texts assigned in, and sanctioned by, their schools. Fan forums offer new opportunities for these conversations. Jenkins (2006a) speculates that fan forums are particularly popular among university students where they can "exercise their growing competencies in a space where there are not yet prescribed experts and well-mapped disciplines" (52). It is difficult to believe that Ashley would show such confidence in her posts to an online forum on a subject more accepted by adults and governed by recognized authorities, such as politics or economics.

Yet, in her conversations on fan forums, Ashley's literacy practices are not only interpretive but evaluative and often analytic. She is confident in making judgments about the quality of a given text and eager to go beyond a simple statement of her likes and dislikes to explore the reasons a given text succeeds or fails:

> I post a lot on the forums. I really like the discussion because you get to play devil's advocate sometimes with people. Like, even if I feel the same way, but now just out of curiosity, I want to see how they're going to react to a different idea of how things happened or why someone did what they did. And you get to play and see the different sides of everything and how everybody thinks. People think, "OK, maybe I'm not so upset about it and I understand it more."

The kinds of literacy practices students such as Ashley engage in on fan forums make explicit the dialogic relationship of text and audience. Rather than wonder what interpretive moves audience members may be making, fan forums allow us to see readers working as a community to make meaning from texts. Members of the audience can now write back to the producer of the text as well as write to each other. The forums display the multivocal and heteroglossic landscape that Bakhtin (1981) imagines as the voices of participants compete, overlap, and offer new discursive resources for the interpretation of texts. While such dialogic exchanges happen in other online spaces such as wikis, fan forums are technically easier to negotiate and more explicit in the dialogic dynamic of writer and audience. Grossberg (1992) argued that, rather than meaning flowing in one direction from producer to consumer, popular culture "audiences are constantly making their own cultural environment from the cultural resources that are available to them" (53). Audience members always bring to texts their own experiences, including their readings of other texts.

Fan forums, however, make this construction of meaning visible and communal. A fan forum, like other participatory spaces such as fan fiction or blogs, creates "a meeting place for what Newkirk (2002a) calls 'the dialogic relationship of multiple worlds' stemming from popular culture, school and academic practices, fans' home and friendship groups, online communities" (Black 2006, 178). It is important to understand that the forums are not just a place where opinions are posted, but where ideas grow from the contact and tension with other ideas. This dialogic making of meaning is very much like what we, as teachers, want students to accomplish in the classroom as individuals try out ideas, ask questions, and weigh responses. Now, in fan forums and blogs, we are able to see the resources individuals call upon to interpret texts, and how those are adapted or rejected or modified and re-employed by other members of the community.

The dialogic and communal meaning making taking place on fan forums is an example of Pierre Levy's (1997) concept of "collective intelligence." Collective intelligence is the phenomenon where members of a community, even a temporary online community, are able to pool their information and experiences in ways that create new knowledge available to the entire group. It is not a matter of everyone knowing all the information all the time but more a matter of individuals being able to contribute what they have to the collective in order to answer questions and make meaning. In an online forum, each post strengthens and increases the collective and creates the possibility for new knowledge to be created. Popular culture is a particularly fruitful arena for the creation of collective intelligence because what is at stake is the interpretation of widely available texts that are not bound to the meanings given them by any particular group of experts or authorities. In addition, some popular culture texts, such as television programs or comics or movie series, offer such vast amounts of information that no one person could be expected to master it all. Instead, the community works together to help answer questions, fill in gaps, settle debates, and speculate on outcomes, with any member at some point potentially able to offer useful information or insights to the conversation. "Everyone could play, contribute their expertise, apply their puzzle-solving skills, and thus everyone felt like they had a stake in the outcome" (Jenkins 2006a, 51). Pleasure and motivation in any endeavor, according to a wide range of psychological research, can be connected in part to the degree of control a person has over the activity and the ability to use her or his skills to meet a particular challenge. Collective intelligence on popular culture forums plays to these aspects of pleasure and motivation.

As Jenkins (2006a) notes, in contrast to fields where experts rule over a bounded body of knowledge, "The types of questions that thrive in a collective intelligence, however, are open ended and interdisciplinary; they slip and slide across borders and draw on the combined knowledge of a more diverse community" (52). Again, such a space is particularly appealing to young people eager to have a place in their lives where they can assert their opinions and feel a sense of control and expertise (Smith and Wilhelm 2002). Certainly having their opinions and knowledge valued as expert is the antithesis of how many students feel about school. Indeed, the collective intelligence of the fan forum is sometimes regarded as a more reliable source of information, even a necessary corrective, to the out-of-touch opinions of "experts." Ted talked about reading film reviews from both professional critics and people who post on forums and blogs but gave more credence to the latter:

> I know that critics are overcritical so that's why I think that if they gave it a C-minus but everybody else (on a fan forum) gave it a B-plus and had good things to say about it, I believe the people who post more because they're probably more like me. So I go see it and then I post on there that the critics, once again, don't know what they're talking about.

Catherine made a similar comment about online forums and comments about music:

> I don't really listen to what the critics say because I don't trust them and, you know, critics are usually experts in the field but just because an expert likes it doesn't mean that it's a good piece of music. It might be, I guess, technically good, but it might not be aesthetically pleasing.

Ted's and Catherine's comments point out that, in the world of popular culture and online forums, the hierarchical, sanctioned system of experts whose knowledge is seen as being more formal and unchanging may be less valued than the more dynamic and fluid ideas and social relationships of the participants in a collective intelligence (Jenkins 2006a).

The Availability of Credibility

The phenomenon of collective intelligence in online settings also shifts thinking about authority and credibility of websites. In the pre-online culture, texts required a significant amount of economic capital to be produced and distributed and this fell to recognizable corporations such as studios or publishers. Credibility rested on the institution and the simple fact of production. If this material was being produced and distributed, it had to be approved by numerous people who were professionals in their field and, after all, they must have known what they were doing.

As has often been pointed out about online environments, however, the ability to produce and distribute information is now broadly available. While the fact of production by a studio or publisher still carries weight, authority is now also often determined by the accumulation of judgment from people who would have once been silent members of the audience. The credibility of a website or video or review increases with the number of people who have viewed or commented on it. People may seek out a video or blog that has rarely been seen, but they are more likely to visit sites that have been visited by others first. They either hear of the site through word of mouth, or check a counter to see how many times the site has been viewed, or check the number of comments. The result is that individuals may grant more authority to a popular site based on the level of audience participation, rather than the credentials or identity of the author. Indeed, as Lankes (2008) argues, the accumulation of judgment as a basis of determining authority, like other aspects of collective intelligence, is particularly appealing for students who face, and chafe at, rigid hierarchies of authority and expertise in other aspects of their lives.

Authors of websites have recognized this shift in authority and sought ways to make the accumulation of judgment more visible to readers. Counters that record the number of visits to a site or comments about a book or movie or the number of times a video is viewed have been common for years. Sites such as *Amazon.com* or the *Internet Movie Database* display the average of user rankings and now offer buttons under user comments where individuals can record whether they found the comment or review useful, and that number is listed at the top of the comment. And the *YouTube* homepage displays a rotating list of the videos currently being watched by others. Many of the students said that they looked to user rankings of music and movies to help them decide. Mitchell said, "If a lot of people have ranked a movie high, then sure I'm at least more likely to give it a chance." And Amy said that sites such as *last.fm*, where users can upload their playlists and see how their musical choices intersect with others', often lead her to discover new artists: "It also gives you a list of the people that share a lot of the same music interests as you, so you can kind of see they like this band that I'm also into, but I've never heard of this band that they are also listening to and I'll have to check them out."

The students, however, were not uncritical of the kinds of choices that could result from following such rankings or the recommendations. Brianna said she looked at ratings, but didn't always follow them. "If they said that movie is horrible, then I want to know why it's horrible so I will usually look at it and make my own decision. I try not to only listen to what everyone says because everyone's different." And Sarah said that the popularity of a site or video could influence her perceptions. "I'll notice someone will say 'Oh this video is so funny' and it'll become this big thing and I'll go and watch it and I won't think it's all that funny. But because everybody has said that it's funny you'll give it more credit than what it probably should be." Comments like Brianna's and Sarah's offer insights into how students are trying to come to terms with the participatory nature of collective intelligence, particularly regarding the accuracy and reliability of information from other members of the audience. On the one hand, the students are wary of recognized authorities and invest authority in the opinions and choices of their peers. Yet they are also recognizing that their peers' preferences may not necessarily reflect their own and they are not always able to figure out how to tell the difference. That many students find authority in online texts on the basis of the accumulation of judgment places the power of credibility in the hands of the participatory audience, rather than in the way that school-based texts continue to invest authority in the published work by the known author.

Learning the Rhetorical Rules

It is, however, important to understand that most fan forums are not formally limited to one group of people, such as adolescents. Instead, the participants in many popular culture fan forums can span different ages, gender, social classes, and so on. What brings the people together in a fan forum is the "affinity space" (Gee 2004) created by their mutual interest in a particular movie or band or celebrity. Although, as I will illustrate at the end of the chapter, affinity spaces in popular culture forums and blogs are still shaped by identity concerns, the demands of negotiating a varied audience through reading and writing are still very real concerns for fan forum participants. Understanding the discursive conventions of an audience is central to effective communication and the creation of meaning and knowledge. For years, as this has happened in terms of popular culture in face-to-face interactions with friends, the discursive demands are relatively easy to understand and learn. Now that such discussions are taking place in print with people who may be miles away and whose other identity characteristics are often unknown, students must learn rhetorical skills that are available only through reading and writing.

Students are aware that when they go online to a fan forum they must contend with a specific set of audience conventions. Brianna said, "You've got to know that the people already posting there have a way of doing things, of getting along with each other and making their points. You've got to figure that out before you just start posting and say something stupid." They also realize that misjudging the audience on a fan forum can have unpleasant consequences. Natalie said, "I've seen people get fried if they start spouting off in the wrong way before they take the time to learn the right way to communicate. I have even done that myself. Started posting as a newbie and been slapped down because of it."

Although, as often happens in student comments, these students do not use the rhetorical terms that are familiar to us, it is clear that they understand the importance of audience when they read fan forums. Students understand that as they read and post comments they must consider the roles of such audience considerations as context, ethos, evidence, and tone. It is also clear that successfully negotiating audience demands can be a source of some anxiety for students on fan forums and lists, as well as a source for a feeling of accomplishment and belonging once they feel they can communicate effectively to others in the community.

First-time visitors to a forum (or many other kinds of participatory online sites) are often called *newbies*. As Brianna and Natalie pointed out, it is important for newbies to understand the formal and informal rhetorical conventions of a fan forum. The awareness that forums are spaces in which there are rhetorical conventions that the audiences expect to be followed, and that these may vary from one forum to the next, is the first thing many students learn. Some newbies research the forum on which they are going to post, usually by *lurking* (reading without posting) and paying attention to how individuals on forums present themselves and their posts (Davies 2006). Increasingly, however, fan forums often post descriptions of the rhetorical conventions that govern the forum. Sometimes these are generated by the owners of the forum or list; at other times they reflect a consensus of the participants. The descriptions can range from general reminders about civility or what topics are considered appropriate for the forum to detailed explanations covering everything from appropriate forms of address to issues of grammar and usage.

The website *Television Without Pity* has extensive forums on multiple aspects of popular television programs. The owners of the site have a lengthy and detailed section of guidelines, advice, and admonitions about posting on the forums. The explanations begin with a description of the function of the forums that makes explicit the connections to the kinds of face-to-face conversations about popular culture that predated online forums:

> Imagine yourself at a friend of a friend's party. You mingle with other guests, strike up some conversations, and generally get along with everyone else even if they might not share the same opinions as you do on everything. You don't go ripping on people for having a different view of something, jumping up and down on the couch and calling them stupid. You'd be shown the door. So it is at TWOP. We like to say "think twice, post once." Be respectful of your fellow posters, agree to disagree when differences present themselves, and never ever make things personal. Otherwise, you'll get a ticket on the Size-Nine Express (*Television Without Pity*).

Not only does the analogy to face-to-face conversation connect the fan forum to previous participants' experiences with negotiating new audiences but makes it clear that there are social sanctions in store for individuals who violate these conventions of civility expected on the forums. Also, the tone of the description models the informal and ironic, but not angry, tone expected in the forums.

Even with explicit guidelines, however, participants on fan forums often misjudge their audiences or somehow violate the rhetorical and discursive conventions of the group. Some forums, like those on *Television Without Pity*, have moderators who will ban those whose posts are deemed objectionable or unfitting. On other unmoderated forums or lists, it is other members who may respond to posts that seem to be inappropriate. Sometimes such responses are constructive and helpful to newbies while at other times the response comes in the form of a harsh or dismissive rebuke that can devolve into name-calling and personal attacks on both sides. One student showed me a post on a forum about the television program *Lost* where a new participant invoked the ire of others by asking a plot summary question, The response read: "If you're just tuning in to the episodes then FOR GOD'S SAKE go read the recaps for the earlier seasons before you start asking inane questions that waste our time and patience." There are many reasons for this kind of discord that occurs from time to time, most of them in some way connected to issues of audience. For example, the capability of online technologies to expand participation in fan discussions can create resentment from more experienced participants toward unfamiliar newcomers. The more experienced participants may not be able to socialize the greatly increasing number of newcomers into the discursive conventions of the community, or the new members may claim new approaches and ideas and dismiss those already in place as outmoded (Jenkins 2006b). The advantage of fan forums and lists, in bringing together a variety of people from a range of backgrounds to discuss similar interests, can also be a weakness. Were we to meet the other members of a fan forum in person at the mythical party the *Television Without Pity* guidelines imagine, we would have other contextual information, from the setting to what people are wearing, to help us interpret the words of others and to moderate our responses accordingly. Yet with printed words as often the only information available, the rhetorical contexts can be misread. Such misreadings can at least lead to confusion. At worst, "flame wars erupt as their taken-for-granted interpretive and evaluative norms rub against each other" (Jenkins 2006b, 142). As research on email has demonstrated, a misreading of the rhetorical context combined with a lack of other contextual information such as gesture or facial expression can mean that irony, hyperbole, and even good-natured kidding can lead to hurt feelings and angry responses. Peter said he could be surprised at fan forum threads that erupted into flame wars: "Sometimes it's like people just go off. Some guy says something that seems maybe the least bit controversial and suddenly everyone is jumping up and down and all hell breaks loose." Even moderators of fan lists and forums cannot predict how participants on a list will respond to reading, interpreting, and composing comments.

The tensions arising from misreadings can be particularly perplexing to participants on fan forums and lists because popular culture is often assumed to be a "common" culture, where texts are assumed to be familiar and have stable, easily discerned meanings. Popular culture is often assumed to be superficial and easy, even among those who are fans of programs. Finding that others read texts in substantially different ways, that they don't like the same film or music for the same reasons that others do, can come as a surprise. In addition, people can have significant emotional investments in particular popular culture texts. Criticisms of movies or television or music can lead participants on lists to defend the pleasure and desire the texts evoke for them. Underlying many critical comments on fan forums seems to be the plea: "How could you not like this program in the same way it has moved me?" Brianna said that she felt she had to respond to criticisms of films she enjoyed. "It may be a movie other people think is dumb. I mean, OK, so I loved *Queen of the Damned* and you may not think it's great. But if you push your comments too far about it, I'm going to come back at you and give you my opinion." Emotions often run strong on fan forums, either in the pleasure of enjoyment or of distaste. "Anti-fan" forums and lists where participants engage in detailed criticisms of programs and movies they detest can be as popular as traditional fan forums (Gray 2005). Finally, because popular culture tastes are often displayed as part of the performance of identity, as I discuss in more detail in chapter 4, a criticism of a movie or show by one person on a forum may feel to another as a criticism of that individual. Sandy said that her enjoyment of a forum once stopped because of the response she received to praising the Natalie Imbruglia song "Torn." "I know they probably didn't mean it, but I was trying to talk about what the song had done for me as a person and then dissing the song because they didn't like the singer still really got to me."

In general, tensions, misreadings, and even flame wars are relatively short lived. On moderated lists, those participants who are considered to have violated the norms of appropriate behavior are often banned. On other occasions, members of the list re-establish order either through persuasion or, at times, what amounts to bullying. This can lead to schisms on lists, with some participants leaving for other forums or for more private conversations. The more positive outcome of such tensions can be a reflection on and clearer articulation of community definitions and goals by members of the forum or list (Davies 2006). More often, civility is re-established rather quickly, though identity characteristics of the majority of participants on a list can make a difference in the response. Bury (2005) points out, for example, that fan lists dominated by middle-class women tend not only to have fewer incidents of flaming and aggressive posts, but show more evidence of participants working positively to maintain civility and socialize new members to the conventions of the list. New members are often given explicit advice about the rhetorical conventions of the forum or list, either through forum posts, or in backchannel communications in private emails (Bury 2005; Davies 2006).

Understanding Ethos in New Communities

Negotiating the demands of fan forums and lists, then, rests heavily on questions of ethos. Issues of civility, belonging to a community, and credibility depend online, as they do in person, on how a person presents him- or herself. Ethos essentially is concerned with whether the presentation of self matches the expectations of the audience for who the person should be. On fan forums and lists, students reported that a credible ethos is established primarily by a combination of the intertextual references made by a writer and the writer's rhetorical moves, most significantly a more measured and detached approach to the subject, the employment of supporting evidence, and conventional uses of style and grammar. Valuing these rather conventional rhetorical moves would sound familiar in most writing classrooms.

For students, the goal of most participants on fan forums should be to be considered credible and persuasive, and certainly those were the qualities the students who were most active in such groups listed most often as important in what they read and posted. Tony, who primarily read sports fan lists, said:

> The intense fans just post a lot of basically, "Our team is better than yours just because we say so" kind of posts. I'm not so interested in those so I don't read them. I'd rather read people who are more open-minded in what they say. You can tell they're more educated on what they're speaking about. They're not just speaking out of pride or out of their loyalty to that particular team. You can tell they gave some thought to what they're saying.

In a similar comment, Genevieve said:

> If somebody makes a really, really strong comment about a video, I don't trust them at all. If they say "This is the worst video ever, I hate this, I hate that about it," I'm like maybe you're not to be trusted because of your personality. So I do, when I read people's comments, I do judge them. And I, I choose who to trust. I trust somebody that looks at the movie or the book as without a bias. Sometimes when you read something, you can tell when somebody has a bias. So somebody who puts forth the image of being neutral until they see, until they're starting to review the movie or book and then present both sides. You know they say some things they like and they say some things that they don't like.

Like Tony and Genevieve, many of the students said they avoided posts that were too confrontational. While they enjoyed humorous posts, their comments indicated a clear preference for posts that reflected a more measured and even detached approach to the subject matter. A number of students used the terms *intelligent* or *intelligently* to describe the posts that they found most credible and useful. Asked to articulate their definition of an intelligent post or participant, the comments usually reflected the ideas of balance and detachment seen in Tony's and Genevieve's comments. Sarah said, "I like people who speak more intelligently. I seem to consider theirs (posts) more than others. You can tell they stop and think about their opinions and about what other people have said and they think about all of that before they write what they think."

Popular culture is often assumed to offer primarily emotional pleasures for students. Indeed, students' descriptions of many of popular culture practices, such as listening to music or playing computer games, centered on the affective responses they derived from these activities. And some students did mention visiting forums to, as Ashley put it, "allow you to talk and kind of vent on it" or find humor or, as Tony said, "just to see what people are going on about. They can be pretty funny to read, especially when it's something you disagree with." By contrast, however, more often students discussed being attracted to fan forums and lists by a desire to gather information from credible, rational sources.

It is intriguing that students identified a more detached, analytical position as the most desirable to read on popular culture forums and lists. Popular culture is often considered to be the domain of immediate and emotional pleasures. Detached apprehension and analysis of an object, Bourdieu (1984) argues, are markers of more elite class status and usually reserved more for what have traditionally been considered "high" culture. As Jenkins (1992) and Bury (2005) have pointed out, fan lists can reflect the discourse conventions of the social class of the majority of their members. Fan forums and lists dominated by socially middle-class participants with higher levels of education often reflect a bourgeois aesthetic of detachment and analysis from texts. Certainly, the institution of education advocates and attempts to reproduce this ideology by training students to remove themselves from the affective responses to any texts and to seek and display more abstract and analytical positions. Students who can frame their ideas as removed from emotion and focused on rationality and balance find that they are embraced by schools and succeed. Often, these are students from more affluent backgrounds with higher levels of cultural capital who have internalized the ability to display a detached apprehension in their lives outside the classroom (Dyson 1997).

Even when such students discuss popular culture in school they take a more analytical stance toward the subject matter, with fewer references to emotional responses than students from less affluent backgrounds, who make as many analytical comments but embed them in emotional responses (Williams 2002).

In the interviews for this project, however, the remarks from students about valuing more balanced and analytical posts crossed boundaries of social class among the students. Though all of the students were in their first year in the university, almost half of them were first-generation university students from less affluent backgrounds. Of course, that they were in the university means they had mastered, to some extent, the kind of analytical position valued by schools. That they were discussing popular culture with a university professor no doubt also influenced how they framed their responses. At the same time, however, many of the same students' other comments during interviews were more indicative of the kinds of affective responses expected of discussions of popular culture.

The distinction students drew between the affective desires of many popular culture activities and the more explicitly rational rhetorical context they valued on fan forums and lists offers insights into how students perceive their literacy practices with online popular culture. Fan forums and lists are still largely dominated by print exchanges, often with relatively limited graphics and images. In addition, the emphasis of the content is on interpretation and analysis of popular culture texts. Fan forums often provide explicit rules that reinforce the importance of balance and reason. Another guideline on *Television Without Pity* states: "Just don't phrase things in absolutes like 'Nobody could seriously believe...' or 'The only possible explanation is....' No matter how sure you are that your interpretation is correct, it's still an interpretation. Leave room for people to disagree" (*Television Without Pity*). Or members of communities may try to socialize new members toward more measured responses. Bury (2005) noted how, on one forum, participants would advise new members about appropriate content and forms for posts, while reassuring them about belonging to the community. As will become clear in later chapters, students' online literacy practices in other venues still often focus more on the emotional and social aspects of popular culture. Perhaps it should not be surprising then, that even when students are reading and writing on forums outside the classroom, they respond to a rhetorical context of print and interpretation by drawing on the experiences and values they have encountered in school about ethos and credibility.

Finding Persuasive Evidence

Along with balance, the use of evidence to support statements and conventional uses of language and grammar—both familiar rhetorical moves valued in schools—were the criteria students mentioned most often in determining which posts they read and trusted. Ted said, "If I'm going to believe what someone has to say about a movie, if I'm going to agree with what they think about part of it, then they've got to show me what they're talking about. Anyone can say what they want, but if you want people to buy it you've got to back it up with examples." On forums and lists, it is not unusual for individuals to provide descriptions of scenes or pieces of dialogue to support their positions. Participants who claim positions without supporting evidence are often asked to provide it by other members. Students spoke of having internalized the need to provide evidence to support their ideas when they posted on forums. Sandy described her approach to posts on movie forums this way:

> I just give my honest opinion. I say "Well, in my opinion..." I'm not really lengthy and I do give examples of what was good and why it wasn't good and I try not to give away the ending or anything. I am very opinionated, but I'll also say, "Yeah, it had good sides, it had bad sides, but overall I think it was a pretty good movie or overall I wouldn't recommend it."

Sandy's conception of creating a credible ethos included both the sense of balance and the need for supporting evidence that so many of the students mentioned. None of the students connected these values to ones that they might have encountered in the classroom, even when asked specifically about any connections between online writing and writing for school. Still, it is difficult to read Sandy's comments and her emphasis on a balance of opinions and examples and not hear the echoes of teachers. At the least, it is clear that, for students reading and writing on fan forums and lists, they value rhetorical conventions that connect to those we hope to teach them.

It is also common for participants on fan forums and lists to copy sections of preceding messages they wish to refute or use for support in their posts. Sometimes, the snippets of earlier posts are meant only to remind readers of the material to which the new post refers. Very often, however, pasting in a portion of another post requires the participant to be more precise with the new message. It is less common to misquote or misrepresent earlier ideas and more common to respond to specific ideas and facts. For example, on a fan forum list for the television series *Dr. Who*, participants were discussing whether a change in lead actors had help or hurt the series. In the following comment, the first lines in italics were from an earlier post to which the later lines respond:

> *Sometimes, there are just inherent Doctor-y bits that David (Tennant) has that connect him to Chris' (Eccleston) version as well, and that's important to me, to be able to see the core qualities of the character across all of the different versions. That's how I got myself used to David, in fact: imagining the stuff being said by Chris. Sometimes, it works surprisingly well, and it did wonders to make me be able to move forward with the change.*
>
> RTD (Russell T. Davies, the series writer) said at the beginning of season two that he wrote the Doctor the same way when DT replaced CE, that in his mind there was no difference because they're both the Doctor. It's just that the two actors perform the scenes differently. I think that as time goes along that's probably less true because they understand how DT plays the Doctor now and can tailor their writing around that. But for the first season of both CE and DT, most of the scripts would have been written before the writers had actually seen either play the Doctor (*Television Without Pity*).

The use of cutting and pasting in ideas from other posts is an explicit illustration of collective intelligence. It is possible to see how knowledge from different individuals increases in value as it is combined with others' ideas as participants build their ideas from the ideas of others. Indeed, sometimes a person embeds two or three different parts of other posts into a message and then responds to each one before finishing with a concluding thought. As Jenkins (2006a) argues, "The new collective intelligence is a patchwork woven together from many sources as members pool what they know, creating something more powerful than the sum of its parts" (140). It also creates a facility with a cut-and-paste kind of writing that I will discuss in more detail in chapter 3. In many ways, the practice of drawing explicitly from other sources to bolster or refute an argument connects to more traditionally school-based rhetorical conventions than many online literacy practices. Engaging in refutation, or including other sources and other voices to support an idea, is a rhetorical skill highly valued in academic writing.

In addition to employing parts of previous posts into their messages, fan forum participants often draw on intertextual material and references as supporting evidence, but also to establish a credible ethos with their audience. For example, on a fan forum for *Battlestar Gallactica*, a participant's reference to a type of story line found on

Star Trek is both an intertextual connection likely to be familiar to others in the audience but also establishes the writer as a person with a knowledge of the history of science fiction narratives on television. Or perhaps a participant on a forum about the television series *Studio 60 on the Sunset Strip*, created by Aaron Sorkin, refers to previous Sorkin series, *The West Wing* and *Sports Night*, establishing credibility with an audience known for following the work of this particular writer closely. Such intertextual references not only demonstrate the knowledge of the writer but also help define the interests of the community through a shared interest in a specific genre, medium, or artist. It is much rarer to find intertextual references that make broad leaps across genre. For example, the *Star Trek* connections would be unlikely to show up on a forum or list for a television series such as *Desperate Housewives*. Again, these intertextual references quickly become part of the collective intelligence of a community and sometimes begin to turn up as a stock reference to a particular character or plot line.

Finally, a number of students mentioned that their responses to the credibility and persuasiveness of forum posts and to the ethos of the writer were shaped in no small part by language use and style. Mitchell, for example, said, "People have to sound intelligent. They have to write in a way that shows me that." Alison's comment was similar: "I'm only going to bother reading things that get posted where the person writes intelligently." The use of the word *intelligent* showed up numerous times in students' responses in regard to the posts and writers they found most credible. When asked to elaborate on what they were describing through the use of the word, students sometimes mentioned balance and evidence, but often described writing *intelligently* in terms of conventional uses of grammar and language. Genevieve's comment was typical: "Largely I pay attention to the word choice or the dialect they put forth. If someone does weird or incorrect punctuation, I think that they are not to be trusted. I want to read real sentences with complete ideas in them, not just a lot of random letters like people are texting." Genevieve's expectations for conventional use of style in posts are also often reflected in fan forum guidelines, such as this from *Television Without Pity*:

> The sad truth is that other posters might skip over your posts if they're too hard to read. Things like proper spacing, capitalization, and punctuation make your posts much easier on the eye, and they make you look like quite the Captain Smartypants, too. Look, we're not grading you. You won't get

banned for misspelling "definitely" or anything. Just try your best to write neat, coherent posts. Don't type "2" for "to," or "U" for "you," or "l8r" or "LOLOLOL!!!!!!!!!!!" or any of that nonsense. Throw in a carriage return now and then to break up the text, and please use proper capitalization. Your computer comes with two shift keys. Use 'em (Television Without Pity).

The use of words such as *neat, coherent,* and *proper* describe not only a desire for clarity in writing but reflect a set of values in terms of social class that are embedded in what are considered conventional uses of language. The values implied in what is considered *correct* or *proper* writing are often the same values that are stressed in middle-class culture, such as neatness and politeness (Bloom 1996). Certainly, unconventional language use and grammar is often used in the larger culture to mark class status, and by implication, education and intelligence. Though online writers, including these students, may sometimes use abbreviations or unusual punctuation, the students clearly paid more attention to writing style that reflected what they considered to be an educated bourgeois aesthetic. Bury (2005), in discussing grammar and usage on fan lists dominated by middle-class participants, notes that unconventional language use or grammar was often either apologized for by the writer or gently corrected, with humor, by other members, or both. The ability to notice and correct such writing underscored "the function of 'good' grammar as form of covert prestige in the community" (115). Such covert prestige translates into a more persuasive and credible ethos for students in fan forums and lists. That students who would write less conventionally in their posts or email still report putting more trust in posts that seemed to them more grammatically "correct" suggests two intriguing implications about popular culture and online literacy practices. First, despite hysterical media reports about the decline of writing in online environments, students are able to code-switch between conventional and less formal styles online, depending on the rhetorical context. In addition, their ability to recognize the appropriate context remains rooted in the identities of their offline selves.

An Online Self/An Offline Self

The connection of online literacy practices and offline identities is a complex one that is the focus of chapter 4. Still, in terms of audiences and popular culture, it is important to consider how issues of identity influence participation and reading and writing. One way to explore these questions of identity is by considering the concept of "affinity spaces." James Gee (2005) defines affinity spaces in part as an online space where:

> People relate to each other primarily in terms of common interests, endeavors, goals, or practices, not primarily in terms of race, gender, age, disability, or social class. These latter variables are backgrounded, though they can be used (or not) strategically by people if and when they choose to use them for their own purposes (225).

Certainly fan forums and lists are prime examples of affinity spaces. Members of the communities are drawn to them first because of their interest in the particular movie or artist or program or computer game. This set of shared interests was apparent and appealing to students. Ashley said, "I've met a lot of my friends on fan fictions and forums because we talk a lot and we have a lot in common about the things that we have passion for, which is the fiction, the novels, the movies, the creativity." It may indeed not always be clear whether a person posting on a list is the same age, race, sex, or social class as the person reading the post. For these reasons, as I noted above, negotiating the discursive and rhetorical conventions of such a potentially diverse group of people can present complications for any writer.

The influence of identity in regard to affinity spaces may be a bit more central and prominent than only being a secondary characteristic. Issues of identity are inextricable from popular culture. Popular culture reproduces, and sometimes subverts, dominant cultural conceptions of identity. At the same time, individuals use popular culture as ways of performing identity and creating community. The affinity for any particular popular culture activity—be it NASCAR, Harry Potter, heavy metal, hip-hop, romantic comedies, computer games—is never separate from how we conceive of our identities. We are drawn to particular popular culture activities and texts in part because we feel confident that in doing so we will encounter others similar to ourselves. Popular culture preferences are ways in which people build common experiences and recognize identities with which they will feel comfortable. As Bourdieu (1984) pointed out, while individuals often speak of cultural preferences as matters of personal taste and individual psychological characteristics, instead taste is a socially constructed set of preferences that reflect social class. Other scholars have similarly illustrated how other elements of identity such as gender, race, and sexual orientation also shape and are reproduced through popular culture. Consequently, identity concerns influence who chooses to enter an affinity space as an initial move before contact is made with others in that space.

Although it is impossible to know the exact composition of any online forum, research (Bury 2005; Davies 2006) illustrates that identity in online popular culture affinity spaces influences who participates. It is also possible to check profile information on forums. Sometimes the identity characteristics are more powerful influences than others. Heavy metal forums and lists, like those on *Encylcopaedia Metallum*, for example, are overwhelmingly populated by young, white, urban and suburban males, making them significantly different from the forum on a *gilmoregirls.org* or *Undergroundhiphop.com*. There are movies and programs with broader demographic appeal for which the affinity spaces are more heterogeneous in some ways, such as *American Idol* or *Harry Potter*.

Still, if we consider the composition of the audience in a popular culture affinity space such as a fan forum, we must understand that identity considerations have already influenced who is reading and writing there and that, in turn, influences the discursive and rhetorical expectations among the community just as identity does in the face-to-face world. When Bury (2005) studied several fan lists where the members were primarily middle-class, college-educated women, she found that the participants employed various "politeness" strategies in their posts that reflected their identity positions. The participants used strategies such as self-deprecating humor, qualifying words to moderate their claims, a more detached bourgeois aesthetic, and a reluctant use of profanity to maintain the discourse that defined their cultural identities. Forums and lists populated by adolescent males often illustrate rhetorical strategies that are more competitive and aggressive, with more personal attacks, less moderating language, and more profanity in posts. In addition, as I discussed above, class status as revealed in the use of style and language also connects to identity characteristics in online affinity spaces.

Consider, for example, two responses to two different, very popular videos on *YouTube*. The first, to a video of the song "Psychosocial" by the heavy metal band Slipknot, wrote: "Yo man. i agree with you endlessly ive never heard of a voice this good and hardcore before i heard sLiPkNoT years ago!!!!!!!!!!!!!!!!!!!!" The unconventional spelling and punctuation and more conversational tone of the comment reinforces a more emotional, informal response that focuses on the visceral pleasures of the band and music (and is one of the few comments not punctuated with obscenities). The other comment responds to a video of opera singer Renée Fleming: "I just listened to both (this video and one of the same aria by Kiri Te Kanawa) again. Amazing. I did notice that Kiri made those high notes with less effort than Renée. Renée was a bit more shrill. What a lovely aria. Puccini's music was studded with hooks, delicious strings of ear candy." This response, with the more detached analysis, focusing on the form and aesthetics, reveals the kind of differences in class response to texts that Bourdieu outlines. While the heavy metal responses, on the whole, were focused on visceral, emotional responses and were highly aggressive to those who disagreed with a participant's point of view, the opera responses were more detached, analytical, polite in disagreement, and made the kinds of intertextual connections valued in academic discourse.

The tensions in discussions that arise in online forums and lists can sometimes be traced to the collision of discourses from participants who come from different identity locations. In the same way that class or culture or gender differences can lead to miscommunication and conflict in face-to-face interactions, they can lead to problems in online forums, exacerbated by the assumption of participants that they are in an affinity space of shared interests where norms of discourse should also be shared. When disruptions stemming from conflicting discursive norms or rhetorical conventions occur on forums and lists, it often results in determining outsider status for some participants who face either adapting to the community or leaving (Davies 2006).

The point of understanding how identity shapes the audiences and discourses in affinity spaces is that we not idealize such spaces as places where students read and write outside of the influences of their offline lives. The same issues of identity that shape literacy practices in face-to-face life can be at work in influence reading and writing in online popular culture spaces. It is just as important that we consider how identity and audience interact with identity when students post and read messages online as when they read and write in the classroom. It is equally important that we help students consider how audience and discourse are at work when they visit their favorite forum or list.

Conclusion

What young people learn about audience from writing about popular culture online has a number of implications for literacy research and teaching. Whether on fan forums or lists or personal webpages, it is clear that students are gaining real understandings of the role of audience awareness in writing and the consequences of misjudging an audience. Even as online technologies have accelerated postmodern conceptions of audience, text, and authorship—where all these elements are now often fragmented, shifting, and unstable—the rhetorical demands of judging audience correctly are still important for effective communication. Students learn through fan forums and other online writing that determining the nature of an audience in terms of ethos and conventions and evidence and style remain important. The degree of understanding and ability to negotiate such audience demands offers encouraging possibilities for literacy educators. We can engage students in sophisticated conversations about audience if we understand the experiences they have had and if we can get them to reflect on those experiences in order to learn from them.

At the same time, it is important to realize that online literacy practices involving popular culture raise differences in the way these students encounter questions of audience. First, students are finding ways to explore these questions of audience in contexts they feel they control and own on blogs, fan forums, and lists. Adapting such genres for the classroom may not be necessary or even useful, but understanding how students perceive ideas of ownership of texts and the role of audience is significant. It is also important to realize that the interactive audiences students encounter online are democratic, if not always civil, and participatory, if not always egalitarian. As such, these audiences challenge our traditional ideas of popular culture and audience and literacy and audience. For these students, audience is an important concept, but it may be a very different concept of audience than many scholars and teachers imagine. In the online world of these young readers and writers, "The distinctions between authors and readers, producers and spectators, creators and interpretations will blend to form a reader-writing continuum, which will extend from the machine and network designers to the ultimate recipient, each helping to sustain the activities of the others" (Levy 1997, 121). For these students, audience has been thought of, and when it is, it is an audience that talks back.

CHAPTER 3

Looking for the Right Pieces

Composing Texts in a Culture of Collage

It is so easy.

As I sat watching, one student after another clicked a couple of times with a mouse, typed a few characters, clicked on another page, and in much less than a minute, a photo or video had been copied from one page onto their personal pages. Their moves were quick, confident, and second nature.

And it is so much fun.

Pat pointed to a video clip she had uploaded to her *MySpace* page:

> Like this guy shaving with a banana. It's the coolest thing ever; you should really see it. It's this guy, he puts on shaving cream and he does a sequence of photos or maybe he does a sequence of shots, I can't remember what it is with a camera. And he puts on shaving cream and then he peels the banana, then he starts shaving with the banana and it actually shaves off his facial hair. And then he puts like music to it and it's a really good video and it lasts for about a minute. And someone told me to go watch it, see this guy shaving with a banana, then later we can talk about how he shaved with a banana, but it's one of those interesting videos that you know you want to see but it doesn't really have a purpose. The minute I first saw it on *YouTube* I knew I had to put it on my page because it is so funny. That's part of what I like about *MySpace*, is being able to put things like this up for friends and then we all have it to talk about.

The online world is a world of collage. Everywhere you look, from *MySpace* and *Facebook* pages to blogs to webpages to *YouTube* to memes, you find pages that combine words, images, sound, animation, and video. It has become so commonplace it barely warrants a remark. But looking closer at the collages that young people read and compose online, you can see that many of the elements are adopted and adapted from popular culture. Whether it is movie clips, CD covers, computer game images, song lyrics, music downloads, or celebrity photos, the material that is often most available and most compelling for students is popular culture. One student's *Facebook* page has, among the many items, favorite quotes from Shakespeare to *Sex and the City*, music videos by Train and Stacie Orrico, and a countdown to the release of the film of *Harry Potter and the Half Blood Prince*. Meanwhile, another student has composed and posted a video on *YouTube* that is a collage of photos and video clips of her favorite moments from the television series *Smallville* set to the pop song "Never Let You Down."

The ability to cut, paste, and compose has created a culture of bricolage and pastiche in which many students read and write with confidence and creativity. The result is that participatory popular culture is altering the conception of texts for students. Rather than experiencing texts as autonomous written products, in participatory popular culture texts are flexible and impermanent collages that are only one link in a larger network. Students' writing and reading practices in the much-discussed "sampling culture" of contemporary life have changed their ideas of composing. In addition, the multimedia capabilities of new technologies and popular culture have given students tools for composing that are changing their ideas about genre, reading, and response. In this chapter, I focus in particular on how sampling, collage, and mosaic, with their juxtapositions of disparate words, images, and video, are appealing to students when they read and write online with popular culture.

Sampling the Culture

The idea that we are in a "sampling culture" is hardly new and has been tossed about a great deal in recent years in both the academic world and in the larger culture. The concept has been discussed most prominently in regard to rap music, where sampling bits of other songs to combine into a new composition is regarded within hip-hop culture as a creative act with a complex set of aesthetic and social conventions (Schloss 2004). In addition, sampling has been an accepted part of grass-roots popular culture such as zines. Outside of hip-hop, sampling has been a more controversial practice and has been criticized in the dominant culture as threatening both norms of individual creativity and intellectual property. Although artists have always borrowed material and motifs from those who have preceded them (look no further than Shakespeare), the rise of the Romantic-era image of the artist as a solitary genius has created the expectation that she or he maintain an illusion of absolute originality when creating new work. Popular culture representations of literary writers are particularly constructed around and reproduce the concept of the solitary genius (Williams and Zenger 2007). Schools often reinforce this concept of creativity when it comes to writing, admonishing students to "do their own work" and threatening draconian punishments for plagiarism for any work not deemed to be sufficiently "original" (while ignoring recent research that complicates such simplistic notions of originality and writing, (Howard 2008). Collage as an artistic approach, however, has been a common practice for more than a century. The examples, from Picasso to Dvorak to Copland, are easy and numerous.

In terms of popular culture, while sampling has most often been connected with rap music, in fact it is easy to find in other genres as well. For example, popular television programs such as *I Love the '70s* or *Talk Soup* are little more than collages of material with commentary and music videos and have often used footage from film and television. The collaborative nature of film and television has, however, made such sampling less of a target for cultural criticism than the work of individual rap artists who challenge the prevailing romantic image of the artist as creating *sui generis* work from her or his own inspiration, an image that gained momentum when the singer–songwriter model of popular music replaced the collaborative Tin Pan Alley tradition of the first part of the twentieth century.

With the spread of personal computers and online technology, however, sampling other work as part of the composing of texts has become increasingly common and increasingly diverse. Not only are individuals making their own versions of existing genres such as music videos or films, but they are combining media and genres in new ways to create forms such as machinima (videos made using computer game software), *YouTube* mashups, and social networking pages. What is new in the way sampling has become part of popular culture, then, is the ease with which new technologies have allowed individuals to participate and play with the words, images, sound, and video of other texts. New media technologies have made images, video, and sound as available and malleable as words as building blocks of creating texts. Students can use multiple modes of communication in composing with the same intent, and just as important, with the same speed, as they use words.

It is popular culture that provides the largest, most varied, and most accessible assortment of images, video, and sound for people to sample as they compose new texts online. The allure of popular culture comes not just from its availability, however. Popular culture content contains embedded meanings that are already available to potential audiences. A photo of a family member has to be explained to strangers. A photo of Britney Spears, while it might have many readings and many different uses, is still immediately accessible without explanation as to who the person is and her general position in the larger culture. Photos of Britney Spears will almost always be employed to generate different meanings than those of Meryl Streep. Consequently, popular culture online, with its ready-made set of meanings and the ease with which it can be appropriated and re-employed, is a rich repository of material for students composing texts.

Sampling popular culture content to use as part of new texts makes explicit the intertextual references that are a part of all writing. When someone writing only with words might use narratives or characters or language that call to mind *The Odyssey* or *Star Wars*, someone sampling pop culture images or video will put the images from *Star Wars* right there in front of you. "The digital remixing of media content makes visible the degree to which all cultural expression builds on what has come before. Appropriation is understood here as a process by which students learn by taking culture apart and putting it back together" (Jenkins et al. 2006, 32). Unlike some forms of cultural expression, however, popular culture engages in and celebrates the routine appropriation and reuse of material. Because popular culture texts are usually not considered to be the high art creations of individual genius, it has long been culturally acceptable to use them and re-use them in playful ways. Advertisements and television shows parody popular movies without worrying about whether such work violates individual creativity. Even in popular music, sampling not only fragments and refashions texts in postmodern ways but demonstrates "rock music's willingness to live off its own history and forms" (Connor 1997, 207). In our own lives, we have long picked up catchphrases of movies and television in daily life or made mixtapes or playlists of our favorite music. The stakes of textual integrity in popular culture are usually low and access to understanding the intertextual references is immediate. People are much more likely to appropriate and reproduce an image from *The Simpsons* than an image by Cezanne. Popular culture is disposable and fun and easy, as well as readable.

Not only is it impossible to pretend that a digital text that uses popular culture content and references is a work of autonomous creativity, new technologies allow for pop culture material used in one text to be appropriated again and again by audience members for their own composing purposes. In a study of online memes—the viral bits of information that get passed around the Internet and often center on popular culture content—Knobel and Lankshear (2007) note that one of the characteristics of the memes they studied was that memes were often not just passed along intact like multimodal chain letters. Instead, the video clip or image or text was often both appropriated and then altered or revised. So that the well-known clip of the *Star Wars* Kid, practicing light-saber moves in a schoolroom was soon superimposed with other pop culture images from *Star Wars* (such as Yoda) or other films such as *The Matrix* or even other memes such as the Dramatic Chipmunk. In fact, the ability to participate in spreading the meme both in copying and manipulating it seemed important to its vitality and popularity.

> In many ways these "mutations" often seemed to help the meme's fecundity in terms of hooking people into contributing their own version of the meme. A concept like "replicability" therefore needs to include remixing as an important practice associated with many successful online memes, where remixing includes modifying, bricolaging, splicing, reordering, superimposing, etc. (Knobel and Lankshear 2007, 209).

What's more, the popular culture content and references that students sample and revise may actually link to other pages that make the text just one collage in a network of ever-shifting collages. Popular culture excels at representing and re-representing material time and again. We are now just participating in the postmodern bricolage and pastiche that has marked popular culture for a hundred years. As Jenkins noted about fan culture in 1992, before most people participated in it online, "Fans, like other consumers of popular culture, read intertextually as well as textually and their pleasure comes through the particular juxtapositions that they create between specific program content and other cultural materials" (37). Yet it is this opportunity for participation afforded by new media technologies that is changing the nature, the project, and the act of composing.

As composing with popular culture online makes explicit the cultural content on which a student is drawing to create new texts, it also makes explicit the dialogic nature of writing. Literacy scholars have long embraced Bakhtin's (1981) understanding that the use of language is dialogic and that each word that a writer uses is already in circulation, its meanings constructed and contested through its uses by others. Such a concept of language can be difficult for students to perceive. The use of popular culture images, video, sounds, and music, however, makes clear the dialogic and shared nature of the material. No one would assume that on a *MySpace* page a Bruce Lee photo or White Stripes song or clip of a kiss from the film *The Notebook* didn't first belong to someone else, rather than springing from the internal genius of the page's writer.

Who Controls Meaning?

In addition to its more explicit intertextual origins, the other significant difference between words and popular culture content, from a Bakhtinian perspective, is that the meaning of the popular culture image or sound is more specifically defined and contextually bound—at least at the start. When we look at a photo of the character of Darth Vader from *Star Wars*, a text that has been sampled, copied, and parodied in many ways, along with the meaning of the text in which it is embedded, we also recognize its origin from the film. This kind of specific, instantly recognizable origin is simply not available for most words in the language. In mass popular culture, the origin is a product of large-scale corporate material production, and as such reflects what Bakhtin describes as the centripedal forces of the dominant culture to control and standardize meaning. Mass popular culture producers go to great lengths to create works that they hope will have as broad and predictable interpretation as possible for mass audiences. They use market research, test audiences, intellectual property law, and advertising to try to produce content that will be as appealing and predictable to as large an audience as possible. Against these efforts at controlling meaning "fans must actively struggle with and against the meanings imposed upon them by the borrowed materials" (Jenkins 1992, 33).

Sampling and re-using popular culture content works against these attempts to mold and control meaning. When students copy, manipulate, and employ material from other sources, they work against attempts to maintain a standard meaning of the original text. Such composing with popular culture content makes explicit the polyvocal discourses that Bakhtin (1981) said provide the centrifugal forces that make the meaning of language and texts always contingent on social contexts. "Alongside the centripetal forces, the centrifugal forces of language carry on their uninterrupted work; alongside verbal–ideological centralization and unification, the uninterrupted processes of decentralization and disunification go forward" (272). Every time someone places a song on a *MySpace* page or an image from an animated cartoon such as *Frisky Dingo* on a blog, the context in which the material is read shifts its meaning. And the next time the same material is used somewhere else the meaning shifts again. Of course the original text remains. A photo of 50 Cent is still a photo of 50 Cent. Though it is also the case that students often manipulate images they find on pop culture sites. Yet composing online texts with multimodal pieces of popular culture is more than quotation, it is more like using a word in a sentence, in which the dictionary meaning of the word cannot account for the malleable nature of the word when it must carry meaning in the social world of writers and readers. Images themselves can be ambiguous and, when placed in juxtaposition with other images and words, can be even more slippery in what happens to the meaning in the exchange between author and reader (Stroupe 2004). So the photo of 50 Cent may be placed in a context in which we are to read it as adoring in one, ironic in another, and perhaps critical in a third.

Because pop cultural content has specific meanings from original texts, however, the photo of a rap star plays differently in the multimodal texts students write than images without specific original public meanings such as a family photo or a drawing of a tree. An image of pop star Miley Cyrus may be iconic on one page, ironic on the next but will still carry with it the meanings connected with the pop singer. When students read and write with popular culture, they are always negotiating the original meanings of the material with the context of the page. They understand that Miley Cyrus on a teen page may be an object of worship and on a heavy metal page may be one of scorn. But they also often read the images, videos, and sounds individually and move back and forth rapidly between the readings.

As I sat at a computer next to Peter, I listened to him as he looked at some *MySpace* pages of friends and acquaintances. I asked him to tell me what he was thinking as the pages opened up and, rather than talking about the person, he began by picking through the popular culture references and content that drew his interest. He began by responding to the song that started to play when the page opened ("Impossible Germany" by Wilco):

> Huh. Yeah that's off, that's from the new Wilco. I'm not really into them so much. The sort of alt-country thing, it's more what some girls are into. Let's see, what else does he have down for music. See, look. Decembrists, Death Cab for Cutie. All too soft for me. Ben Folds, too. At least he's got Bob Marley. (Looking at an image from a film). *Shaun of the Dead*. I loved that movie. I mean, it's really rare that you've got a movie that is scary but cracks you up completely. I saw it like the day it came out and didn't know what to expect but it's definitely on my top ten.

Peter went on to talk about other images on the page of movies, computer games, and references to movies in the lists on the page. In each instance, he referred back to the original film or band or computer game and discussed his response to the film or music, rather than what it made him think of the person who put the information on the page. In addition, while he compared popular culture within categories, for example, noting that the bands listed were too soft for his tastes or that there were several horror films listed on the page, he did not link film and music and computer game references to make any judgments about the page's author. It was not uncommon for students to respond to popular culture on social networking sites or blogs by discussing their own relationship to the work, particularly if it evoked strong emotions in them. Our responses to popular culture content are often inextricable from our experiences and memories of when we first encountered the texts (Jenkins 1992) and consequently can have powerful emotional resonances. We're all familiar with the experience of hearing a song and being transported back to the memories of the summer when that song was popular. The students often maintained an awareness of where an image or song or video clip had originated and how it fit into its original text. When students made such intertextual connections they were almost always about popular culture, rather than about literature or politics, for example.

Responses to popular culture content that respond to the original content rather than the new context are particularly interesting when we consider that, when talking about composing their social networking pages, many students said they used the popular culture lists to tell friends and others about themselves. Sarah said, "When I'm making my page, I'm thinking about people I know and plan to meet. So I think about what the lists and stuff are going to say about me and I want it to be right, to be accurate but not too limited. But I put those things on there for a reason." A number of students spoke about designing their pages to show their particular popular culture interests. Andy, for example, pointed out that he had multiple images and references on his page to the university's sports teams, from a background of a cowboy hat with the team logo on it to images of well-known athletes to links to other sports-related pages. In contrast, Lisa pointed out the posters from plays she loved as dominant images on her pages.

Yet the reason that Sarah and others use popular culture on their pages is not necessarily to remind readers of their connections or opinions about a particular song, film, or television program. The already existing meanings of popular culture texts provide what students often hope will be a convenient shorthand for their blog or social networking site—as well as something fun and entertaining— yet sampling and using such content also allows readers to focus on the original text at the expense of the meaning intended in the new composition. Although some students seemed to sense some of the tension created for them as writers by the use of such meaning-laden popular culture content, none of them focused on it or could articulate the tensions clearly. (They were more able to talk about the tensions they felt in their performances of identity, as I will discuss in chapter 4.) It is clear, however, that the ability to sample and use popular culture easily as a regular component of writing raises different rhetorical challenges for writers and readers than even the already slippery challenge of writing with words.

Just as quickly as students would read popular culture content for the meanings of its original context, they could turn and read the sampled material in its new context. Peter, for example, after reading the page where he discussed the popular culture only in its original context, clicked to another *MySpace* page where the music was hard rock and the movie and computer game lists were oriented toward action and adventure. The author of the page had loaded the results of two online personality quizzes: "Are You Alien or Predator?" and "What Type of Unicorn Are You?" (with the answers being "Alien" and "Blue Sea Unicorn"). Peter laughed and said, "I love it when someone surprises me with something like the unicorn quiz, 'cause it's all sweet and girly. You know it's there for a laugh. Like anything to do with Smurfs. And having it next to the alien is even better be-

cause, you know, what's an alien going to do to a unicorn, right?"
Several factors came into play in determining whether students were
more likely to read popular culture content in the context of the page
or by making connections to its original context. Material and references that surprised the readers, that seemed incongruous with the
purpose of the page or the general tone of the rest of the material—
like a quiz about unicorns—were more likely to draw students' attention to how the content was being used in the context of the overall
page. In a similar way, material that provoked intriguing juxtapositions, such as one page where a video clip from *SpongeBob SquarePants*
was placed among references to more dramatic film and television
using images of DVD covers from *The Wire* and *Lost*, drew a comment
from Catherine when she saw it. "OK, why SpongeBob? All the rest of
this is so serious and dramatic. And it's not even a SpongeBob parody
like the Chinese SpongeBob. It definitely makes me stop and think
about the person and what is going on," she said. Students often click
quickly through webpages, bypassing the mundane in search of the
novel. When they come across startling or unusual juxtapositions, I
will see them slow down, even if only for a few moments, and take
time to try to make some meaning from what they were seeing. Even
if they do not comment on the juxtapositions explicitly, it is clear that,
in an online world bursting with images, video, and sound, it is these
startling or unusual juxtapositions that can break through the flood of
information to engage readers.

Personal pages, whether on social networking sites or by themselves, were more likely to get varied readings. Popular culture content on websites about particular genres or subjects was read more
consistently in the context of the page. A website about a band such
as Coldplay that one student visited obviously was read in the context of the explicit focus of that page. On personal pages, however,
whether popular culture content was read in the context of the page
the student was viewing depended sometimes on whether the reader
knew the author of the page. Students reading pages of friends often
talked more about the material in terms of the context of the page
their friend had produced. Looking at pages of strangers or people
they did not know as well was more likely to produce comments
about the original text, particularly if the reader had a strong connection to the original work. It is not surprising to note that strong connections to the original work, be they emotional or intellectual, also
influenced how people read the images. Someone who liked the *Lord*

of the Rings films was more likely to talk about the original films when seeing an image from them, though not necessarily to the exclusion of talking about the content on the page. Conversely, a *MySpace* page that opened with a song the reader hated could also result in comments about the band as well as the author of the page.

Showing Your Hipness

The interpretation of the material also depended, predictably enough, on whether the reader was familiar with the popular culture content that had been sampled. Sometimes popular culture is sampled and reused because it is broadly understood "common culture"—an image of Darth Vader or Mickey Mouse, for example. Other times, however, popular culture is used to determine insider or outsider status of individuals. For young people who are often obsessed both with the social status and a desire to appear "cool" (or at least not "uncool"), sampling an obscure but hip song lyric or movie clip can be a statement of identity and a test of sorts for the reader.

As Knobel and Lankshear (2007) point out with online memes:

> The playfulness seen in most of these online memes—whether absurdist or aimed at social commentary—taps into shared popular culture experiences and practices. This in turn helps to define certain affinity spaces...by semiotic nods and winks to those "in the know" as it were. "Outsiders" to these spaces will often have difficulty seeing the humor in or point to many of these memes (217).

The cultural shorthand provided by popular culture content is short-circuited by obscure references, which by contrast provide a means of displaying iconoclasm or hipness. Sarah said that inside jokes were sometimes the point of particular quotations because they did establish a sense of status about insider–outsider status and popularity:

> It's kind of an unwritten thing that you want people to see your quotes from movies and from friends because it kind of looks like you—this sounds bad—have more friends and stuff. "Oh, I have inside jokes with this person because we've been quoting this line from this movie and thought it was hilarious and you think that's not funny and you didn't get it." It kind of shows how popular you are sort of. I mean no one ever says that but it does.

Most of the time students skimmed past material with which they seemed unfamiliar, unless it was particularly odd or provocative. One student, Kevin, coming across the skull-like image of the character Killface from the animated series *Frisky Dingo*, wrinkled his brow and said, "What is *that*? That's weird. Why would you put that on your page?" Because unfamiliar content could not be traced backed to its origin, when students did comment on it, their comments focused, like Kevin's, on the context of the page and often the motivation of the author.

Indeed, some students composed pages in hopes of confusing or troubling potential readers. Though some students such as Andy and Lisa described using popular culture themes such as athletics or theater to provide consistency for their pages, others described sampling and composing their pages with an intent to make the pages difficult to read. Angela said the popular culture quotations she put on her *Facebook* page ranged from:

> Serious quotes that I think should be taken seriously and that I believe in. And then there are funny ones, too. Like this one from John Candy or this one from *Saturday Night Live*. I don't want it to be too simple for people to think they know me. I have 450 friends on Facebook and anybody can read my page and some people I know better than others. If they read my page, I want them to have to think about all the parts of me, not just reach a quick conclusion.

The elements that students arrange on their pages contain meanings that are often simultaneously personal and social (Weber and Mitchell 2008) and just as often in tension with each other. Students such as Natalie demonstrated that they understood both the power of the popular culture content but also the rhetorical power of how best to arrange the material on the webpage. Natalie had at the top of her *MySpace* page a grisly image of a tongue being pierced and mutilated, an image taken from a goth heavy metal video. When she opened the page for me, I couldn't help but gasp, prompting her to say, "Yeah, that's what I'm looking for when the page opens. I want to shock people, make them sit up and notice. When I first put it up there I was in a bad mood and I just thought it was cool. But I've decided I like it there, so if people can take this, they can take me and I want to know that." Further down the page, however, she also had images of fairies from an online role-playing game in which she participates, an animation of a bat, gay pride logos, and a video clip from the animated comedy series *Family Guy*. As she scrolled down the page, she had this to say:

So here are some fairies from my game, because I am such a fantasy geek, and to show I'm not completely dark and brutal. I want people to have a sense of all my different interests. Here's my gay pride stuff and I have some weird stuff. Here's my bat, her name is Glowstick and you feed her. And then here is a clip from *Family Guy* that makes me laugh. Peter and some random other person go into the stalls of a bathroom and they start farting out some weird little tune. It's just funny. I figure if you got this far down the page you should get to laugh too if you want.

Natalie's comments reveal an awareness not only of the power of the images she is using on the page but also her awareness of the uses of arrangement, collage, and juxtaposition as rhetorical strategies. As Gunther Kress (2003) has pointed out, new media technologies and the multimodal communications they enable have placed an emphasis on the creation of meaning through the arrangement of elements on a page, or more significantly, on a screen. "Placing something centrally means that other things will be marginal, at least relatively speaking. Placing something at the top of the space means that something else will likely be below. Both these places can be used to make meaning" (2). Where words in print must be read linearly, one at a time, to reveal meaning, multimodal communications on webpages emphasize arrangement in space to create meaning (54). On a webpage, for example, what is visible on the screen when the page opens is considered to be more important than what can be revealed as one scrolls down the page.

Natalie, with her shocking piercing photo at the top of the page, understands the impact this will have as the largest and first image the reader encounters as the page opens. She also understands—and indeed counts on—that some people, shocked by the image, will leave the page quickly. For those who withstand the initial shock, she has constructed the page to offer new clues to her identity and even, in her mind, rewards for taking the time to get past the initial images. Clearly, she understands how each screen of images will look and has composed the material to have a particular meaning in each screen. In addition, she understands both the convention of how webpages, and specifically *MySpace* pages, are read with casual users often only checking out the initial images but more interested readers scrolling down the page bit by bit to discover more about the author. Finally, she realizes that the juxtaposition of different popular culture elements on the page will have particular meanings for the readers. For example, she understands that having the images of fairies and the *Family Guy* video further down the page will soften her identity and be a relief to the reader, just as surely as she would understand that having the fairies as the first images on the page would create a fundamentally different focus for the page.

While students such as Natalie have certainly not abandoned an affection for linear narratives, it is clear that they have also learned how to compose multimodal, associate collages online. For years, proponents of hypertext have urged us to take advantage of new media to teach students how to write in associative, multimodal ways. What students such as Natalie illustrate is that the students have learned how to write this way, think about such writing rhetorically, and are learning it largely outside of school through using sampling and popular culture content. As with any kind of composing, some students were more adept with and reflective about their work than others. But most demonstrated at least a basic understanding that popular culture material had meanings outside of their texts, could be used because of those intertextual connections to carry embedded meaning, or conversely be used to create exclusive social bonds. The students I spoke with and observed used popular culture as the building blocks of collage by consciously using the intertextual connections afforded by the sound, images, video, and print.

Mosaics of Meaning

A useful metaphor for considering these multimodal literacy practices of students is the creation of mosaics of meaning. Although collage is also a useful metaphor, mosaic can differ from collage in that the different pieces are arranged into particular patterns to create meaning. The patterns of mosaics are less free-form than those of collages. In terms of these literacy practices, the patterns that shape the mosaics emerge both from the templates of pages but also from rhetorical patterns.

Barry Brummett (1991) argues that individuals create mosaics of meaning from the swirl of contemporary popular culture they inhabit. In a mass-mediated culture, the model of gathering information from a single text with an identifiable author has been replaced with a mosaic model in which we arrange "bits" of information into mosaics, into patterns, that offer meaning to us. On a given subject, such as global climate change, for example, we take information from multiple sources—television, websites, emails, chatroom comments, radio, newspaper headlines—and pull them together into a pattern that creates for us a coherent narrative about the issue. Indeed, ask a group of people, such as a classroom of students, about an issue and you'll hear them voice their opinions based on the mosaic of the bits they have gleaned from just such a mixture of sources. When we apply such a metaphor to personal pages on social networking sites, we must see the subject of the mosaic as the individual's performance of identity. The bits that students draw on are more often than not popular culture and the rhetorical patterns are what they are learning from friends and the culture at large about what is acceptable to place on such a page.

Attempting to track the nature and origin of all the bits of information in an age with so much information that is shifting all the time is impossible in our contemporary mass-mediated culture. What is possible, Brummett contends, is the investigation and analysis of the patterns we have available to us that enable us to form the bits into meaningful messages. Popular culture content and patterns offer "reservoirs of ways to manipulate signs, of the logics one might use to make meaning; (they demonstrate) patterns for ordering mosaics" (77). This is the way we make meaning from the incessant flow and use of information, particularly online.

If we consider what Natalie and other students are doing when they compose their multimodal pages, we need to be aware that it isn't freeform. They often are conscious of both the sources of the bits of information they appropriate and of the patterns they employ to create new meaning from the pieces they've sampled. To call what these students are doing *cutting-and-pasting* implies a simplicity of action and thought that does not capture the thoughtful and complex nature of these literacy practices. Instead we need to pay attention to the skills students are employing when they sample and compose with popular culture content:

> Appropriation may be understood as a process that involves both analysis and commentary. Sampling intelligently from the existing cultural reservoir requires a close analysis of the existing structures and uses of this material; remixing requires an appreciation of emerging structures and latent potential meanings. Often, remixing involves the creative juxtaposition of materials that otherwise occupy very different cultural niches (Jenkins et al. 2006, 33).

Rhetorical patterns of participatory popular culture provide a foundation for the students' decisions about what materials to sample and use and how to arrange the elements. Of course, on social net-

working sites, the template provided by the site shapes the composing choices, as I will discuss further in chapter 5. Yet even within such
templates, students have to make decisions about how they arrange
the elements on the page and what rhetorical effect that will have on
their readers.

Reading for Plunder

To appropriate and reuse popular culture content through sampling
and mosaic necessitates a different way of approaching the texts as
readers. As I noted in chapter 2, new media technologies have
changed the relationship of audience members to popular culture by
allowing them to respond to producers and other audience members.
The same technologies are changing the popular culture reading practices of many students. For some time, reading in print culture was an
activity that made meaning from a text but did nothing to the text itself, recognizing the autonomy and authority of the writer to create
the text. Readers could interpret and analyze the meaning and structure of texts but regarded the texts as coherent wholes that should
remain that way. New media technologies, however, have resulted in
reading activities that are better described by ideas of textual poaching and bricolage.

Michel de Certeau (1984) argues that it is not enough to study representations of culture separately from individual behavior. Instead
he maintains that we must be aware that "everyday life invents itself
by poaching in countless ways on the property of others" (xii). In
other words, we not only interpret texts in various media to determine their meaning, but we appropriate pieces of the texts and make
new things from them that serve our own interests and experiences.
A simple example is that we might take a phrase from a television
program and make it part of a conversation we are having that will
produce a different meaning than in its original context. We've not
only understood the quotation in the original text, but we've employed it for new meanings, perhaps sincerely, perhaps ironically,
that integrate it into our own experiences to serve our own needs.
This is not a new activity, as anyone who has quoted Shakespeare to
make a point during the past four centuries could attest. But as de
Certeau points out, we might say, "once more unto the breach" (perhaps without ever having seen a production of *Henry V*) in a conversation with a friend as we head to work in the morning, but our

ability to appropriate and reuse pieces of text has until recently been limited by our limited means of production and cultural power. Being able to create and widely distribute a text was the province of individuals or groups who had the cultural and economic capital to print novels, make movies, or create television programs. Consequently, producers and other institutions of the dominant culture—such as schools—not only controlled the production of texts but worked very hard to control the interpretation and uses of such texts. Such efforts at controlling production and meaning continue today. Schools and teachers work to inform, and test, students on specific interpretations of texts, for example. As de Certeau notes:

> Reading is as it were overprinted by a relationship of forces (between teachers and pupils or between producers and consumers) whose instrument it becomes. The use made of the book by privileged readers constitutes it as a secret of which they are the "true" interpreters. It interposes a frontier between the text and its readers that can be crossed only if one has a passport delivered by these official interpreters who transform their own readers (which is also a legitimate one) into an orthodox "literality" that makes other (equally legitimate) readers either heretical (not in conformity with the text) or insignificant (to be forgotten) (171).

The students I talked to still usually considered this the approach to reading that dominated their lives throughout school. Kevin, echoing the words of many, said, "Reading for school is more nerve-wracking and less interesting because you've got to get the way you read it right to satisfy the teacher. Otherwise, your grade is down the tubes." Individual readers, including students in school, are not completely powerless in the face of the efforts of the dominant culture to control meaning. De Certeau reminds us that individuals often continue to read texts for pieces they can "poach" and incorporate into their own experiences for their own ends. Even more explicitly, they may engage in "tactics"—small gestures of creativity and resistance that allow them to take dominant texts and gain some control over them in their own lives. In school, for example, this might be as simple as students sitting at a lunch table coming up with crude parodies of poems they have been assigned in class.

Jenkins (1992) drew on de Certeau's ideas about readings to theorize the activities of fan fiction writers. These fans, who adopt the characters from popular movies and television programs for their own narratives, "appropriate popular texts and reread them in a fashion that serves different interests, as spectators who transform the experience of watching television into a rich and complex participatory culture" (23). Rather than relying either on the producers or culturally recognized "experts" to establish a stable meaning for a text, fans were both reading the original text while at the same time drawing from it to create new texts that would satisfy their own individual and social needs. In a struggle to make these popular culture texts more satisfying and meaningful, "only by integrating media content back into their everyday lives, only by close engagement with its meanings and materials, can fans fully consume the fiction and make it an active resource" (62). Popular culture offers itself more readily to such activities because it is perceived as culturally insubstantial and common. Students have often been drawn to such activities because authority figures such as parents and teachers dismiss popular culture and so do not attempt to teach and assess students on "correct" readings.

Yet the fan culture Jenkins described in 1992 still required a level of commitment and effort to produce fan fiction and other fan texts that was unappealing to most people. Now, however, new media technologies have enabled all audience members to read with an eye toward textual poaching. So students read not just to get meaning in one text as they would in school, but they are, to use de Certeau's metaphor, like nomadic poachers roaming across texts hunting not just for meanings but for pieces they can incorporate and reuse in their everyday lives. Peter described the behavior this way: "I don't usually look around for specific stuff to put on my pages; well, sometimes I want a picture of a band, a specific band. If something hits my eye then I will grab it, even if I didn't go to the page looking for it. That's some of the best stuff—the stuff you find by accident." Natalie's comments were similar: "If I have a goal in mind for what I want to do with my *MySpace* page, then I'll hunt around until I find the right picture or animation to make that happen. But I've always got my eyes open for things I can use when I'm looking at other people's pages." These comments, and many others like them from students, point out another difference in how these students engage in textual poaching from Jenkins's (1992) descriptions of fans. The fans in Jenkins's study tended to focus their participatory reading and writing practices around specific texts, such as a television series like *Star Trek: The Next Generation*. Such texts create the affinity spaces in popular culture that continue to draw varied individuals together around a common interest, as I focus on with fan forums in chapter 2 and fan fiction in chapter 5. The difference for the students I interviewed, when it came to their social networking site pages or their blogs, was that any site they visited could be a potential site for sampling and reusing the material. They often looked for specific images or music to add to a page but just as often composed their pages from what they happened to come across that they found funny or intriguing, or felt would represent some part of their identity. Like hunter–gatherers, they were always reading with one eye scanning for what could be taken and reused for themselves.

Reading as textual poaching, in addition to interpreting texts, is an important element of the process of mosaic that students engage in with popular culture. Textual poaching makes it clear that, while serendipity can play a part in the material students sample, like mosaic artists who must often find the best colors to fit particular patterns, students often search purposefully for the right piece to use on a personal page or blog. At the same time, like mosaic artists who may be limited by the stones and colors available to them, students who could mine the entire online world for material for their pages tend to return to familiar themes, images, and sounds that are meaningful within their social groups. Consequently, video of Maria Callas or quotes from Milton or images of Louis Armstrong are rare objects of student sampling compared with the familiar and quickly readable content from the most popular movies, television, computer games, and music of the moment. The mosaics that students compose, then, are both patterned by the social and discursive forces of mass popular culture and yet made into coherent designs by the students who "fragment texts and reassemble the broken shards according to their own blueprints, salvaging bits and pieces of the found material in making sense of their own social experience" (Jenkins 1992, 26).

Who Owns the Pieces?

How these students put the material that is available to them to their own uses brings to mind de Certeau's description of bricolage. Rather than being helpless before the definitions of the dominant cultural ideologies reproduced in popular culture, these students appropriate pieces as they go along that help them define themselves. Lisa, for example, takes rainbow images from children's websites and uses them as symbols of her lesbian identity on her *MySpace* page. The students make do with what they have to create small moments of resistance to the dominant cultural forces. Even student sampling and reuse of material in ways that are not as explicitly resistant as Lisa's can still be regarded as bricolage in the ways they challenge the concept of ownership of popular culture content. The efforts of the popular culture industries to protect their intellectual property in the face of the sampling and file-sharing possibilities of new media technologies has been much discussed in the popular media over the past decade. Actions by corporations to protect the images and characters of popular franchises such as *Star Wars* and *Harry Potter* from appropriations and use by audience members have been particularly heavy handed and punitive (Jenkins 2006a). Yet, in the face of such efforts, the students I spoke with continue the textual poaching and reuse of images, words, music, and video. Other research has found similar activities in students creating zines (Knobel and Lankshear 2004) or fan fiction (Black 2008) or machinima (Lowood 2008) or mashups and ezines (Willett 2008). To a person, the students brushed off the concerns of intellectual property if they felt they had found material that would help them express themselves, either seriously or ironically.

When I asked Peter if he had concerns about intellectual property issues when he downloaded popular culture content onto his pages, he said:

> I know it matters. I understand the whole file-sharing issue and I know that people who create music or make movies need to make money on what they do. I get that. But to be honest about it, if I find something that works for me, I'm probably going to copy it. The reason for that is that the people who make movies or music, those people, they're going to make their money. I mean it's not going to cost them anything for me to use a picture from a movie. To be honest, it will probably give them more publicity.

The tension in Peter's comment was present in many students' responses. Most had an awareness of some of the issues at stake in intellectual property rights and yet at the same time noted the power of the corporate producer of popular culture as at least a partial justification for their actions. Ashley said, "Sometimes people have gotten in trouble for loading some things on their pages. I've had songs on my *MySpace* page disappear because the artists had a fit. It's no big deal; there's always more songs you can find out there for a page."

Some might regard such comments as Peter's and Ashley's as evidence of a significant moral gap, and it may be so. But before leaping to that judgment, it is important to recognize the resistance in their comments. Students did not see sampling as always justified.

For example, most said they would not copy from another student's blog without mentioning where the text came from. On the other hand, students regarded the producers of popular culture as largely unresponsive and greedy corporations who were fair game for more subversive activities. They enjoyed the material that popular culture producers created but felt that small-scale resistance, the kind of bricolage de Certeau describes, was justified and empowering to them. Ashley said, "I'm not like 'Oh, I'm going to be a huge rebel today and download files.' But I do hate the way the movie studios try to control everything to death and I think those of us who are fans sometimes have a purer sense of the characters and the stories and we have the right to use them too." As Jenkins (1992) notes, poachers don't merely hunt, "they trespass upon others' property; they grab it and hold onto it; they internalize its meanings and remake these borrowed terms" (62). Movies, television, and computer games were regarded by the students as common, unauthored texts, controlled by corporations. Music, with its cultural links to singer–songwriter authorship and artist status was more likely to raise questions of authorship for students. Also, as Buckingham (2008) and others have warned, we should not over-romanticize the resistance of youth to mass popular culture. There is no doubt that students still find pleasure in consuming popular culture and that it has significant influence on discourse, ideology, and identity. It was clear, however, that while not their primary motivation, students recognized a subversive pleasure in sampling and reusing popular culture content.

Fast and Fresh

Another change that new media technologies have brought about in students' sampling and reuse of popular culture content is the speed at which such activities can happen. If textual poaching is easier now than it was fifteen years ago, it is also much faster. Decorating a school locker with photos of pop stars—finding the photos in magazines, cutting them out, taping them to the door—is ponderously slow compared to the ability to click on an electronic image, copy it, and paste it on a webpage.

Mass popular culture has long depended on speed for part of its appeal. Delivering content quickly and keeping it fresh has been promoted by producers and rewarded by audience members since the early days of film and radio. Technological innovations such as television remote controls have only intensified audience members' willingness to roam quickly looking for something rewarding and new, and resulted in faster editing of television programs to keep the audience from zapping away (Gleick 1999). The conventional complaint about popular culture is that has led to shorter attention spans. Yet such a complaint does not seem accurate when placed against the evidence of young people sitting through three-hour movies such as the *Lord of the Rings* or *Harry Potter* films or spending hours on end playing a computer game. What has changed about these texts is not their length but their speed. Comparing the number of edits in a contemporary film, even a drama, with a film from fifty years ago reveals how the pace of presenting information has changed much more than the length of texts. Our attention spans have not become shorter but faster (Williams 2002). We have become accustomed to an increased speed of images, speed of delivery, and the speed with which common vocabularies and icons arise in the culture at large.

Students who are aware of their own preferences for fast and fresh material as audience members and readers incorporate such values into their online composing. One illustration of this is the frequency with which they revise, or "tweak," their pages on their social networking sites. Angela said she tweaks her page several times a week, sometimes daily:

> When I first set it up, I didn't put a lot of time into it because I didn't want to put too much information on it because I was still wary about how it would work and who would be able to see my profile. But now I update it pretty regularly. You know, I find a new interest or a movie I like or a new quote I think is funny, I'll just go there right away and update it.

Brianna made similar comments: "I could be updating all the time or sending people stuff like a punch or a drink or a flower. I have to really be careful or I could be updating my page all the time." While most students did not report tweaking their pages as regularly as Angela or Brianna, they did say that they tried to keep their social networking pages or blogs fresh. Kevin said, "If people are going to visit your page, you want to make sure they have something interesting to look at. Nobody wants to be boring," and Amy said that if she went to a person's blog several times without seeing any updated posts, she would stop visiting the site. "There is so much to see that I don't have time to be checking in on places just to see that nothing has changed. That's really boring. If you're going to have a blog, you've got to keep it going or you're going to lose anyone who's interested."

These student comments reflect the same kinds of concerns about keeping an audience interested and entertained that preoccupy mass media producers. The same concerns that keep media producers putting new movies in theatres every week or editing television programs to keep people from zapping away keep students tweaking and revising their personal pages and blogs.

Popular websites such as *Amazon.com*, *YouTube*, and the *Internet Movie Database* constantly rotate the images and features on their homepages. They know that they have only seconds before people visiting the page decide they have seen the information already and click away. Students demonstrated a similar understanding of the stakes of having their readers regard their pages with been-there-done-that disdain. Mitchell said, "Even if it's only my friends, I don't want my page to bore them. They might stop coming back." As Susannah Stern (2008) notes, students' response to audience needs of freshness and entertainment is similar to that of mass media producers:

> By appropriating music and images and incorporating links to retail and media sites they indicate that consumer culture provides accessible and appealing tools not only for self-preservation and subcultural affiliation, but also for entertaining the audience. And they try to keep content new and fresh in order to keep audiences coming back for more, considering frequent updates a sign of a good page or blog (109).

The desire for speed and novelty is easy to see online, such as the flash-fire popularity of many viral videos or memes. For several days or perhaps even weeks, everyone may be talking about—or at least sending links for—a video of a person shaving with a banana or a Lego version of "Thriller." Before that particular video or meme begins to fade in popularity, a new set has emerged. Students understand that freshness, newness, when a page was updated, and how it capitalizes on the latest trend or application is particularly important to keep their audiences interested. A need to be "cool," to be in on the "in-jokes" as I noted previously, or at least not to be "lame" is a long-standing concern of adolescents that has transferred easily to the world of social networking sites (boyd 2008). Concerns about staying cool or hip play into the consumer culture strategies of mass popular culture and are subsequently adopted as rhetorical moves on students' webpages and blogs.

The need to address audience desires for freshness and speed—or "endless originality" (Goldhaber 1997)—contributes to an online "attention economy" where the flood of information online results in ever-increasing efforts by individuals to "attract, sustain, and build attention under new media conditions" (Lankshear and Knobel 2003, 109). Different strategies are emerging and evolving online to catch and hold the attention of readers whose commitment to many websites they drop in on may be tenuous at best. Certainly, keeping a site updated, fast, and new is an important strategy. Flashing ads, animation, invitations to participation, and familiar templates are among the many ways online writers try to draw and keep the attention of readers (Lankshear and Knobel 2003). What also works in terms of getting attention, and what students have figured out, is the use of popular culture content. Advertisers long ago figured out that using celebrities or other popular culture content and references would draw attention to their products. Students decorating lockers with photos or wearing a T-shirt with a band name or catchphrase on it were seeking attention as they were making statements about identity. Popular culture content draws attention, evokes emotions, and, if it is new enough—or old and ironic enough—establishes your hipness.

Clearly, students employ popular culture content while composing blogs and personal pages, among other reasons, as a way of drawing and keeping attention. For example, Mitchell has a large photo of Godzilla atop his blog, Jeff has a cartoon image of a character from *The Incredibles* he uses as a signature when he makes blog comments, Natalie has the bloody pierced tongue from a music video on her *MySpace* page, Jenny has a *YouTube* video of the "Evolution of Dance" at the top of her page, while Tony has a flashing background of a university sports logo. When asked about why they chose these items to place where they did, all of these students included in their reasons the ability of the material to draw the attention of others. They talked about being conscious that they wanted material on their pages that would make people stop and pay attention to the rest of their pages. "I use it like a movie commercial. You get people to notice and wonder and then maybe they read more. And if it's my friends, at least I get them to laugh," Mitchell said.

Blurring Lines of Reading and Writing

Students' sampling and use of popular culture content as they compose webpages and blogs has several implications for the ways in which we think about their literacy practices.

First, the practices of textual poaching and mosaic blur the distinctions between reading and writing. De Certeau (1984) argued that readers who read as poachers neither simply accepted or rejected the author's meaning and position but instead gathered fragments from readings and combined them with their own experiences to make new meanings. What Jenkins noticed dedicated fans doing almost twenty years ago was taking the process de Certeau describes and turning those new meanings into texts: "Fans do not simply consume preproduced stories; they manufacture their own fanzine stories and novels, art prints, songs, videos, performances, etc." (45). What is clear about students today is that as even the most casual of fans are sampling and reusing popular culture in their own texts, it is difficult to know where reading ends and multimodal writing begins. As I noted at the beginning of this chapter, students can copy and use popular culture material with the same ease and facility with which they type words—and sometimes the typing is even slower.

The students I interviewed read most online popular culture texts with one eye on appropriation and composed their blogs and personal webpages the same way. I watched Amy reading music blogs she liked to visit and when one of them had a link to a *YouTube* video of an obscure band she liked, she clicked to the site, watched the video, clicked three more times, and added the link to her own blog, which had been open the whole time. "Cool," she said to no one in particular as she began to write on her blog about why she had added the video and what she thought of the band. To label these literacy practices as *multitasking* misses the way the work is focused on reading and writing. Amy may not be composing in a single sustained effort at her computer, but she is doing more than just surfing the web. Literacy scholars often talk about the connections between reading and writing but must pay more attention to the practices of these students whose fluid movement between the two practices can be so rapid as to make the actions almost indistinguishable. The literacy practices of reading and writing with popular culture, focusing on intertextual connections and speed, are not familiar to many literacy educators.

The second implication is the way in which creating texts from sampled popular culture material further destabilizes cultural conceptions of authorship. The still-powerful cultural images of the author as solitary genius creating unique and stable print texts does not hold up well in the face of sampling, mosaic, collaboration, and constant revision. Postmodern theorists have for years discussed contemporary writing as a product of pastiche and of the contemporary writer as a person just assembling pieces of already existing texts. But students' online textual poaching and writing show how the explicit practices of such theorists have become an integrated, normalized part of their lives.

The students I interviewed and observed knew that the texts they were creating were simultaneously theirs and yet not completely theirs. Mitchell said it best: "When I put up a *South Park* picture on my page, sometimes I wonder if it belongs to me now because I'm using it the way I want, not the way they want. Like, I know it's still theirs. Though I didn't get it off their page. It really belongs to both me and them." Though students such as Mitchell understand that they are the ones composing the pages, they also are aware that much of the material on their pages was created by others in other contexts. Like a more explicit expression of the heteroglossia theorized by Bakhtin about the novel, the students realize that there are multiple voices at work in their texts at any moment. But they also feel the desire and the permission to make such content their own, in the same way that people alter memes before passing them on (Knobel and Lankshear 2007). As authors, then, students are consciously composing with pieces created by others that they find and reassemble to make their own meanings. In addition, they realize that the pieces they have used are fair game for someone else to use and so the elements of their personal pages or blogs may end up on countless pages of people they may never meet.

Finally, the networked environment of online writing enables students to collaborate with and receive feedback from others with ease and speed. Such collaborative capabilities of online communication have been discussed by many scholars in both home and school contexts. What the consideration of popular culture sampling brings to these considerations is how much of the collaboration, particularly on social networking pages, happens with popular culture. Students send each other links to videos, or links to images they think a friend will like, or share songs with their friends. On *Facebook* now students send each other pieces of *flair*—buttons with messages that are a parody from the film *Office Space*—or bumper stickers with popular culture images and funny phrases on them. When it comes to sharing content, only personal photos rival popular culture material. Building a personal page, then, may become a collaborative effort as content is gathered by the student author but also provided by friends.

Friends, and often strangers, also provide comments on pages and blogs that at the least let the author know someone is reading and at the most lead to revisions, more writing, or conversation. Weber and Mitchell (2008) and Willett (2008) maintain that this kind of response not only leads to rethinking and revising texts but also encourages students to reflect on the work they produce and the identities they perform. Such reflection makes many of the students much more self aware of their reading and writing processes than we might expect. Of course, not every student thought deeply about the rhetorical choices involved in sampling and writing with popular culture content. Yet, as the comments by the students in this book make clear, students do think about how they compose with popular culture and reflect on the product of their work and the responses it engenders. Again, such comments may not always be phrased in rhetorical terms we value, but they do demonstrate students' concerns with the effects of what they read and write.

Conclusion

As the means of production of popular culture have expanded from those with substantial financial resources to potentially any member of the audience, the sense of authorship and ownership of popular culture texts have also changed. Now that online technologies have made the production of popular culture both affordable and relatively effortless, any person can take part in it by mashing up images and songs, creating machinima, or even just putting a soundtrack to one's identity by choosing a song to play when a *MySpace* page opens. Who among us, after all, has not dreamed of having our own personal soundtrack? They "possess not simply borrowed remnants snatched from mass culture, but their own culture built from the semiotic raw materials the media provides" (Jenkins 1992, 49). The desire to take ownership of a text regardless of its author, and the confidence and authority to do so, is another mark of convergence culture. Interactive media have not only created the opportunity to appropriate texts and reconstruct them but also the confidence and expectation within students to take such control of texts. Although it may not always be accurate, they experience a "strong sense of their own autonomy and of their right to make their own choices and follow their own paths" (Buckingham 2008, 17). This participation, however, is not always solitary and more often than not is connected to communities of participatory audience members who either can respond to any text or connect their interests and knowledge with other fans.

If students are writing with popular culture content, if they are sampling and reusing material, if they are composing with an awareness of rhetorical patterns, if they are aware of its intertextual connections and the push to keep information fresh, then we need to be paying attention to the ways in which their literacy practices are transforming. The ways in which they are engaging in these practices outside the classroom are fundamentally changing how they perceive reading and writing. If they are changing their attitudes and practices in terms of how they poach from other texts or how they perceive authorship, then whether they are making the connections or not, this influences how they are thinking about literacy when they enter our classrooms. It is essential that we engage in genuine and respectful conversations with students about how they are going about the new work of composing.

CHAPTER 4

"Which *South Park* Character Are You?"

Popular Culture and Online Performances of Identity

If I handed out sheets of paper with the heading "About Me" on them to a group of writing teachers and asked them to fill them out, I've little doubt that most would fill the page with expository passages about themselves, their backgrounds, accomplishments, family descriptions, and so on. Every *MySpace* page has a section titled "About Me" where the person creating the page is invited, similarly, to write expository, biographical descriptions. Yet the "About Me" sections on the *MySpace* pages of university students are often among the least used, least detailed, and least informative parts of the page.

> Here is Tony's: "Hey! How are ya? Well a little about me. I'm a pretty laid back guy for the most part. I enjoy hanging out with my buds and kinda just relaxing. I just like to go out and have fun, but I know my limits. But feel free to talk."
>
> Or Jenny's: "Oh, you know me. Just a girl who likes the sun on her face and the smell of popcorn. Say 'hi' if you want. Maybe I'll answer. Maybe not."
>
> Or Ashley's, which just has her name in glittering type.

The brevity of these "About Me" entries might lead a person unfamiliar with *MySpace* to believe that the pages reveal little about their creators. But the truth is that the pages are filled with information that the writer of the page has composed to construct a performance of identity. This information is drawn from multiple media and, very often, directly connected to popular culture.

In this chapter, I focus on *MySpace* and *Facebook* pages and the students who created them. When I interview students, their answers to questions of intent, audience, and rhetorical choices vary, but what is common on these students' personal pages is their reliance on popular culture content and references they can appropriate from other sites to enable them to compose their identities and read the identities of others. They use popular culture icons, catchphrases, music, text, and film clips in postmodern, fragmented collages that present selves that seem simultaneously sentimental and ironic. The construction of these pages illustrates how popular culture practices that predate online technologies have been adopted and flourished with new technologies that allow content to flow across media as well as increase the ease of audience participation. The intertextual nature of popular culture texts creates opportunities for multiple readings of social networking webpages in ways that destabilize the identity students believe they have created. These multiple readings create ambivalence for students who realize that their practices in composing pages online may be in conflict with how they read other pages, and how their own pages are read.

Identity on the Page or Screen

Issues of identity have been important areas of discussion in both literacy and popular culture. Composing texts, whether in print or in multiple modes, requires deliberate decisions about how identity is going to be communicated, just as interpreting texts always includes making decisions about the identity of an author. Though the cultural contexts may vary, we are always negotiating identity when we read and write. Even when writers try not to reveal explicitly personal information, the audience then reads the text to a default identity according to the cultural context. For example, for scholarly writing that attempts to be detached and impersonal, the default identity remains the white male in the lab coat (or in the humanities and social sciences, perhaps it is the tweed jacket). In the choices we make about audience, how we choose and arrange words and images, what we choose to disclose about ourselves, we are making choices that both emerge from and shape identity.

Accepting that literacy is a social practice is to accept that identity is central to both how texts are created and how they are interpreted. What we perceive we are allowed to write and read, the resources we can employ in our reading and writing, the ways in which we present identities in texts are all shaped by the social and cultural contexts in which we live. As Barton and Hamilton (1998) maintain, literacy practices are influenced by social rules. Such rules

> Regulate the use and distribution of texts, prescribing who may produce and have access to them. They straddle the distinction between individual and social worlds, and literacy practices are more usefully understood as existing in the relationships between people, within groups and communities, rather than as a series of properties residing in individuals (7).

Ethnographies of literacy practices (Heath 1983; Street 1995; Barton and Hamilton 1998; Gregory and Williams 2000; Pandey 2006) have offered extensive evidence of the complex and powerful interrelationships of literacy and identity. Rather than reveal a single authentic "self," such research has emphasized that our performances of identity through literacy may be shifting and are always contingent on the cultural context. Context determines our ability to make meaning from language, as well as the material and cultural resources to create and interpret texts (Gee 2004). Regardless of the genre or the technology, when a literacy event occurs an identity is performed and it is important to consider the possibilities and effects of such performances.

What Gee (1990) says about "Discourse" is also appropriate to questions of literacy in that reading and writing act as "a sort of 'identity kit' which comes with the appropriate costume and instructions on how to act, talk, and often write so as to take on a particular social role that others will recognize" (142). Online writing is deeply connected with social roles and identities, even more so for secondary and university students who are in particularly important and often turbulent years of social and emotional development. Adolescents are struggling toward understanding their sense of "self," in both physical and psychological terms. Their performances of identity and their relationships with social groups are under constant negotiation and often significant alteration. It is not unusual to see adolescent identities shift remarkably over a single school term as social and personal circumstances change (de Pourbaix 2001).

As adolescent identities shift, so do their perceptions of literacy practices. Where almost any form of reading and writing is praised in young children, by middle school and beyond, the cultural and institutional limitations on how literacy is defined become more pronounced. Literacy in school and the larger culture, very often, is restricted to the reading and writing that accomplishes work. Reading a textbook or a literary novel is acceptable; reading a romance or science fiction novel is not. Schools then reinforce larger dominant cultural attitudes about literacy that are based largely on issues of social class and cultural capital. Writing and reading that emphasizes detachment and aesthetic or analytical appreciation is valued, and writing and reading that evokes emotions or is sentimental is not. Consequently, most people would see reading a textbook or writing a research paper as evidence of literacy but not writing Christmas cards or reading a comic book.

As the last example illustrates, literacy practices connected to popular culture—unless they are detached analytic critique—are dismissed by school and the dominant culture as frivolous (Newkirk 1997). Even as students described their online reading and writing about popular culture with much more enthusiasm and authority, when asked to define literacy, they did not include this pleasurable, emotional, out-of-school reading and writing for which they were highly motivated. Distinctions of race, gender, and—perhaps most of all—social class contribute to the gap in what is considered legitimate literacy practices. Reading and writing that evokes emotions or uses images or video or takes a more explicitly personal approach to a text is regarded as being "easy" and lacking the detachment and rigor of the work assigned in schools. As I pointed out in chapter 2, detachment and aesthetic appreciation of texts are perceived as demonstrating a higher social class status (Bourdieu 1984). Mass popular culture is almost always regarded as the domain of those from a more common and less intellectual social class. When they are in school, many in our culture, including students, are encouraged to discount and apologize for the direct pleasure and emotion they find in popular culture.

Like all literacy practices, then, those connected with popular culture are formed and perceived through our cultural constructions of identity. Often, issues of race, social class, gender, and sexual orientation are explicit in popular culture. For example, the computer game industry and audience has been overwhelmingly male and this has been reflected both in the kinds of games that have been created, such as first-person shooters, as well as in the way young people approach and interact with the games. Though students such as Natalie who is an avid player of a fantasy only role-playing game called *Furcadia* illustrates how the gender balance of gaming culture is changing. Also, as I noted in chapter 2, people are drawn to online affinity spaces, then interact with others on fan forums and lists based on shared identity expectations.

Locker Decorations and T-Shirts

Issues of identity and popular culture certainly predate online technologies. Mass popular culture has led people to make statements or judgments about identity and taste based on the popular culture references of those they met. A person might ask new acquaintances about the movies they had seen or look through their record collections as a way of evaluating potential social relationships. Similarly, people appropriated popular culture images and references in their daily identity performances. Part of the allure of mass popular culture has always been the identification of audience members with celebrity as people performed identities through public appropriation of celebrity images. For example, students decorated school lockers with photos of celebrities or wore rock concert T-shirts to connect the attributes of the popular culture reference to their own identities. Consequently, the high school girl with the preppy pop star's photos pasted all over her locker and the boy walking down the hall wearing a heavy metal band T-shirt might give each other one glance but, on seeing the popular culture references they had appropriated, not bother with a second.

The performance of identity obviously is always a social phenomenon. Thus, popular culture has not only been an element of identity construction but has also been a central part of creating community in contemporary society. Clearly, mass popular culture has created common cultural references that are shared by millions of people who may have never met. Joshua Meyrowitz (1985) noted that the casual discussion of popular television programs has served the same social function as conversations about the weather in terms of providing material of which everyone could have both some knowledge and an opinion. Popular culture has also provided the basis for social activities (groups that get together to watch television programs such as *Sex and the City* or parties that took place when it was revealed "who shot J.R." on *Dallas*) or shared social interests.

In the general population, such casual interactions with popular culture have been widespread. More intense, inter-media and interactive uses of popular culture such as fan clubs or fan magazines existed before online technologies, though they were the province of a much smaller group of devoted "fans" back when that term and such behaviors had more derogatory connotations. Before the advent of interactive online technologies, writing fan fiction, attending a fan convention, or belonging to a fan club required a commitment of time, emotion, and resources beyond that of more casual members of the audience. Still, such devoted fans existed and did engage in such interactive activities of textual poaching (Jenkins 1992) in regard to mass popular culture texts. The activities of fans were motivated both by the desire to appropriate control of the popular culture text as well as the opportunity to become part of a "collective identity, to forge an alliance with a community of others in defense of tastes which, as a result, cannot be read as totally aberrant or idiosyncratic" (23). As people have read and adopted popular culture texts to their social contexts, popular culture has long served functions of both identity construction and community building.

Finding community through shared popular culture interests is, again, a long-standing phenomenon for young people. People have identified communities through their statements and interests about popular culture. Liking particular movies or television programs or bands created spaces through which people could not only identify shared interests but also could perform identity through the popular culture texts. For example, young people feeling particularly alienated may be drawn to punk or goth bands and fashions. Other young people connected more to books than sport may be drawn to the *Harry Potter* books and movies as texts that celebrate school and learning. Popular culture communities are also created by exclusivity and rejection. A group of people may find common ground by deriding a particular band or program, particularly if it has become largely popular in the culture. The preferences of people for their own popular culture preferences over others may become intense—so that Rolling Stones fans disdained the Beatles or *Star Wars* and *Star Trek* fans argue for the superiority of their favorite science fiction franchise. Even university professors engage in such identity performances by professing to ignore all popular culture except public broadcasting.

The elements of inter-media and interactive popular culture that Jenkins (2006a) emphasizes as central to convergence culture existed before online technologies. Consequently, online technologies did not create the desire for such activities but rather provided opportunities and media that enabled more people to engage in such activities more easily. It is not difficult to see that fan webpages seem so like fan clubs or that online fan forums seem like larger watercooler conversations.

Online and new media technologies have not only expanded the abilities of people to participate in popular culture by making it easier and faster for everyone to engage in activities once the province of the most committed fans but also created the possibilities for performing different identities at the same time. One element of online activity that has fascinated people from the first days of electronic bulletin boards is the opportunity it offers for playing with identity. As it was so neatly encapsulated by Peter Steiner (1993) in his famous cartoon, where one dog at a computer says to another dog, "On the Internet, nobody knows you're a dog." When they are online, people can discard or transform many of the "semiotics of identity" that define their daily lives and portray themselves as somehow other than they are in their daily lives (Thomas 2007). Online, people can alter identities and do for a variety of reasons—safety, play, disguise, harassment, or hiding the fact they are fans. In participatory popular culture, some of the more popular activities, such as fan fiction, fan forums and lists, online game playing, and posting videos and comments on *YouTube* often involve people using pseudonyms or otherwise transforming their identities. For example, on fan forums, people sometimes use a title that pertains to the program or film or band about which they are writing, say "fanoffrodo" for *Lord of the Rings,* or just one that strikes their fancy, such as "gossipguerilla." There is often a profile link through which people can provide some information, such as age or nationality, but just as often the profile spaces are not filled out.

As with the famous Internet dog, it can be difficult to determine the identity characteristics of people who post online or to verify whether the information people do provide is accurate. A student posting fan fiction might alter her age on the profile to look older and get different readings of her work. On multi-user role-playing sites, such as *SecondLife* or *World of Warcraft,* the larger point is to create avatars that play with identity. Yet when the point of the site is not to play with identity, such as a fan forum or fan fiction site, people often want to protect their full identities but at the same time be honest about their ideas and emotions. As Genevieve put it, "I did conceal some of the stuff because I didn't want people to look at it and judge me....The type of stuff I put in there was really limited. I didn't reveal a whole lot about myself because I didn't want people—a certain type

of person—to contact me, you know." For the readers of the posts or
narratives, however, there is no way to determine who the person is
except for discursive and rhetorical cues that may or may not be accurate for placing a person in terms of identity characteristics. People
may try to create digital bodies, to write themselves into being using
words and images and video, but such "digital bodies are fundamentally coarser, making it far easier to misinterpret what someone is expressing" (boyd 2008, 129). We might imagine that a writer of a post
using aggressive language and unconventional grammar and spelling
is male and has less formal education, but we could also be very
wrong in our assumptions.

As *MySpace* and *Facebook* pages make clear, however, to say that
people can play with identity online does not necessarily mean that
their play is detached from their offline lives. As Angela Thomas
(2007) argues, composing identities online through the semiotic resources is inextricable from our embodied reactions and emotions.
Our desires and anxieties over what we compose online as well as our
emotional responses are very much part of our embodied identities.
Other research (Stern 2008) has indicated that students can use posting online or composing personal pages as an outlet for expressing
powerful emotions in a cathartic or therapeutic way. What writing
and reading with participatory popular culture online does is connect
such emotions not only with representations of self but also with intertextual representations of popular culture content. In this way, the
individual's identity is mediated through the texts he or she com-
poses by drawing on and appropriating a variety of other resources,
as I illustrated in chapter 3. For example, the photos on a *Facebook* or
MySpace page of the author with friends and family are read with the
images of movie or music stars to create an identity through the juxtaposition of the images. If the images of a female student are accom-
panied by images of female pop stars or athletes, for example, the
celebrity photos can be read as "an extension or projection of their
bodies, a desiring or coveting of another's appearance" (Weber and
Mitchell 2008, 31). It is not as simple as drawing a simple line between
online and offline identities. Indeed, for many young people, "there is
no dichotomy of online and offline, or virtual and real—the digital is
so much intertwined into their lives and psyche that the one is en-
tirely enmeshed with the other" (Thomas 2007, 163). For students
composing identities online, then, there is both the familiar and
strange, the embodied and the detached, all of which can create ten-

sions as they struggle to determine how their online texts will be received.

Social Networking Sites and Templates of Identities

It is well accepted in the rhetoric and composition community that both definitions of literacy and performances of identity are complex social phenomena situated in cultural contexts. Those working with online technologies have extended these ideas to the performance of identities on webpages that are instantly accessible to people across town or around the world. The emergence of *MySpace* and *Facebook* has created an explosion in the number of people posting personal webpages. The ease with which the templates of these social networking websites allow individuals to create personal sites means that such expressions of identity have suddenly become available to anyone, not just people who can write HTML code or even use point-and-click web writing software. Although the templates may be criticized for the limitations they place on composing texts (and I will discuss the role of templates in student literacy practices more fully in chapter 5), there is no doubt that the ease and predictability of the templates have encouraged wider creation and consumption of such webpages with both *MySpace* and *Facebook* claiming users in the multiple millions.

The *MySpace* and *Facebook* pages of many high school and college students include the kinds of material that have regularly shown up on personal webpages in the past, such as photos of friends and family; they remind us how online texts draw from preceding genres such as locker doors or yearbooks or diaries. What is distinctive about the webpages on these social networking sites is how much more material and emphasis there is on popular culture. Most of them have a great deal of popular culture-related content, often comprising more than half the information presented on the page and often numbering between fifty and seventy-five distinct popular culture elements.

The templates that shape *MySpace* and *Facebook* pages raise a chicken-and-egg question about the influence of popular culture in the performance of students' identities online. The templates ask people to think of their identities in terms of popular culture references with the requests for lists of favorite movies, television programs, and books, with the capability to choose a song to play when the page opens, and with the capability to load images and video from other

do you think social networks is beneficial for students?

sources. We shouldn't be surprised; that's how people respond to the templates. Still, it is easy to see why these social networking sites set themselves up to emphasize popular culture content if we again think about how popular culture texts serve as the common cultural touch-stones by which we first judge other people. If when we initially meet people we often ask about their tastes in movies or music or we scan their bookshelves, it is a natural move by *MySpace* and *Facebook* to replicate such information on their pages. Students such as Sarah talked about using the pages to gather just such information about people before meeting them in person:

> I think you can learn a lot. At least more than you could if I just met you, you know....If you're going to meet someone, if you're going to go on a date, that gets annoying. What books do you like, what movies do you like? What's your favorite quote? That's not stuff that people say anymore, I don't know if they used to but we don't really talk like that. So it's good to already have that information and then if you are going to like meet someone the first time it does start conversations because you already know what type of music you like, I already know what type of movies you like and I can always bring that up and I've done that before. Been like, "Oh, I saw that you like this on *Facebook*, I love that movie."

The popularity of the sites indicates that the decision to construct the templates around popular culture contents resounds with users who are comfortable with this approach. I've yet to see a student's *MySpace* or *Facebook* page that does not have the popular culture lists filled in, though I'm sure they exist. Even when other forms of identi-fication are asked, like political or religious affiliations on *Facebook*, they are not filled in as regularly and, perhaps more significantly, they offer users only a few predetermined choices on drop-down menus rather than the ability to create an individual list. Nor are there options available for other lists that might be used to construct identities, for example, "most important social issues," or "places I have lived" or "childhood illnesses."

In addition, on both social networking sites, lists of popular cul-ture references are linked so that, for example, by clicking on the name of a band on *MySpace*, one can connect to the band's page or, on *Facebook*, to others who have also listed the band. Such linking en-courages thinking about popular culture preferences in terms of communities of others who share the same tastes. The capability of online technologies to facilitate the affinity spaces around popular culture texts is a key element of convergence culture that influences the reading of personal pages, as I will illustrate later in the chapter.

What also makes the lists of references on social networking sites different than conversation one might strike up with a new acquaintance is the capability of online technologies to publish the information for a broader audience. This is another instance where media technologies and popular culture practices converge to create new concepts of performing identity. The popular culture content and references on social networking pages are available for others, casual acquaintances, or even sometimes strangers, who encounter it in contexts that perhaps lead to significantly different interpretations than the authors intended. Students creating webpages on social networking spaces do so with the expectation that others will not only visit the page but respond to them and the page's content. Just as they often will respond to the popular culture content they encounter, students expect friends to make judgments and comments about their choice of songs, images, or video or to respond to fan forum ideas or fan fiction stories. The question of how the presence of an audience beyond the local influences how students regard identities on these sites is an important one to consider in thinking about convergence culture, and one that can provoke students' anxieties as I will discuss later. Such performances of identity through popular culture content that reach beyond the local are changing the way students compose and read their identities on such pages.

Reading Friends and Strangers

Ashley's *MySpace* page is a fairly representative example. As is true with many pages, a song plays when her page is opened; her page's song is by pop musician Josh Groban. She has lists of favorite movies (*Pirates of the Caribbean, Star Wars, Madagascar, Dirty Dancing,* etc.), music (Josh Groban, Justin Timberlake, Nickelback, Nichole Norderman, Green Day, etc.), books (the *Harry Potter* series, *The DaVinci Code, the Bible*), and television (*Charmed, Veronica Mars,* etc.). Embedded in the lists are images of some of the films and television series she mentions, such as *Eragon, The Lord of the Rings, Pirates of the Caribbean,* and *Charmed*). The two largest images on the page are under the heading of people she wants to meet. There, you find a large photo of Orlando Bloom reclining on a couch, shirt unbuttoned to the waist, and Johnny Depp in *Pirates of the Caribbean*. In addition, Ashley has downloaded from another site a questionnaire about personal preferences that includes popular culture questions such as her favorite CD or favorite candy bar. The page also includes other images, such as an American flag, and a statement of support for U.S. soldiers; the page's background is an image of an angel with a rosary draped over its shoulders.

Other students' *MySpace* pages have other forms of popular culture content in addition to the kinds on Ashley's page. For example, Mitchell's page includes the results of online personality quizzes he has taken on sites such as *Quizilla*. These quizzes allow him to download the image and description of his results. He has, among others, the results of "What *South Park* Character Are You?" (Kyle), "What *Pirates of the Caribbean* Character Are You?" (Barbossa), and the kind of rock star he is most like (punk rocker). Jenny's *MySpace* page includes downloaded music videos, including the video of Fatboy Slim's "Weapon of Choice," and the video of "The Evolution of the Dance," which became hugely popular on *YouTube*.

I first asked students how they read the *MySpace* and *Facebook* pages of their friends and people they had only just met. Although the responses varied in terms of what students looked at first, they were surprisingly consistent in the way the students interpreted the authors' performances of identity. Shannon, for example, paid particular attention to the song on a person's *MySpace*:

> As for their song, I listen to music a lot so that tells me a lot about them. What kind of song they would like. Maybe more is that it tells me what kind of song they would put up on their page for me to see. Because if it's more of a rap song, then it's not so much for me. You can tell a lot about a person by the song.

Although Jenny also paid attention to the song, she mentioned other items that also helped her interpretation of the page:

> You can tell from their quotes if they have a perverted sense of humor, depending on what their quotes say. Or music-wise you can tell if you like the same genre. If someone has a lot of rap listed, I won't get along with them as well because I'm not the biggest rap person. Rap or country. Usually, I think by figuring out what a person listens to, you can figure out more about them. There are some things you can just tell in an instant. If they list a lot of Disney movies, it's going to be a little weird to talk to them.

Though the popular culture elements that drew students' attention varied, they all mentioned that it had an influence on how they read the page owner's identity. The only other element mentioned by a significant number of the students were personal photographs placed on the page. Popular culture influenced how people read identities on the pages, and also the judgments such readings led them to make about others. As Jenny and Shannon mention in their quotations, their judgments about someone they did not know well could be shaped by the popular culture content included on the page. Some of the students even mentioned the shock of looking at a friend's *MySpace* or *Facebook* page to find popular culture preferences that surprised them or seemed inconsistent with the person they thought they knew. Brianna said:

> I was looking the other day (at a friend's page) and they had Lil' Wayne on there and I was like "Wow, you wouldn't even have thought they liked Lil' Wayne." I was like, "I am so sorry but seriously like, I said look at her!" It was a girl too, she doesn't even look like she like even knows who Lil' Wayne is. It was like her number one favorite artist, she was obsessed with Lil' Wayne, I thought it was so funny.

Another student likened such revelations to "guilty secrets," and Shannon noted that "Some of the people I've known since long before *MySpace* have things on their pages that I can hardly believe and I think 'What is that?' or 'That doesn't make any sense' or 'I don't like that.' I try not to let it make me like them any less, but it makes you think twice about them anyway."

Again, the judgments people make about the popular culture preferences of others are nothing new. We have all been shocked at the revelation that a movie we loved is one a close friend loathed. Yet as I noted previously, in the past, those judgments were made most often in face-to-face interactions, one person at a time and usually only about one form of popular culture at a time. The performance of identity though popular culture forms on *MySpace* and *Facebook* pages, however, happens in a virtual space, to an audience that may or often may not be known to the writer, and offers multiple pieces of popular culture content that are read both quickly and in relation to each other.

James Gee (2004) has noted how interactive popular culture has allowed for the creation of "affinity spaces." These affinity spaces, which Gee argues can be virtual or physical such as websites or fan magazines, bring people together by a shared interest or activity. Affinity spaces allow individuals "to any degree they wish, small or large, affiliate with others to share knowledge and gain knowledge that is distributed and dispersed across many different people, places, Internet sites, and modalities (73). Interactive popular culture has allowed the creation of multiple affinity spaces for any single popular culture text or interest, such as the television program *Lost*, where those with an interest in the show have the opportunity to engage in fan forums, fan fictions, online games, and so on. These online affinity spaces can be easily accessed and so demand little commitment, though they also often allow levels of commitment that become habitual and defining for the individual. Popular culture content on social networking pages creates small affinity spaces demanding minimal commitment; an image or a song may result in a comment from a visitor to a page but usually little in sustained discussion. Though the image or list of favorite movies may be linked to further content that broadens the affinity space. Even so, the popular culture content on these pages creates opportunities for affinity spaces between the owner of the page and the user that are sustained by the popular culture content, not necessarily by age or gender or educational level (Jenkins et al. 2006). What is different with these spaces in contrast to a fan forum for a television program is that the popular culture is not the motivation for visiting the page. Yet once visited, the popular culture content mediates the relationship between writer and reader. The identity of the page owner cannot be read without making connections to outside popular culture content.

The Anxiety of Real Audiences

The students' affection for using the images, songs, and templates of social networking pages to make quick judgments about others, including friends, stands in contrast to their awareness that the identities they were creating on *MySpace* or *Facebook* were incomplete and could result in incomplete or inaccurate readings of their identities. Tony, for example, realized that the incomplete representation of identity could be misread by others, particularly those who did know him face to face:

> I would say that my friends are the audience. But I know they're not the only ones who look at it. But on here I guess it's almost a surreal kind of thing. People who are looking at *MySpace* aren't real. It's almost like they don't exist as people, like they're not going to look at my profile page and think that is what they should think about me and think that is me. Which really they probably do. But my chances of knowing who these people are is slim to none so it doesn't really bother me how they view me as a person.

Students like Tony displayed an understanding of the slipperiness of representation that would make any postmodern theorist proud. Tony makes the distinction between the people who might read his page online and the people he would know face to face. In part, this understanding comes from the different perceptions of the audiences of the pages. It also, however, comes from the understanding that the audience in such situations is double, regardless of the website. Although Amy said that she hoped her audience was like her, she had to admit, "I really have no idea...I wonder how many people actually come to mine because there's no way to really tell." Students like Tony and Amy understand that while they may be constructing an identity for their friends, the nature of the online text is that it is extended to an audience that is beyond the knowledge and beyond the control of the writer of the page.

The practice of using popular culture images to create an identity or proclaim an affinity extends back as least as far as those decorated school locker interiors many of us remember from our youth. Unlike the locker, however, the webpage is not just seen by friends or even passing acquaintances but by anyone who can access the page. The removal of face-to-face interactions also means that, as I noted previously, identities can be falsified or altered, even on personal webpages. Students displayed an acute awareness that the identity they might be seeing performed on someone's page—particularly someone they didn't know face to face—might very well be constructed in ways the students would find misleading if they knew the person offline. Genevieve's skepticism was typical:

> I think that people put those (lists of popular culture references) down a lot to put forth an image so I don't trust them as much because you can control what's on there. If I knew that I wanted to be in a group with everybody who liked AC/DC, you know if I really liked this group of kids, then I'd put on my *MySpace* page music, AC/DC. So I don't really trust the music, movies, and books because I think a lot of people put down stuff they don't like just to put an image forward.

And Kevin said that the only way to be certain about identity was to limit his online friends to people he already knew. "Anybody can put anything up there and try to portray themselves as something they're not. You have to go onto the pages realizing that." But he said he tried to make his page an accurate portrayal of himself so that "if someone that I don't know well looks at it, it would create an interest in learning more about me, about the real me."

The affinity that those visiting the page feel for different popular culture content may be in conflict from one person to the next. Davies and Merchant (2007) note in their research on blogs that the tensions between known readers and unknown readers often create anxiety for writers and result in surprising and often disruptive responses from readers. Students who had not set their page viewing preferences to private, or limited to friends, quickly realized how they might be read in different and disturbing ways by others online. The realization that others were reading their pages struck some students as if the notes they were passing in school for an audience of friends had suddenly been posted outside the school. Several of the students talked about having had confrontations with their parents over content on their personal pages, particularly while they were in high school. Students with public settings also reported receiving unwelcome and often deeply disturbing messages from strangers, particularly on *MySpace*, at least until they changed their settings. These kinds of messages, particularly for the women, made the kind of detached position that Tony assumed toward his unknown audience much less available to female students. As Ashley said:

> There's kids the age of twelve on there (*MySpace*) and they try to act like they're teenagers. They try to act like they're in their twenties, the way they dress, the way they act, their profiles. And people wonder why these thirty- and forty-year-old psychos who are on there end up finding these girls because they (the girls) don't know better than to not say something.

Even students who had set their preferences to private realized that, while it might make them uncomfortable to think about, they could be read by friends of friends of friends, or people they might only meet through a social networking site, and who would be reading their identities only through their pages.

For some of the students, this raised questions and concerns about their intent in creating their pages and the reality of being read differently than that intent. Brianna pointed out that she had changed the background on her *MySpace* page, even though she had liked the image: "I had Mickey Mouse. I love Mickey Mouse and Mickey Mouse was my background. But I finally changed it because I thought people would think it was really childish." And Jenny said she began to think about the self she was composing as she looked at the music she was listing as her favorites:

When I fill out my own I try to think, "This is what I do like, this is what I don't like." But when I take a step back from it, I think, "Does that really describe me or not?" It kind of makes you think, "Oh wow these musicians I'm listing have a lot of dark music. Is that really me? I just like the music."

Jenny's thoughtful reflection on how her page is representing a particular identity is indicative of the kind of care many students put into the choices of popular culture content they employ in composing their social networking pages. Though there may be many audiences that students are aware of, it is clear that the primary audience that frames their composing is that of their peers. They want to appear as attractive and "cool" in their online performances of identity for their friends and potential friends as they do in their face-to-face lives (boyd 2008). Though they may dismiss the pages as frivolous or fun in their initial comments, during the course of an interview, it was not uncommon for students to report spending many hours *tweaking*—a verb that can mean either minor or substantial revisions—their pages and thinking about how these pages and their images, references, and songs will be read by friends, acquaintances, and strangers. Catherine said that when she began to list her popular culture preferences on her pages, it was "really hard for me to sit down and write about myself like that. I remember constructing my list of like favorite music or whatever and I'm sitting here for hours. I have like days of music in my, you know, music library…but sitting down actually writing that down was really hard for me to focus on." Angela Thomas (2007) calls this kind of attention and revision of identity online "a close editing of self" (9), and it illustrates how the commonly held belief that social networking pages are composed without thought or even anxiety is about as believable as thinking that university students don't pay attention to which clothes to wear.

Jenny's comment also illustrates the tension a number of the students mentioned about how their pages might be open to multiple readings they did not intend. The source of the anxiety in her comment can be traced in part to issues of competing and conflicting contexts in the use of popular culture content. Although the templates and conventions of the sites guide interpretation, the intertextual connections created through popular culture content can be greatly varied. We often think of popular culture as a set of communal texts with which we are all familiar. While this commonality may have been more accurate in years past with few television networks to choose from, in today's convergence culture of multiple popular culture sources that flow across media and invite participation from audience members, the interpretation of any popular culture text is necessarily more situated and dependent on the specific context. The context of a social networking site personal page, and the juxtaposition of different popular culture content on such a page, creates multiple meanings of the kind that concerned Jenny.

The Multiple Readings of Popular Culture

As I mentioned previously, the popular culture content on individual pages varies widely. What is consistent across student pages, however, is that the popular culture content is almost always displayed without comment or explanation. The writer of the page offers little guidance about the way the various popular culture elements are to be interpreted or why they have been placed on the page. The meaning, then, must be arrived at through the reader's intertextual connections to the popular culture references and the juxtaposition of these popular culture elements on the page.

The question of context is crucial in how popular culture content is written and read on social networking pages. Take, for example, on the *MySpace* pages I described previously, a single image from Ashley's page and Mitchell's page. Ashley has, under the heading of "Who I'd Like To Meet," a photomontage of Johnny Depp in *Pirates of the Caribbean*. On Mitchell's page, he has an image of the character Kyle from the television program *South Park* as the result of an online quiz he took on "What *South Park* Character Are You?" The image has this caption: "You are clever, and often come up with intelligent and funny comebacks to other people's stupid remarks."

Each image exists on the page as one element within the template of the page. Obviously, putting the Depp photos under the heading of who Ashley would like to meet asks us to read them as an object of romantic fantasy, whether humorous or not. It also could indicate a preference for dark-haired men with beards. The image of Kyle and the caption ask us to consider that Mitchell thinks of himself as smart and funny or that he perhaps sees that conception of himself as ironic. It also indicates an interest in animated television programs. What is just as important in how we read the images on the page, however, are our connections to the popular culture content that extend beyond the page. Because these images are adopted from larger popular culture texts, how we respond to them will be influenced by our relationship to the original text, and the original text's position in the larger culture. Thus, highly contextual affinity spaces create contexts for interpretation that may provide one set of meaning for those within those spaces and another for those unfamiliar with the texts.

If we look at an image of a *South Park* figure without a knowledge of the television series, it is just a crudely constructed image of a young boy smiling. Our knowledge of *South Park*, however, can change our reading. If we see *South Park* as juvenile and offensive, our reading will be different than if we think of it as irreverent and creative satire. *South Park* has a reputation in the larger culture beyond that of a simple animated television series. It has been the focus of numerous public debates about offensive material on television and written about in mainstream media many times. At the same time, its popularity can be charted in the T-shirts, posters, and catchphrases from the show that float through the culture disconnected from specific episodes. Consequently, an image from *South Park* can be read as a reference to more than a television program; it becomes instead a synecdoche for a particular popular culture sensibility of subversive, transgressive humor and cultural critique.

The reading of a *South Park* image becomes even more complicated if we know the characters on the show. Kyle is smart and funny, so we might see Mitchell's posting of the image on the page as in some way a sincere reflection of the identity he is constructing. Had the character posted been Eric Cartman, the selfish and bigoted character from the program, we might see it as a more ironic statement. The fact that either character is the result of a "personality quiz" from a page that has countless parodies of such quizzes also would influence our reading. Such quizzes, on everything from favorite ice cream flavor and favorite movie monster to which television characters people resemble are hugely popular on *MySpace* and *Facebook*.

Similarly, Ashley's image of Johnny Depp is read not only as an image of an attractive young man. Our reading of the image will also depend on whether we have seen the movie from which it was taken and how we felt about the film, as well as our knowledge of other of Depp's films and even our knowledge of his public life as a celebrity. How differently might an image from Depp's film *Ed Wood*, about the cross-dressing cult film director, be read on the page? Even with the image on Ashley's page, do we assume that Ashley is aware of Depp's roles in other films when she includes it, or is it his image in only one film that appeals to her?

Convergence culture has allowed individuals to use popular culture content to compose identities on social networking sites with unprecedented ease. Students have taken advantage of this opportunity to use such content to create texts that they feel represent themselves in some specific way because they feel they can count on readers understanding the meaning of the popular culture references. They count on readers of their pages sharing affinity spaces and understanding which references should be read seriously or ironically. Yet because popular culture texts have meaning outside of a personal page, the way photos of family or friends do not, the intertextual layers of meaning in popular culture texts can undermine or at least be read far differently than the writer of the page intended. A few students noted an awareness of how intertextual connections of popular culture content opened up interpretations for readers. Genevieve said, "If you don't write something in the 'About Me' section, if you put up a bunch of pictures (of celebrities) instead, then it's like you're letting people draw conclusions for themselves." But more of them said they would assume their audience understood the meaning behind the content. This is but one way the changes in technology that allow media convergence have altered the relationships of audience members to each other. A member of the *South Park* audience, for example, now has ways to perform his or her identity to other members of the audience by using images from the show in ways that may or may not be dialogic but certainly influence interpretations of identity.

The use of popular culture content and references to compose an identity online inevitably raises complicated questions about the role of consumer culture in the process. Popular culture content is also consumer culture content. After all, regardless of their artistic merits, movies are made to put paying customers in the seats, television programs are meant to keep eyeballs occupied until the commercials come on, computer games are made to be bought or rented. And for all the discussion of the democratic and liberatory possibilities of the Internet, it has also quickly become a consumer culture machine. From the viewpoint of the producers of popular culture, convergence culture offers the opportunity for greater marketing and greater profits. Students now in adolescence may have been on popular culture websites such as *Pokemon-* or *Harry Potter*-related sites—designed as part of the marketing apparatus for the films, books, and other materials—since they were young children (Mitchell and Reid-Walsh 2002).

It is perhaps a truism that consumers of popular culture are also consumed by it, but certainly what happens when students use popular culture content to define and perform identities reflects this idea. As students use popular culture to compose identities, they place themselves in the service of the consumer demands of that culture. Every movie star, every CD or book cover, every list of favorite television programs, every song that starts playing when a *MySpace* page opens is not only an illustration of preferences but is also an advertisement for the further consumptions of the popular culture. Just like young people wearing T-shirts sporting corporate logos, personal pages on social networking sites turn individuals into billboards. As personal pages also function as advertisements, they reproduce and reinforce the ideology of material gain that accompanies consumer culture. The choices that students make in determining what images or songs to put on their pages are not only a result of aesthetic or personal preferences but are influenced by the ideology perpetuated by consumer culture. For example, a person putting an image of a *Star Wars* character on a page may be in part responding to narrative and character but has also no doubt been influenced by the marketing machine that has made *Star Wars* a ubiquitous brand. No one would deny that consumer culture is a relentless force in affecting the fashions and tastes of young people—or all people. While we should resist seeing the power of consumer culture as inescapable for young people, we also must realize that if identity is embedded in consumer culture in our daily lives, then it is also a present and substantial force in popular culture and online identity. In the same way that a student will dress or listen to music in part because marketers have succeeded in making it cool or desirable, the same consumer culture forces will influence which images, sound, and video students put on a personal page.

A further wrinkle in terms of consumer culture is the way in which audience members have become the content providers in participatory popular culture. On the one hand, individuals in the audience now have the opportunity to respond to programs, talk with other fans, and create new content with sampled material on personal pages. At the same time, however, by posting this material, the audience is providing the content that makes profit for the websites. If people didn't have personal pages on *Facebook* and *MySpace*, then those sites could not make money from the advertising they sell. Yet the people posting on personal pages or blogs or fan forums are not receiving compensation for their work, even as some of these sites become profitable enough to be purchased by other corporations. (The purchase of such sites has not been without controversy, as several students said they had closed their *MySpace* pages once the site was sold to Rupert Murdoch's News Corp. because they opposed his conservative political positions.) This is another way that the consumers of popular culture become the consumed in convergence culture.

When I raised the question of consumer culture to students, either as an influence on how they constructed their pages or in terms of the content they provided for sites, most of them brushed off the question. Either they hadn't thought about it or they did not believe that it was relevant to them. The only comments were along the lines of Greg's, who said, "I don't care if they make money off of it. I mean, that's capitalism. But it's not going to matter about what I do with my page." The lack of interest in questions of consumer culture is not surprising. Students are not encouraged either in school or at home to look critically at the mechanisms and ideology of consumer culture. What's more, in a culture such as the United States, where the mythology of individual agency is powerful, students resist the idea that their choices might be in any way subject to social forces. Even when they express skepticism or cynicism about advertising, for example, their comments are usually couched in terms of how it might manipulate others but that they would never fall prey to it themselves.

Bonding the Self with Social Groups

The question of authorial intention in creating social networking personal pages is, of course, a slippery one. Even for the students I spoke with, different elements on the page reflected different levels of interest. Tony had many images of college and professional sports logos and athletes on his page and talked at length about how central his interest in sports was to his life. Also on his page, however, was a favorite *South Park* character that he said he had included on a whim. "I have my favorite *South Park* character, even though I've probably only watched *South Park* about four times. But I saw a friend had one up on his page and I thought it was really funny." There was nothing on the page to indicate these differences, however, so a reader of the page might see the *South Park* reference as an important part of the representation of his identity.

It is important to understand that students often see these pages as created for friends, as online extensions of face-to-face social relationships. This is reflected in the personal photos, quotations, and jokes from friends posted on the pages. Indeed, one common reason given for creating a personal page is what the author's friends have done (boyd 2008). The pages not only allow friends to post messages, either privately or on the public page, or share photos or other content, they allow users to form social groups. The groups cover interests including politics, sports, and local social organizations, or just playful ideas ("Because I Am Senior, That's Why!" or "Treehouse Lovers"). Popular culture, again, provides the focal point for many of these groups. Some are organized around a specific movie or show while others focus more on a genre of music or film. Each group then has a page where comments, images, videos, and so on can be posted. Some groups, particularly the sillier ones, tend to be fairly short-lived fads. But other groups, including some of the popular culture groups that have a broader focus, have longer life-spans. How involved students were with groups varied. Some belonged to few or none while others belong to fifty or more.

The *Facebook* popular culture groups Pat belonged to included "Dane Cook is Awesome" and "I Understand Monty Python Jokes." He said, "I don't go to the groups all the time but every now and then, just for fun. And sometimes I find out something I didn't know or I'm reminded of something. But mostly I just see who is there." For other students, popular culture groups occasionally provided affinity spaces through which to gain information, though most students—if they talked about making use of the collective intelligence of online communities—talked of doing so through fan forums and lists. In general, however, the participation students reported in the popular culture groups on *MySpace* and *Facebook* was much more about belonging and community. Like Pat, students went to groups to see who else was there. Or, perhaps even more tellingly, a number of students said they rarely visited popular culture groups once they had joined them. It was the joining, the declaration of an affiliation to the group that would be a visible link on the personal page, that motivated most students' choices to join. Once again, the performance of identity through proclaiming group affiliations enters into how students read and write these personal pages. As boyd (2008) notes, "For better or worse, people judge others based on their associations: group identities form around and are reinforced by the collective tastes and attitudes of those who identify with the group. Online, this cue is quite helpful in enabling people to find their bearings" (130). Angela said, "If I don't know the person I scan their groups. I can sometimes get more than a lot of other things about them through their groups. I can even get a sense of humor." Like all popular culture statements of affiliation, identity with the community is created both through inclusion and exclusion. By stating which groups a person has joined, and which a person has not, students add important elements to their pages. Does the person have a lot of groups that seem like fads, one-time groups that may soon fade such as "Paris Hilton for President"? Or are the groups more obscure, making statements of hipness and cool through their esoteric and limited appeal?

As group membership indicates, popular culture content is often an extension of social relationships. An image from a movie may reflect a shared interest in that film with a particular group of friends who may have watched the movie together. A catchphrase from a television series may reflect a social discourse specific to one group of friends who use that catchphrase as part of sharing a particular affinity space. Such a catchphrase is an extension of daily activities used to reinforce social bonds.

But a person with a social networking page is connected to multiple social groups whose interests, and relationships to the multiple popular culture texts on a page, overlap and conflict with each other. These overlapping affinity spaces mean that some readers of the page may be drawn to certain images or videos or songs and simultaneously puzzled or even disconcerted by others. This is why even close friends when encountering the multiple popular culture texts on a page can respond with surprise and consternation about the identity represented.

One quick example of how the slippage between daily social life and the content of social networking pages can lead to misreadings comes from Jenny's *Facebook* page. She has, among her quotations, one from the film *Forrest Gump*. When I first read the quotation, "Run, Forrest, Run!" I assumed she was a fan of the film and was drawn to the quotation because of the way, in the film, it represents the title character's quest for independence and dignity. I also assumed she enjoyed the film and that led me to assumptions about the kinds of movies she liked and what that indicated about her personality. When she talked about the quotation, however, she said, "I'm on the rugby team and my nickname is "Forrest." I am supposed to run, apparently, so they nicknamed me "Forrest" and yell that at me when we play." Clearly, her teammates visiting her page would understand the reference and appreciate her attempt to reinforce her bonds with them. For others reading the page, however, the social context is lost and replaced with the context of the original popular culture text and its meaning in the larger culture. Such misreadings, several students said, also resulted in parents not understanding popular culture references or whether such references were meant ironically, and responding with concern or puzzlement.

The result of the multiple popular culture references or content on a page is more than the creation of multiple and overlapping affinity spaces where one person might like *Pirates of the Caribbean* while another likes *Charmed*. Obviously, these multiple images, videos, songs, and lists do not exist in isolation but are regarded in juxtaposition to each other. On Ashley's page, for example, we do not see Johnny Depp without also seeing images of Orlando Bloom, *Eragon*, *The Lord of the Rings*, *Pirates of the Caribbean*, *Charmed*, the American flag, and an angel with a rosary draped over its shoulders. This collage of images is also juxtaposed with lists of favorite songs and movies and a downloaded song. Some of the juxtapositions may seem complementary, such as the image of Bloom and an image from *The Lord of the Rings* films in which he acted. Other images, depending on our readings, may seem contradictory—Depp as a critic of U.S. foreign policy next to the U.S. flag—or puzzling—the angel as the background to all the images. For the writer of the page, as I demonstrated in chapter 3, these multiple images may seem like different aspects of identity or may only represent different motivations at different moments. Either way, however, the juxtaposition of disparate popular culture elements shifts the meaning of each as it arranged with the next.

Culture and Identity on Personal Pages

Finally, a discussion of identity performance would be incomplete without a consideration of how these pages are composed and read in terms of larger identity constructions such as gender, sexual orientation, race, and social class. Popular culture preferences often reflect cultural identities. Say *country music* and the default audience is expected to be European American and rural; say *hip-hop* and the default audience is expected to be more urban and African American. A list of romantic comedies would be more likely to indicate a woman's page and a list of crude sex comedies would indicate a man's. Clearly, there are exceptions to all of these statements—and the exceptions students highlight raise interesting questions—but the reality, supported by years of research too lengthy to list, is that popular culture is often a vehicle through which people both perform identities and make judgments about others in terms of these larger identity characteristics. If students use popular culture content and references to compose identities on their personal pages, then they are also making statements about how they position themselves in terms of social identities. When Sandy said about her *MySpace* pages that "Here's my music. See, I like anything but rap. (She reads a label on her page) 'Rap Stands for Retards Attempting Poetry' Yes, I found it clever." Although Sandy seemed slightly embarrassed at showing me the language on her page, her statement about rap also helps her perform her identity as a white student from a small rural community. These final thoughts on the complex influence of culture on performances of identity are admittedly brief, though the subject will come up again in chapters 6 and 7.

Students' identities on their personal pages are, of course, first determined from the photos at the top of their pages. On most pages, the age, sex, and race of an individual are quickly apparent. What can be discerned from the photos is fairly limited, however, leaving the popular culture content to complete the representations of identity. More often than not, the representations reflect what would be considered fairly conventional identity constructions. For example, men's pages tend to have more action and horror movies, such as *300* or *Dawn of the Dead*. Women's pages had more comedies and romantic dramas such as *The Notebook* or *The Sisterhood of the Traveling Pants*. Of course, not all references are as revealing of identity. Still, in general, if you removed the name and personal photos from most personal pages on social networking sites, you could use the popular culture content and references to make a fairly accurate determination of at least the age, sex, race or ethnicity, social class, and nationality of the author.

When I asked students how they thought their pages represented their identities, most of them deflected the question by saying they did not think about such issues when composing their pages or, even more often, saying their pages represented only themselves, not any larger cultural identities. This is not surprising, particularly in the

United States, where, again, the dominant mythology is that individual agency is unfettered by cultural or social forces of any kind. The students I talked with resisted the idea that their ways of representing themselves might be influenced by culture just as they resist such conversations in the classroom, and indeed just as the larger public resists such conversations. The exception to this position from students was when they felt they had put something on their page that they felt would defy the dominant cultural expectations. Sometimes such moves were meant to be rebellious. Natalie, who mixed goth images with fairies on her page, said, "I would never want people to think that I'm too girly-girl. I want to keep them guessing." Other students pointed out references or material they felt was inconsistent with their cultural identities to explain the incongruities. Greg, for example, had *Pride and Prejudice* listed under his favorite movies and pointed to it saying, "That's just on there because it's my girlfriend's favorite movie."

The students I talked with were more willing to consider cultural identities when reading the pages of others, however. Catherine said that she sometimes looks at pages with "lots of sports stuff or action movies all over it and I'm like 'God, what a guy page. Dial it back a notch, will you?'," Or Genevieve noted that how pages are read could be dependent on gender. "You know, if I go and see a bunch of pictures of beautiful women and Britney Spears on some girl's page, I think that she has self-image problems. And then again maybe if a male would look at the same page, he would say she really idolizes beauty, you know she wants to be beautiful." As so often happens, the students were willing to see culture as an influence on their peers, even as they denied its possible effect on them. Given the judgments that students make about the pages they read, and—as I discussed in chapter 2—given the ways that identity influences popular culture tastes and affinities, it is easy to see that students use identity characteristics to make decisions about the pages they visit and the ways they evaluate the authors of those pages.

Another intriguing issue of popular culture and identity that social networking sites raise is the ways in which different sites appeal to different groups of students. Among the university students I spoke to, there was a common narrative in which they discussed having had *MySpace* pages in high school but having migrated to *Facebook* once they entered university. Amy said, "*MySpace* is getting more and more ridiculous. So *Facebook* is more aimed toward like the college audience and people that are of college age at least." Francesca had a similar response: "I got it (a *MySpace* page) my sophomore year (of high school) but I don't get on it. It's just, I don't know, it's silly. It's more like stupid junk stuff all the time than anyone actually having a conversation with anyone." Over and over again, students described *Facebook* as more serious, more mature, or cleaner and easier to use. They also talked about preferring the more exclusive nature of *Facebook*, which at the time was limited to university and high school students, to the more open environment of *MySpace*. This is interesting in light of boyd's (2008) research that indicates *MySpace* memberships cut across economic, gender, and racial lines. What the student response may reinforce is boyd's (2007) speculation that *Facebook* has become identified with more affluent, college-bound students while *MySpace* is seen by these students as the province of a younger, more marginalized, and less affluent population. Not only are different populations drawn to the different sites, but boyd points out that while *MySpace* has flashy imagery more reminiscent of Las Vegas, *Facebook* cultivates a clean and modern look more akin to websites and publications that target affluent audiences. Of course, it is difficult to raise the possibility to students that their choices may be grounded in class status and aspirations because, again, they dislike thinking that their choices are influenced by culture or that the United States as a society has powerful class divisions. Such responses are not limited to students, as can be seen when boyd's blog entry on this subject, which was careful and nuanced as a piece of initial theorizing on the subject, was subjected to fierce and angry responses that revealed how sensitive social class is as a subject.

Conclusion

Online media technologies have allowed students to construct new performances of identity and yet also reinforce existing social identities from their face-to-face relationships with all the excitement—and anxiety—that accompany such activities. Online media have also allowed, and encouraged, students to appropriate and reuse popular culture content and references as resources for composing and revising their identities on a daily basis. Students' use of popular culture to compose identities online is not a haphazard event but instead is a conscious process of self-inquiry and self-editing (Thomas 2007; Stern

2008) and as considered and reflected on as what clothes to wear and which group to sit with at lunch.

The use of collected elements to create a collage of meaning has been interrogated in different settings as a move characteristic of authorship in a postmodern culture. The use of unexpected juxtapositions and associative meanings composed from appropriated texts has been addressed in such contexts as the creation of zines (Knobel and Lankshear 2004), memes (Knobel and Lankshear 2007), webpages (Alexander 2006), and new video (Stephens 1998). According to Stephens, new identities can be created not only through the linear exposition of print texts but also "through the deft juxtaposition of carefully selected aspects of surfaces" (217). As I discussed in chapter 3, the students I spoke with were comfortable and confident about the creation of identities through the composition of fragmented, associative collages of popular culture texts. Immersion in popular culture, as discourse, as epistemology, as a text for creating identity is the everyday life of both our students and ourselves. Added to the already pervasive nature of popular culture are the technological capabilities of online communication that have not only made easier this kind of appropriation of and composition with popular culture texts but have often made the cutting, pasting, and creating with such texts easier and faster than composing with print (Lewis 2007). It would, indeed, be more remarkable if students bypassed popular culture as a means of composing personal pages than that it has become the foundation for such performances of identity.

CHAPTER 5

A Story of One's Own

Social Constructions of Genre Online

The television listings in my newspaper in the United States indicate that *Heroes*, the popular fantasy series, will be broadcast at 9:00 p.m., Monday. There was a time when, if you wanted to watch the program, you would have to be in front of a television at that time and stay there until it was over. Those were the days in which people talked about "appointment television" and arranged their calendars around their favorite programs. The listing was not only all you needed to know to watch the program, it was all you could know. The narrative was limited to what was broadcast, the discussion largely to what could be talked about with friends the next day or perhaps read about the actors in magazines. In similar ways, movies were limited to the times they were shown in theaters and what appeared on the screen and music to the albums bands produced.

The contemporary situation is very different. Sure, *Heroes* is still on Mondays at 9:00 p.m. But of course I am no longer limited to watching it then. I can record it on tape or digitally, or I can just go to the *Heroes* website and watch it there. What's more, I'm no longer limited to just watching the show. The narrative of *Heroes* is not confined to what is broadcast each week. If I go to the official website, I can find the usual accompanying material such as trailers, interviews with the writers and actors, and character biographies. But I can also read a graphic novel about the characters that offers new story lines and information not in the broadcast series, I can watch videos made for the web with new characters, I can play an online game involving the characters that reveals information not seen on television. In short, I can extend my experience with the narrative and the characters of the program in multiple directions. As the site for the online game *Heroes Evolutions* puts it, "Take the next evolutionary step forward by joining *Heroes Evolutions*. Explore the *Heroes* universe, unravel new mysteries, and go beyond your TV to become part of TV's greatest adventure" (*Heroes Evolutions* 2008). Going beyond the TV, or the movie screen, or the CD is reshaping what genre and narrative mean for young people as they read and write.

Each text I can read or interact with on the *Heroes* page gives me more content than the program itself. The graphic novel, for example, is more than a retelling of what has been on television; instead, it is separate but related content. Mitchell said he had read some installments of the graphic novel, "And I get some background to the main characters so I understand why they do things better or I find out what happened exactly that they only talked about in the series." What's more, because as a viewer of the show and visitor to the website, I can choose among the various texts and because there are too many for most people to choose them all, my experience with *Heroes*, my reading of the narrative, will be unique. Though I could only watch the television series and have a satisfying narrative experience, the graphic novel and other texts offer layers of information and story lines that provide a more complex reading. Jenkins (2006a) calls this *transmedia storytelling*, where each piece one reads offers new perspectives, characters, and narrative lines to enrich the narrative. "The whole is worth more than the sum of the parts" (102). The consequence of story lines and characters that exist simultaneously on different media has been a change in student expectations of narrative and genre. They are becoming more and more accustomed to fragmented narratives on multiple media that they can access and read as they like.

Not only can they read what pieces of the text that they like, but convergence culture allows them to participate in the narratives. Some students participate through commentary and fan responses such as blogs or fan forums or making lists for social networking pages. But there are others who take the narratives themselves into their hands by creating fan fiction, fan films, mashups, music videos, and machinima. In addition to new media technologies creating more fragmented collages of narratives, students now often approach the narratives created by mass popular culture producers with the expectation that they can intervene in them, take control of them, and remake the meaning and the narrative. Not all students produce fan fiction or music videos, but the overwhelming majority I spoke with were familiar with them and found their existence a normal and expected part of their popular culture lives.

In this chapter, I focus on how the new technologies and literacy practices of convergence culture influence how students perceive concepts of genre and narrative. Genre and narrative have been central and powerful elements of popular culture for more than a century. Participatory popular culture has allowed individuals both to borrow from and remake the genres and narratives that they enjoy. Practices such as fan fiction or mashups demonstrate how they learn to read and write in the genres. In addition I will examine how the popular culture genres that predated online technologies continue to influence what students read and write. Finally, I will discuss how online technologies themselves are shaping students' ideas about genre, such as social networking site templates, and how students adapt popular culture content and rhetorical forms to respond to these new forms.

Widely Shared Expectations

Before discussing online technologies, it is important to remind ourselves how genre and narrative have shaped mass popular culture over the last century. Genre is a powerful concept in mass popular culture that allows producers to work within particular narrative characteristics at the same time it allows audiences to approach new texts with certain expectations. In literacy practices, genre can be thought of as particular kinds of literacy artifacts and events that allow producers and audience to communicate through shared expected patterns of style, form, or content. Genre is central to the way mass popular culture operates as part of consumer culture. When movies or television programs or bands create work that meets certain genre expectations, then a larger audience can consume the product, confident of what it will be buying. Popular culture producers also realize that if they do not meet these genre expectations, they may disappoint their audiences. Indeed, the material realities in terms of production and distribution costs of mass popular culture mean that creating works within established and popular genres becomes a series of economic rather than aesthetic decisions. The result is that genres that have proven to be financially lucrative—such as action films or reality television programs—get repeated over and over until they become so worn out and predictable that the audience loses interest, as in the case of cowboy movies.

The shared producer–audience expectations of genre are what make mass popular culture both widely consumed and widely predictable. We've all gone to movies where, before the first reel is over, we can predict what is going to happen in the narrative, if we haven't already figured it out from the trailers and posters. What specifics happen in the narrative of the genre movie or television show may be less important than that the text meets certain conventions. It doesn't matter really what happens to the heroine in a romantic comedy as long as the movie hits all the right conventions of theme, image, and plot (Altman 1999). Consequently, popular culture genres can be more about referencing other texts in the genre than they are about referencing real events. In other words, action movies are less about real terrorist plots or police departments than they are about arrogant, heartless villains and the final confrontation between the hero and his nemesis, as we have seen them time and again in other action films. Still, popular culture genres have to walk the narrow line between predictability and novelty. If a movie, for example, is too formulaic, too predictable in repeating genre conventions, it becomes boring or ridiculous; yet if the film pushes genre conventions too far, it can confuse or disappoint the audience. "Too much originality, then, can be risky and dangerous, once a successful formula has been established" (Welsh 2000, 168). The point at which genres become too formulaic in adhering to conventions is usually the point at which parodies of the genre emerge.

In general, however, our familiarity with genres leads us to hold on and reward popular culture texts that conform to conventions. When new technologies emerge, the power of genre is such that we often try first to adapt existing genres into the new technologies (Stephens 1998). For example, early movies were essentially just filmed versions of plays until a new way of thinking about narrative, editing, and camera use created a genre to match the new medium. Similar cycles of development occurred with radio and television. Early webpages tended to look like newspapers or other familiar genres. In part because it takes time for new genres to match the opportunities offered by new technologies, and in part because change always provokes anxieties, the genres that develop with new technologies often draw criticism and resistance. As Stephens notes, "We rarely trust the imposition of a new magic on our lives, and we rarely fail to work up nostalgia for the older magic it replaces" (32). In the eighteenth century, novels were often condemned as being mindless and addictive diversions, potentially harmful to young and impressionable readers. In the nineteenth century, newspapers were often criticized for providing too much cheap entertainment in too unsophisticated a form (Paine 1999, 283). The complaints about television are numerous and include Federal Communications Commission Chairman Newton Minow's famous 1961 denunciation of the medium as a "vast wasteland."

Such responses to new technologies and genres illustrate that while tradition always plays a role in forming and reproducing popular culture genres, technology has also played a role. The shape and size of Renaissance theaters influenced how Shakespeare could construct his plays, the length of film reels and the number of showings needed to make a profit helped shape movie narratives, as the duration of 45-rpm records did for pop music. With computer technologies, processing speed, memory, and bandwidth have most obviously shaped the form of computer games and online role-playing games. What is also clear, however, is that the power, and limits, of computer technology is also affecting other popular culture genres as online video and audio become more central to people's popular culture experiences.

Like the rest of us, students are well acquainted with popular culture genres. The long and varied experiences they have with popular culture texts have allowed them to encounter mainstream genres time and again. In this way, they have learned what to expect from the genres and have many texts to draw on as examples. Asked to define mainstream genres such as science fiction, romantic comedy, sitcom, horror, country, or hip-hop music, they can easily come up with a description of a given genre and a list of its characteristics. The characteristics might be connected to plot, production style, character, or other elements. In addition, students have learned how to use genres to structure their readings of popular culture texts. For example, students can discuss how the conventions of television genres, such as the creation of a series around a central character, shape the narratives of individual episodes. To quote a student from an earlier study, "There was one episode of *Buffy* (*the Vampire Slayer*) where she was losing her powers and she was about to get stabbed and you know they're not going to kill her off. They can't do that. So you know she's going to be okay" (Williams 2002, 57). As I have argued before (Wil-

liams 2002; 2003), the genres students learn from popular culture media such as television influence how they respond to reading and
writing print texts. The emphasis on plot and the resolution of narrative conflicts on much of television—including reality and news programs—makes such texts easier for students to interpret while they
struggle more to read or produce print texts that emphasize character
or argument (Williams 2002).

New computer-related genres such as computer games have had
their own effects on student reading and writing. It was about ten
years ago, when I was talking with a primary school student about
the story he had written, that I noticed how, rather than a conventional plot-driven narrative as one might see in a film, it was a description of a series of perils with no sense of resolution. I realized
that I was seeing the effect on narrative of the boy's experiences with
computer games with their levels of increasing challenges, an insight
that has been confirmed by other scholars (Newkirk 2002a; Beavis
2007).

Fragmented, Multivoiced, and Multimodal

Among the most persistent claims for online literacy practices over
the past twenty years have been the assertions that they encourage
fragmented and multivoiced texts. Online reading and writing, it has
been argued, allows for easier construction of texts that challenge the
unitary, stable conception of texts privileged in the modernist thinking of the early twentieth century. Instead, online literacy practices
promote postmodern aesthetics in which texts are multi-authored,
flexible and changing, fragmented, and multimodal (Mackey 2006;
Selfe and Hawisher 2004). Online texts have been celebrated for the
ways in which they promote associative, non-linear reading. Rather
than read one word after the next with all the text in one location,
such as a book or an article, the texts that can be written for online
reading, through the use of links and connected texts, provide readers
with multiple ways of making meaning from a text in which no two
meanings may be the same for any reader or reading. In addition, as I
pointed out in chapter 3, new technologies allow for the kind of sampling and composing that uses and reuses other texts' multiple modes
of print, image, video, and sound. Online texts also create the opportunity for easy collaboration and participation by readers and writers.
In this way, as I noted earlier, they provide a more explicit construc-

tion of the kind of multivoiced text theorized by Bakhtin (1981). But more to the point here is that this heteroglossic text, with multiple voices and intertextual connections, strains the boundaries of the concept of text as a single-authored, unitary form. In even the most mainstream online texts, such as *Amazon.com* or *The New York Times*, the presence of multiple voices discussing, arguing, joking creates a Bakhtinian dialogic exchange "of multiple voices, or the cacophonic subversiveness of the 'carnivalesque' in language in which the careful social hierarchies and boundaries of language are inverted or effaced" (Connor 1997, 229). Finally, online texts are rarely unchanging, and often altered multiple times a day. In this way, the concept of the single-authored, stable, print text as the most important form of communication in our culture has been strongly challenged.

Although I would avoid breathless labels such as "digital natives" for a generation of young people with such varied experiences, I do think that many students' conception of a text is broader than the single-authored, print-based, linear, stable artifact they are so often presented with in school. Certainly, they recognize the single-authored print text as privileged by schools, but that does not mean it has the same status for them. Instead, their daily literacy practices are more likely to involve social networking sites, which change constantly, invite multiple voices, reference other texts, link to outside sources and groups, and use a mix of print, image, and video to present a representation of a person that the reader very well knows may not reflect the "real" person who created it. It's hard to imagine more thoroughly postmodern texts.

As with online literacy practices, popular culture has been widely discussed in the ways it enacts postmodernist theory. Popular culture has been noted by many scholars (Borgmann 1992; McRobbie 1994; Connor 1997) for the way it employs postmodern concepts and tactics such as parody, pastiche, collaboration, fragmented narratives, self-referential texts, and textual instability. Indeed, what Connor (1997) says about television could easily be adapted to online texts: "we seem to have arrived at a view of TV as constituting the postmodern psycho-cultural condition—a world of simulations detached from reference to the real which circulate and exchange in ceaseless, centreless flow" (190). Genre in popular culture, disrupted as it is through flow and irony, often represents a particularly postmodern sensibility. As an example, film genres and television genres have been discussed in terms of the ways they progress from fresh concepts to establishing mainstream and dominant sets of conventions and intertextual conventions, before eventually exhausting themselves in intentional parody and unintentional self-parody. Students are not only able readers of popular culture genres but are increasingly able at combining, blending, and responding to both existing popular culture genres as well as the new genres that are emerging online.

The convergence of media that is now possible with online technologies has only accelerated and intensified the postmodern pressures on genre. It has become more and more difficult to speak of genre and narrative in terms of stable texts and clear authorial intentions. It has also become increasingly difficult to confine a genre and its characteristics to a particular medium. It is the multiple narratives on multiple media that surround a particular story—like the multiple narratives around *Heroes*—that make impossible a single, unified, stable text from a single author. It is the combination of these multiple narratives and the opportunity for the audience to participate in and alter the narratives that are of particular interest when we consider how students encounter and imagine genre.

Jenkins (2006a) calls such multiple, converging narratives transmedia storytelling (124). Although he notes that creating content in a different medium about a movie or television or band is not new (*Spider-Man* lunchbox anyone?), in the past most of these efforts have been marketing strategies by popular culture producers. The producer licenses the rights to characters or images to be produced on T-shirts or created as toys for fast-food children's meals. But such licensing has traditionally been limited to reproductions of the original film or television content and has been designed to keep control of the narrative and characters in the hands of the producers.

The difference with transmedia storytelling is that the narratives that are created in different media do not simply replicate the narrative or characters of a central text on television or film. Instead, like the online graphic novel for *Heroes*, the content is connected to the narrative of the program, yet also exists as its own narrative. Incidents that happen in the television series are alluded to in the graphic novel, but each exists as different narrative threads of the same imaginative world. The online game operates in the same way. Jenkins (2006a) points out that *The Matrix* series of films explored this concept by having goals in the computer game and a series of short films connect to, but not repeat, narrative points in the movies. For example, in the computer game, a player can help a character through a series of battles and obstacles to arrive in time to help other characters in a car chase that will be seen in one of the movies. Both the film and game could be played separately but offer new insights when connected.

Though this approach bewildered and even angered many mainstream film critics, it revealed an approach to genre and storytelling in which the flexibility of the narrative is matched with the most appropriate medium and genre. As Jenkins quotes one game creator, "I've got my world, I've got my arcs, some of those arcs can be expressed in the video game space, some of them can be expressed in the film space, the television space, the literary space, and you are getting to true transmedia storytelling" (124). Like Cynthia Selfe's (1999) arguments about how best to approach teaching students to compose texts with new technologies, the creators of transmedia storytelling understand that different media offer distinctive affordances for expressing narratives and ideas most effectively. Computer game creators are not the only people with this vision. From participants in online role-playing games (Thomas 2007) to fan fiction writers (Black 2008) to those creating online video remixes (Knobel and Lankshear 2008), it is clear that young people often move back and forth between several different media to express ideas about the same characters or narratives. Many fan fiction writers, for example, also create and post fan art of their favorite characters. Students involved in these activities are also making decisions about where to express their ideas and narratives based on what medium will best serve their interests.

Whether the creator is a mass popular culture producer or a member of the audience, transmedia storytelling means that the text is no longer a single identifiable genre. The writers and readers of graphic novels conform to conventions of that genre in terms of images, print, and the ways the narrative is arranged. The fact that the graphic novel in this case is an online publication creates an additional set of genre expectations and constraints in terms of how the novel is arranged on the page. The television episodes have a different set of conventions guiding them, many of which are temporal instead of spatial. The episode is constrained by time, patterned by the need to insert commercials, and structured around the need to complete at least some part of the narrative in one episode while making it consistent within the larger series. A computer game has its own set of genre conventions of participation, images, control toolbars, advancement within the game and so on. For transmedia storytelling to be successful, then, the creators have to understand different genre conventions and what material works best within particular genres and media. Readers have to understand how different the narratives created for different media will conform to particular genre expectations and not expect a computer game to provide the same kind of narrative content and arc as a film.

The Search for Multiple Narratives

Students understand that they can go online for more material and information about the popular culture narratives that interest them. For many of the students, such activity is limited to searching for reviews or reading fan comments or fan forums. An increasing number, however, are finding the complementary story lines for the films and television series that interest them. Greg, for example, said he had become an avid reader of the *Heroes* online graphic novel. "At first I just read it because it was different. But then I started to realize that every week you were getting more and more stuff about the characters that you were not getting on TV." For Greg, the realization of what the graphic novel was providing him as a reader became clearer when he talked with friends who were only watching the broadcast episodes. "I would say things about characters in the show and other people were like, 'Huh? How do you know that?' and I'd tell them about scenes I'd read (in the graphic novel). I knew so much more than they did." Greg said that then some of his friends began reading the online material as well. He said he felt as if he had a better understanding of the story line, but also that it was "cool to be able to read more about the show. I am totally into it and I could have more to think about in between episodes." Greg also said he had one friend who had not seen the series but was a graphic novel reader who started reading the *Heroes* graphic novel after hearing Greg talk about it but never did move on to the television series.

I asked Greg what, in addition to the content, he noticed as differences between the television episodes and the graphic novel. He replied, "The graphic novel chapters are tighter. There's not as much time for what you can put into a TV show, unless you made them (graphic novel chapters) a lot longer. I also don't mind cliffhangers as much on TV as I do in a graphic novel. I want those stories (in a graphic novel) to finish up." Mitchell, who had also seen the *Heroes* graphic novel chapters and the television series, when asked a similar question had a more detailed answer:

> There are ways in which they're a lot alike. The flow of images is the same. And you can see the images, see what they were imagining, just like on TV. That makes it different than a print novel like you were talking about. Probably what is the most the same is the paths of thought they both make you take. When you see a page on a graphic novel of people in action or talking and you see it on film it's really a lot alike, the movement of the story and the thought. That's why things like *V for Vendetta* and *Road to Perdition* can make good movies. But it's not exactly the same. The movies have music and real movement to them, but you just watch them a few times. But the graphic novels I can read over again when I want. It's different.

In the replies of both Mitchell and Greg, we can see how students are recognizing not just the differences in content across media in transmedia storytelling but how they are coming to an understanding of the ways different media play to different genre conventions. Both students' comments demonstrate a knowledge of how material must be shaped to different media strengths and limitations but can still deal with the same characters in compelling narratives. The tension between spatial and temporal organization is evident in both students' comments. They recognize overlap between the graphic novel and the film or television program but also realize that space constrains and shapes the book in the same way as time does the film. Yet it is also clear that they both have certain genre expectations for both genres in terms of image, movement, and narrative style that they expect to be fulfilled and that they either like or dislike. In Mitchell's final comments about watching the films or reading and re-reading the book, we also can see a student understanding that his reading practices are being shaped by the genre of the material with which he is engaged.

Students who are participating in transmedia storytelling also show an increased tolerance, and perhaps even preference, for fragmented, incomplete narratives. Ted, a fan of *The Matrix* films and computer games, said he had realized when he began playing the computer game *Enter the Matrix* that it was more than just a re-creation of the movies. He said for a while he would go back and forth between the movies and the game, trying out different scenes and different narratives. "I started getting things out of order just to play with it. It was sort of fun to play the game one way that would make the movie maybe mean something different." When I asked if he had seen the series of animated short films, *The Animatrix*, that introduce still other characters and narrative lines, he shrugged and said he hadn't. "I know they're out there, but I don't feel like I have to have seen every single thing. Maybe I would understand more about the movies if I had seen the animated ones. But I don't mind sometimes there being things that don't completely make sense. I like being able to bring my own meanings to it." Clearly, though, Ted did not expect the movies to be the single stable text of *The Matrix*.

Ted and Greg also talked about seeking out other online material for shows and movies they liked as a way of finding new narratives or filling in narrative gaps. Ted talked about how his older sister started watching the television series *Lost* and so he began watching it too:

> But what I found out that she didn't know was that there were all kinds of fake websites. There was an Oceanic Airlines (the name of the fictitious airline in the series) website where you could put in numbers and get clues to the show. And there were others I started to find too that were about the show. It was pretty cool. I don't know that it added too much to the show, but it gave me more to think about and I liked the puzzles. My sister didn't have a clue either.

Ted also talked about how he began to look on fan forums and wikis about the show to find more fictional websites created for the show.

This is yet another example of the kind of collective intelligence that I discussed in chapter 2. In this situation, however, there is more at work than just discussing popular culture texts. Instead, finding more narrative material creates what Neil Young, a computer game producer, calls *additive comprehension* (Jenkins 2006a, 123). In other words, the online content provides clues, information, or narratives that enhance or alter the perspective of the audience member. The additional material does not change the entire narrative but may in fact significantly shift the interpretation. For the television series *Lost*, for example, there are also now short videos, created for online viewing, that offer more background and development of key characters. At the same time, online collective intelligence means that no single audience member need feel responsible for tracking down, or keeping track of, all the possible material being generated. As Jenkins (2006a) points out about *The Matrix* narratives:

> Across a range of fan sites and discussion lists, the fans were gathering information, tracing allusions, charting chains of commands, constructing

timelines, assembling reference guides, transcribing dialogue, extending the story through their own fan fiction, and speculating like crazy about what it all meant. The depth and breadth of *The Matrix* universe made it impossible for any one consumer to "get it" but the emergence of knowledge cultures made it possible for the community as a whole to dig deeper into this bottomless text (127).

As more and more transmedia storytelling emerges, where the content online is as important as that on the movie or television screen, then students will be encountering and regarding narrative as fragmented but also as under their control as to which fragments they choose to read.

As students read multiple texts across media, they are learning how to distinguish between the genre conventions for the same material. Mitchell said, "I just wouldn't expect the show and the graphic novel to be just alike. What would be the point in that?" Instead, they are learning how to read similar characters and narratives across multiple media and pull from each the information they need to create a compelling, complete story for themselves. In addition, as they read transmedia stories, they are less likely than previous generations to privilege one genre over another. While they understand that print novels are the narratives that matter to teachers and schools, they do not afford them a more privileged cultural position. Among the students I talked to, there was no single narrative form that they would point to as more important, credible, or powerful than others. While the majority of students talked of going to or renting movies, they also talked about television programs with the same enthusiasm and thoughtfulness. And more than half of the students also played computer games and held the view, as summarized by Ted, that "Games used to just be a laugh, and not nearly as important to me or as complicated as movies. But that's changing. Games are changing." If we want to understand how students read texts in convergence culture, then we need to understand how they negotiate the multiple media and multiple genre conventions and expectations to form a complex and sophisticated narrative for themselves.

Parody and Mashups

As Jenkins (2006a) comments about the collective intelligence surrounding *The Matrix* narratives reminds us, participation is key to understanding how students experience and learn about genre in online popular culture. As I pointed out in earlier chapters, students read popular culture texts online not simply for interpretation, but also with expectations of response or appropriation. Again, the text in such circumstances is no longer a stable, single thing but exists to be modified or added to by readers. Not only does this indeed blur the line between reading and writing, it also adds to the sense that texts will be fragmented, multiple, and multivoiced.

Such a hybrid, participatory approach to reading texts affects awareness of genre as well. If you expect to respond to a particular text, either with critique or creative work, it is important to understand the genre conventions of the original text. Fan fiction, as I will discuss in a moment, is one example of such writing. But other direct examples of the necessity of such genre awareness are fan-produced film parodies and machinima. Sites such as *YouTube* and *Metacafe* are filled with fan films and film parodies. No sooner does a popular movie become part of the general cultural conversation than parodies of it begin showing up on *YouTube*. Sometimes the parody is a reenactment of a pivotal or iconic scene, sometimes it is an animation, sometimes it is a mashup or edited together scene or music video from a popular film. Regardless of the kind of film, in each instance the film, like all parody, relies on a dual knowledge of genre. First, the conventions of the original film genre must be well known so that when they are commented on or distorted in some way the audience realizes it is funny. Without a knowledge of the conventions of the movie Western or disaster film, parodies such as *Blazing Saddles* and *Airplane* are nonsensical. In addition, however, there is a genre to parody films themselves that has conventions, such as the rhythm and frequency of jokes or the insertion of competing and incongruous genre elements—such as the Count Basie Orchestra in *Blazing Saddles*.

Individuals creating and posting film parodies online are well acquainted with the need for both kinds of genre knowledge. For example, the animated parody series of alternate film endings on *howitshouldhaveended.com*, imagining how the films should have ended, depend on genre knowledge. You need an understanding of superhero movies to get the joke in the alternative ending to the film *Superman*, where Batman asks Superman what he did after defeating Lex Luthor and Superman replies, "Oh the usual. Made sure they put Luthor away. Made out with Lois for a little bit. Flew out into space, smiled at the camera." A similarly popular site with students is *angry-alien.com*, which offers 30-second-long, highly abridged, animated versions of popular films such as *Titanic* or *Brokeback Mountain* with the main characters as bunnies. "I love the thirty-second movies with bunnies," Angela said. "And the thing is they get everything right in thirty seconds, every important line, every scene you remember." Angela understood not only the films that were being parodied, but also how the parodies themselves worked. Parodies abound online, from the countless parodies of well-known films such as the *Matrix* or *Star Wars* series to other films such as *Silence of the Lambs* or *The Godfather*. Many of these parodies are produced by high school and university students who clearly understand both the genres they are ridiculing and the genre of film parodies themselves.

While parody is a popular form of participation, new media technologies have also resulted in new genres, such as mashups or machinima, created from the blending of media and genre. Sometimes called *mashups*, though the students I interviewed just called them *Internet videos*, the creators bring together video from television or movies and then remix the sound or music. They also usually re-edit the video, making creative juxtapositions of the existing material. *Machinima* are videos in which the creators have used the tools and images from video and computer games to create films with original narratives and dialogue and soundtracks. Mashups, machinima, and other combined genres are prime manifestations of convergence culture.

In mashups, these individuals have taken scenes from movies and television and created new narratives or new experiences by blending in new dialogue and music. Sometimes such videos are homages and re-creations of the mood or message of the original film, such as a video that mixes a montage of still photos from the film of *The Sisterhood of the Traveling Pants* with the Ace of Base pop song "Cruel Summer." Some machinima videos are also music video tributes to the game or to the song involved. Other mashups re-create favorite scenes from films such as *Titanic* with animated Legos or Claymation or just friends acting in a house, and some machinima use computer game engines to re-create scenes or create new narratives from television series such as *Star Trek: The Next Generation*. A recent genre that has developed is low-tech homemade re-creations of films such as *Jurassic Park* or *Star Wars* based on the style of re-creations in the film *Be Kind Rewind*. The creators of the fan films even label the videos as "sweded" versions of the original film, as the characters in *Be Kind Rewind* do when they try to pass their versions off as having been made in Sweden. It is intriguing to see a genre of fan film emerge from a portrayal of fan filmmaking in a studio movie. While the videos are amusing as they stand, the intertextual connections to *Be Kind Rewind* reward viewers who have seen the film and are in on the joke.

Then there are the mashups and machinima that are not specifically connected to the narrative of a film or program but create an unusual juxtaposition of image and word or even a new remixed text. One example of this would be video of the Monty Python "Knights of the Round Table" song to images from the original *Star Trek* series. Ted said he had heard of the video from a friend and then emailed all his friends the link. "You had to have watched both the (film *Monty Python and the*) *Holy Grail* and the TV show (*Star Trek*) to get it. But if you did it was hilarious because it got the characters so right and then made the song funny in a whole new way." The reimagining of texts, of creating a new vision with the available pieces from popular culture, so that the new text reflects the creator's sensibility, is what appealed to students about these videos. One of the most popular machinima series is *Red vs. Blue*, which uses characters from the computer game *Halo* to create a new narrative. In this situation, the armor-clad, faceless soldiers from *Halo* stand about lamenting their meaningless lives and assignments in a comic cross between *Clerks* and *Waiting for Godot*.

And even new mashups can get mashed up. The video of "Why Is the Rum Gone," which remixes images and dialogue from the film *Pirates of the Caribbean* to a techno beat to create a new piece of music and video (and includes sampled images of the Teletubbies, Pikachu, and the Terminator) was itself sampled and remixed many times with films ranging from *The Transformers, The Lion King*, and the *Harry Potter* films. The continued sampling and remixing illustrates the importance of participation to convergence culture genres. As Knobel and Lankshear (2008) note, "Participation (in remixing online popular culture texts) signals solidarity with the spirit of the phenomenon ('I get it; I'm part of this' or 'I am like you') rather than any particular attention to the information value of the images" (29). A central convention of online popular culture genres, then, is participation; they are not simply meant to be read, but they are to be responded to and re-created time and again.

As with the multiple texts students encounter in transmedia storytelling, the mashups and machinima students read make them comfortable with the juxtaposed, multimodal, multivoiced text. Angela, who said she probably watched videos on *YouTube* and other sites more than she watched television, said that she usually found things to watch through the recommendations of friends, either online or by word of mouth.

> One of my co-workers, my manager, she told me about this *Mario* (mashup) video on *YouTube*. It's like a *Mario* video put to this really sensual song and she said it was hilarious. So I went and saw it and it was funny because you just wouldn't have thought of those things together. People put the weirdest things together and sometimes it's just weird. A lot of the time. But it also stretches your imagination because you didn't think about putting those different things together like that and then you see both of the originals differently. Everyone likes to be surprised and that's what makes things funny.

The juxtaposition of incongruous texts and the challenging of genre conventions, along with the participation either in new remixes, or recommendations to friends, or comments on the websites, appealed to these students and created for them new concepts of genre. As I will discuss in chapter 6 on irony and emotion, students also liked the subversive nature of parody and irony.

A final point about the emerging genres of mashups and machinima is that they demonstrate again how technologies shape genre conventions. Machinima is an obvious example in that the limitations of the game engines constrain what a creator can do. Similarly, video cameras and editing software have certain limitations. But there are other limitations that also have had an effect on these emerging genres. For example, bandwidth has had a substantial impact on the way mashups and machinima have developed. Because of the limited amount of data that can be transmitted to computers, online video was created to be shown on a small screen for a short duration. Most of the videos on *YouTube* are made to be viewed on a screen only slightly bigger than a couple of credit cards laid side by side. In addition, the image resolution is often less than crisp. Consequently, the most successful *YouTube* videos are ones with close-ups of images or people rather than long shots of landscapes and crowds. In addition, bandwidth limits, and the fact that people still mostly watch online video sitting at a computer rather than lounging on a couch, means that online videos have been relatively short. The videos on *YouTube* and other sites are mostly less than five minutes long. Like the limits imposed on pop musicians by the 45-rpm record, creators of online videos have responded to the technology with specific genre conventions. The bandwidth limits for online videos have led to a genre that emphasizes short films with large images and fast editing. Students are aware of these genre conventions for online video. Jenny said:

> I do look at *YouTube*. I found this one thing about Diet Coke and Mentos that it lasts for so many chains and I thought it was amazing watching that. But mostly I just look at things people tell me about. It's just, not like some people I guess, I don't have time to just search and search for videos I like on *YouTube*. But if people tell me about them then I know I can watch them and I can watch it fast and it will be like a fun break that I can do and get back to work.

Like Jenny, other students said they used online videos for brief breaks or at least expected them to be short and usually not dramatic. "It's not like I'm watching *YouTube* for Shakespeare," Ted said. "I expect it to be quick and funny. That's it. It's not like the commitment of two hours I'm going to make to go to a movie." Although students did not mention bandwidth specifically, several did note that the screen and image constraints of online video limited how much they would watch. Jenny said, "I can watch a few (videos online) but I get tired fast of the poor pictures. I wish it was better." And Brianna said, "It's not comfortable to sit at a computer and watch a whole TV show. I can't imagine a movie. And you have to do it alone. Can you see me and my friends hovering around a computer screen to see a tiny picture? I need a big TV and a big chair so I can lean back and enjoy." Brianna echoed the comments of other students who said that movies and television programs were best watched on bigger screens because of issues of clear images, comfort in watching, and the ability to watch shows and movies as a social activity.

Fan Fiction, Response, and Genres

To get a sense of how the cross-media and participatory convergence culture influences what students learn about genre, I want to look briefly at three examples: fan fiction and fan film communities, computer games, and the templates that organize social networking sites.

Fan fiction, as a form of participatory popular culture, has been the subject of rich and persuasive research since Henry Jenkins's (1992) *Textual Poachers* was published. As Jenkins's book illustrates, fan fiction, like many aspects of fan behavior, existed before online technologies but with far fewer participants. As with so much of participatory popular culture, new media technologies have expanded the scope of fan fiction writers and readers by making it so simple to write, post, and read these texts. Jenkins has continued his study of fan fiction (2006a; 2006b) as it has moved online, focusing in particular on the struggle between individuals writing fan fiction and mass popular culture producers trying to protect their intellectual property rights. More recently, other research has included Rebecca Black's (2005; 2007; 2008) extensive and important study of the literacy practices of English language learners who use fan fiction as a way of engaging both popular culture and new linguistic challenges, as well as research by Ito (2006) and Wright (2008).

The most obvious way genre operates in fan fiction is that the writers need to learn the genre conventions of the larger texts that they are adapting. There are different genre conventions in the narratives of *Grey's Anatomy* than in those of *Star Trek* or of *CSI*, which people writing fan fiction need to follow. In addition, fan fiction writers must learn certain literary moves necessary in fan fiction that make it different from the movies, television programs, computer games, or comics from which they are drawing characters and inspiration. Writers have to learn to write short stories or novels but ones in which the characters and setting are essentially known and require less exposition than conventional novels and stories. Clearly, students involved in fan fiction are thinking about these popular culture genres and how they adapt them to their own writing. Ashley, who is an avid fan fiction reader and writer, talked about what she and other writers had to learn to write effectively about the *Harry Potter* characters. She said she not only had to know the information in the books well and to feel she had an understanding of the motivations of the characters but that she also had to "fit the same kind of mood as the books. It's got to have the same feel. You can't like decide 'OK, I'm writing a romance novel,' even if you're writing about romance. It still has to be like Harry Potter." What Ashley is clearly talking about is the need to conform to the conventions of both plot and description, but also of style, of the J.K. Rowling novels. She said the best fan fiction writers learn the conventions so effectively that their work begins to blend with the original novels:

> You really do. I would read series over and over waiting for the next book to come out so I'd know I was prepared for the next book and what was supposed to happen in the next one. And sometimes you get confused. Was this a fan fiction I read that I'm remembering? Was this the book? Because

you get so into those (fan fiction stories) and they are so much like the mood of the book that you realize you have to read the book over and figure out what's what. And you read it and it's like "All right, I like what this author online said that happened during this time period that the book doesn't tell you."

Ashley was quick to point out that none of them copied Rowling and that each writer did try to develop "a sort of unique way of writing that people could recognize," but that it was important to connect to the conventions of the books and films.

Yet rather than repeat all the insights gained in previous studies of fan fiction, I would like instead to focus on how fan fiction literacy practices online illustrate the conception of genre as a social activity. Fan fiction, as it has developed online, is not just produced by writers but is actively responded to by readers. This active and dialogic online environment influences the development of fan fiction genres as surely as the conventions authors draw from in their narratives.

Gunther Kress (2003) notes that the development of genre is dependent on social relationships. He regards genre as the structure and shape that we use in social interactions to allow predictable and coherent communication and that texts produce representations of these social interactions. "The significant point is that social actions shape the text that is a result of such actions. If the actions are relatively stable and persistent, then the textual forms will become relatively stable and persistent. At that point generic shape becomes apparent" (85). Once stable genre forms emerge, there arises within a discursive community expectations that certain conventions be met in that form; there can be criticism or confusion if they are not. A genre, then, requires a community to be able to communicate and replicate the conventions of the text until they become the expectations of readers. For mass popular culture genres in the twentieth century, the communication from audience to producer came indirectly through attendance or viewership or purchases—and later perhaps through focus-group research. But in the online fan fiction community communication from writer to reader and back again is easy, quick, and direct.

In her research, Black (2008) demonstrates how integral response and critique is to online fan fiction. Although the content of different responses varies, she notes that much of it is focused on critique of a writer's narratives as well as constructive comments intended to help the writer improve her or his work. In general, the kinds of comments readers provide are couched in supportive and non-confrontational language. "Most readers are careful to avoid flaming the writer and instead work to temper constructive critique with appreciation for other aspects of the writing and encouragement for the author" (112). It is clear, however, that in the online fan fiction world, response is expected by both writers and readers. Whether the response is straightforward encouragement, critique and comment, or what Black calls "editorialized gossip," the convention is that writers and readers engage in dialogue. Indeed, for some fan fiction participants, a story with multiple chapters and no responses is evidence of the poor quality of the text. It is in this dialogue, along with other comments on aspects such as usage and mechanics, that there is often a substantial conversation either explicitly or implicitly about genre expectations and how best to meet them.

To get a sense of how things works, consider again Ashley. She began writing fan fiction when she was in middle school on the *Harry Potter* website, moving to *FanFiction.Net* when she was in high school because she felt it would accommodate a more adult theme and reach a broader audience. She said:

> Fanfiction.Net is usually motivated toward people of the age of 15 and older. There is a little more in detail and probably what a lot of people consider more graphic. You get lost in it, like you do in a book. It's not just "OK, here's the situation and just a story." It's a lot more detailed and I write like that. I write more in detail and I write longer.

Ashley understood that the audience for the website helped shape the genre conventions of the pieces posted there. Not only could she deal with more mature themes on *FanFiction.Net*, but she could engage in more stylistically complex writing. She said she had learned about *FanFiction.Net* through the comments of one of her readers on the *Harry Potter* site who said Ashley might find a more receptive audience to her work there.

Ashley was writing two different fan fiction novels, working on the fifth chapters of both. She said she had read countless stories and was currently keeping up with thirty to forty stories; she received email notifications of updates for another 100 stories. Ashley said she liked the way fan fiction offered new perspectives into familiar stories:

> I love seeing how everybody can spin what's already written and say like, "OK, we don't like how the author did it. We're going to switch it." Or "This whole book doesn't count; we're going to do it our way." It is quite interesting to see the different views that people think. A lot of people think

that one character in the book—"Oh, he's evil." But what if you want to make the main character turn evil with him, instead of being the good guy? It's really interesting to see the different spins that everybody puts on it. 'Cause a lot of people view the same thing, but they put their own little bitty details on it and then it's like, "Wow, I never thought of that," and then it gives you your own ideas to do things. It's how you get ideas.

Yet, as Ashley described it, the alternative narratives only worked if the writing worked within the genre for which it was written. "You have to know when you're writing that everyone has read every book so many times and seen every movie. We all know what the characters are like, what the places look like. So you can't just say, 'Hogwarts isn't a castle' or you can't change the basics of stories. It's got to fit." In these comments, Ashley outlines the productive tension that defines fan fiction. To be successful, fan fiction must cover recognizable territory both in terms of the genre conventions of the narrative—*Harry Potter* stories, for example, must work within the genre conventions of fantasy or coming-of-age stories—and yet not simply cover territory already well explored in the books and films. In many ways, this is the challenge presented by any genre: meeting conventions while introducing novelty. The genre expectations of fan fiction readers can be much more demanding, however, and they will have the opportunity to respond to the writer. Ashley said that when she or other writers begin to stray too far from the genre conventions, that is one of the first things to which readers respond.

Black (2008) points out that comments and mentoring about genre conventions extends even to the Author's Notes that many writers put at the beginning of a story. When one writer wrote an Author's Note that contained an extended list of thanks to readers who had helped her with her writing, some readers criticized the length of the list as being inconsistent with the genre of the Author's Note, while others then defended the practice.

This kind of response and learning begins in fan fiction with "beta readers." Beta readers are individuals who read and comment on a text before it is published on the website for the public. Beta readers are highly valued in the fan fiction community and the writer–reader relationship that develops between author and beta reader is often long-term and quite intimate. On *FanFiction.Net*, you can browse a list of beta readers who fill out a profile listing their strengths and weaknesses as readers (such as whether they are strong copy editors or stronger at character development or genre and character consistency and so on), as well as the genres of narratives they prefer to read.

Ashley said her beta reader had been invaluable to her. "She lets me know when I'm getting out of character or with plot holes. She's really good at finding plot holes." In return, Ashley acts as a beta reader for other writers. "I have beta'd for a few people. In high school, a lot of my friends who might have writings they had to turn in for English classes, they'd ask me to proof it. So that got me started on fan fiction reading for people. So that helped. It's a neat way to meet people and improve your writing." The social aspects of fan fiction reading and writing are clear in Ashley's comments. She is both learning to work with genre as the kind of social function of communication through predictable textual conventions and also using that as a way of maintaining and developing social relationships. Sustaining social relationships, whether through fan fiction, fan forums, or social networking pages, comes back time and again as a significant motivation and effect of participatory popular culture.

Ashley said that, in addition to responses from readers, there were resources on websites about how to write better fan fiction (and there are similar sites about making fan films or machinima or video blogs). The advice on the sites includes standard writing advice, such as not relying too much on a computer spell-check or telling about action rather than showing it directly. Yet a significant amount of the advice on such sites is either explicitly or implicitly about genre. For example, on the site *How to Write Almost Readable Fanfiction*, Jane Leavell offers more than thirty pieces of advice, including many that are specifically about genre. There is advice about narrative consistency with the original popular culture text, "Watch the show. Watch it over and over again. Base your characterizations and dialogue on the show" (Leavell 2008). But there is also a great deal of advice about the genre of fan fiction writing itself. For example, Leavell (2008) writes:

> Write about the actual character, not your fantasy, unless you label the story "AU" or "alternate universe." Many Sentinel fans picture Blair Sandburg as a frail, delicate flower, but if you watch the show, you'll note that the character is quite short but also quite solidly built. He is not fragile or slender. He does not have thin wrists or thin shoulders or thin anything. Similarly, don't have Joe Dawson of Highlander kneel by anyone—Joe (like the actor who plays him, Jim Byrnes) lost both legs just above the knee and wears prostheses. He CAN'T kneel.

Such advice reflects a common theme in the genre advice of experienced fan fiction writers and readers. Members of fan fiction communities often caution or admonish writers to stay true and consistent with the original popular culture text and not indulge in personal fantasies that are not part of the original film or television "canon" of texts.

A particular genre convention of some fan fiction—the Mary Sue character—comes in for particular criticism. A Mary Sue character is "a character representing the author of the story, an avatar, the writer's projection into an interesting world full of interesting people whom she watches weekly and thinks about daily" (Pflieger 2008). Mary Sue characters, as Leavell notes, are broadly condemned in fan fiction communities. "You may write a Mary Sue story—again, all writing is good practice—but if you post it or print it, be prepared to either be flamed or laughed at, even if a few people profess to like the story" (Leavell 2008).

Whether in beta reader profiles, comments to writers, or pages such as Leavell's, it is clear that the dialogue in fan fiction communities between readers and writers works to reinforce and reproduce the textual characteristics of genre. This social construction of genre works quickly and efficiently for students such as Ashley to initiate and integrate new writers into the established conventions of the community.

Learning Conventions While Playing Games

Among the forms of mass popular culture in which students engage, computer games are often the ones least familiar to their parents and teachers. While older generations may have some idea what students are experiencing with movies or television programs or music, they are often neither players of games nor involved in conversations about them. Thus, discussions of the genre conventions of computer games are completely foreign territory. Those familiar with computer games are also familiar with the development of distinct computer game genres such as first-person shooter, god-games, RPGs (role-playing games), and MMORPG (massive-multi-player-online-role-playing games). And, like a television series or movie, a computer game might fit in several genre categories depending on the classification criteria. For example, a game might be a multi-player, role-playing, science-fiction game for the X-Box, with each of those classifications defining a different set of genre conventions (Burn and Carr 2007). Though the style of gameplay is often the genre category most often used when discussing games, discussions among players often move among different categories when commenting on conventions of a given game (Burn and Carr 2007). In addition to the development of genres with recognizable characteristics, genre hierarchies have developed among many game participants. For example, in print fiction, romance novels do not carry the same cultural capital as so-called "literary" fiction; similarly, computer games based on popular movies are looked down on by many gamers and assumed to be of poor quality.

Because they have developed as part of convergence culture, it is not surprising to see in computer games many of the genre characteristics I have described previously. Computer games are multivoiced, multiple, and multimodal texts. In addition, they are, by definition, participatory texts, which means that they are unstable and always changing every time they are played by an individual. There is a growing and significant body of research on literacy and computer games that covers such aspects as learning, (Gee 2003), narrative (Mackey 2006), identity (Thomas 2007), and interpretation and writing while playing (Carr, Buckingham, Burn, and Schott 2007; Garrelts 2005). Also, like other forms of popular culture today, computer games are the subject of convergence culture practices such as fan forums, fan fiction, sampling, and uses of social networking pages Again, however, I choose to focus in this chapter on what students playing computer games are learning about genre.

Like students reading and writing fan fiction, computer games can emphasize how genre is constructed through social communication and relationships. Young people playing the online, role-playing game *World of Warcraft* move back and forth between talking as their online characters and talking as themselves. When they talk as themselves, their comments include both social dialogue and mentoring conversation. The latter covers tactical advice as well as advice and feedback about genre and character conventions (Carr 2007; Bennerstedt 2008). Natalie, an avid player of *Furcadia,* another online role-playing game, said that she both gave and received similar comments while playing.

> I've been playing for six years and sometimes, when new people will play the game, it aggravates me because they're not into the definition of Furcadia. They don't know the commands. They don't know how they're supposed to talk and get everything to work. And they just sort of make me mad because they are using these little sentences that's like "walks over and

sits in a chair" instead of like defining their character like how they walk and what they're thinking.

As with fan forums, gaining insider status is part of the appeal of online games. Once accepted into the community, participants then have to decide whether to try to integrate newcomers by explaining genre conventions or instead try to ostracize or ignore them. As Thomas (2007) points out, students new to games quickly try to adopt the proper conventions, including their writing styles. One participant in her study, playing a game in which his avatar is a warlord in ancient China, learned that to be credible he had to alter his writing voice. "To do this I read a lot and see how people of my character's 'stature' and 'personality' talk and I simply pick and copy pieces into Zhou Wei's speech" (Thomas 2007, 54). Natalie's position, which is not unusual among gamers, illustrates how embedded computer game texts become in social practices and hierarchies.

Natalie said that her willingness to help new participants in the game learn the genre conventions varied. Like other participants in fan forums and games, she wanted new people to get involved but was wary of having what she considered her hard-earned enjoyment of the game ruined by those who did not seem to understand the conventions. She contrasted *Furcadia* with the more popular *World of Warcraft* by noting that the conventions in her game were both more difficult and more rewarding:

> (In Furcadia) you actually have to be your character and not just run around and click something. So you actually have to be your character. Since I've been playing for six years, I probably help when I feel sorry for someone (new to the game) if I'm in a good mood. When I'm in a bad mood, I'd just tell them to go away but if I'm in a good mood I will show them like how to use the commands and stuff and help them out a little bit, give them a little leeway since they're new. But after about a month of playing, I get harder on them since you've had a whole month to learn how.

Natalie said that she had learned the conventions of the game through "keeping quiet and watching carefully" but also acknowledged that she had been helped by other players from time to time. She said that she thought it would be almost impossible for a new player to truly understand the conventions of the game without explicit help from a more experienced participant.

For *Furcadia*, as with many computer games, many supplemental resources are available online, including blogs, wikis, reviews, databases of characters, online art galleries, fan forums, programming instructions, and so on. For other online games, supplemental resources include history webpages, music, and poetry (Thomas 2007). *World of Warcraft* resources include places to trade skills, learn spells, and exchange money along with fan fiction and machinima. Such resources exist for non-online computer games as well. Although some resources are professionally produced, such as the television show *X-Play*, which reviews new games, many of the resources such as lists of "cheats" or "walkthroughs" that provide intricately detailed information on to how to succeed at a game, are created and posted by individual game players. In terms of collective intelligence, this vast and varied set of resources provides game players with seemingly endless amounts of information to read and contribute to.

In addition, however, much of the supplemental material for computer games either implicitly or explicitly involves questions of genre. For example, advice on designing an avatar for a game often includes comments on how the character will be received if it does or does not conform to certain genre expectations. Actions in online games that violate genre conventions, such as when a group holding a virtual memorial service for a real participant who had died was attacked and slaughtered by another group, generate passionate discussion and debate about the appropriateness of the actions given the expectations of other players. The agreement on genre conventions of online games—and the degree of agreement becomes clear when violations of conventions occur and generate widespread condemnation—is particularly interesting given the international constituency of most online computer games. Although Natalie said that there were online forums for *Furcadia* and other websites with advice and other resources, she believed that the only way to become adept at the subtleties of the game would be through being mentored by other players. The linked and participatory nature of gaming culture, which has developed alongside computer games, illustrates how the social aspects of genre construction are even more integral to the creation and reproduction of game genres than for genres of movies and television programs.

Genre awareness in computer games involves more than the actions taken while playing, however. Computer game players also develop genre awareness of the textual qualities of the games. For example, on fan forums or online reviews, participants will discuss such textual features as the camera angles in the game that either offer a good or poor view of the action, or the "physics" of a game in terms of how physical objects do or do not seem to act as they would in the material world, or the quality of the narrative—including cut scenes—that shapes the location and challenges of a game. Textual conventions such as these often transcend individual game genres. On the other hand, some game genres, such as single-player role-playing games, may emphasize an underlying narrative and cut scenes while a sports game may not. Greg said that when he had started playing games he paid no attention to the textual qualities of games, but that changed when he started watching *X-Play*. "I never thought about camera angles or if the controls made sense, I just played it or didn't like it and gave it up. I've figured out (through *X-Play*) what made a game good and I know what to read on forums before I get one. I think reviews have helped me waste less time," he said. Once again, as discussions of these textual characteristics circulate online and in magazine and television reviews, they reinforce what are accepted as important and stable genre characteristics.

Increasingly there are instances where teachers are connecting students' familiarity with computer game genres to game-building software so that students can experiment with composing their own computer games. On the one hand, students involved in such projects often draw on their experiences with existing popular culture forms such as television and movies to create narrative lines and characters (Burn 2007). At the same time, they have to draw on their experiences as game players to meet genre expectations such as the location of the game, whether there will be cut scenes, and what kinds of challenges will be presented to those who play the game. The students are also introduced to new ways of combining print, image, and video into multimodal texts. Perhaps most distinctive, however, is the necessity for the students to understand and incorporate genre characteristics unique to computer games such as "economies"—the resources in the game that the game designer decides will be available to players such as health or weaponry (Buckingham and Burn 2007).

Templates and Individuality

Students designing computer games can use some existing templates but then find ways to create their own distinctive texts within those templates (Buckingham and Burn 2007). The widespread use of templates in creating online content has allowed the explosion of participation in popular culture online. Rather than having to learn to write

HTML code, now people can plug their information into relatively simple forms to create pages or participate in discussions or collaborations on existing pages. Indeed, the ease with which templates now allow participation sometimes causes an overestimation of some students' new media capabilities when much of what they actually know is how to fill out forms.

On the other hand, many students who begin with templates then bend and push at their constraints or at least experiment with how best to express themselves in distinctive ways through the templates. Weber and Mitchell (2008) use the analogy of construction toys to discuss how students work with existing materials to create new media texts. Students may begin with the initial templates and available materials but then work, either by themselves or in collaboration with others, to find ways to compose distinctive texts. "Suggested blueprints and models may be included with both toys and media design, but individual and collective uses and interpretations of them may differ; negotiation, subversion, and adaptation are commonplace" (39). Students use templates to help determine and work within genre conventions, but their literacy activities with the templates also indicate their willingness and desire to challenge and modify genres.

The genre implications of the use and revision of templates is easily evident on social networking sites. The development of easy-to-fill-out templates has been central to the success of sites such as *MySpace* and *Facebook*. "I'm not going to take the time to learn how to make webpages from scratch," Francesca said. "I do *Facebook* because it's so easy. You just fill in the blanks or say 'OK' to applications you want to add. If I had to do more than that I wouldn't spend my time doing it." Indeed, many students fill out the templates on social networking sites and do little more with them. For these students, participation is the key, not necessarily creating a distinctive look for the page. Yet students talk about quickly understanding what the constraints are of the templates and how to use them most effectively. Angela said:

> There's millions of different kinds of backgrounds. Some of them are pretty racy. Some of them have bands, sports teams. Mine is just stripes with stars on it. Others have patterns. But if you see one that has, like, Heidi Klum on it, then you know they're interested in Project Runway or fashion or models or if they have the New York Yankees, you know they love the New York Yankees 'cause it's their background.

Angela, like other students I mentioned in chapter 3, also acknowledged that she used her knowledge of templates to arrange material in places where it would draw more or less attention. She said:

> On Facebook it's set up so that at the top it has their relationship status, gender, sexual orientation, religion, political views, what you're interested in. I just go down the page. Then there is the contact information, what activities, music, books, quotes, and then about me, and then there's wall quotes. Everyone will just read down the page and you know that when you put stuff on the page.

What Gunther Kress (2003) notes about the importance of arrangement and multimodal texts is also relevant to how students think about the genre of social networking sites. Because the templates arrange the information in particular ways, students learn to read and write the texts with an eye toward which parts social practice has determined will be read first and which will be skipped over.

For other students, however, creating social networking pages is more than just filling out the existing templates. They work to manipulate and push against the templates to create pages that are distinctive. Some students on *MySpace* use the editing software or ready-made layouts that can be found online and adapted to a personal page. Others manipulate the conventions of the page, such as colors or backgrounds, to personalize the pages. Genevieve said she had seen one page where the "background was black and then she has a bunch of text written in black which you don't know and all she has was her horoscope that was written in blue. And so I thought that was interesting that she kind of wanted to conceal something but if (you) highlighted it you could read everything and also all her images were kind of askew." Although *Facebook* templates are less flexible, students can still edit how pages are arranged or play with the conventions of the pages. For example, one category on *Facebook* pages is for "Activities." Most students list half a dozen or so items such as cycling or cooking. But on one page, a student has the words "study, eat, sleep" written over and over again more than one hundred times, creating a large and distinctive block of type.

The different qualities in the *MySpace* and *Facebook* templates also create genre differences in how students perceive the two most popular social networking sites. In general, *MySpace* was regarded as a more playful and perhaps riskier site. Tony said, "*MySpace* is more goofy. *MySpace* you can make it your own. You can make different backgrounds, you can put music videos on there and music. You can have pictures actually on the page itself." *Facebook*, with its greater reliance on print text and its connection to college life, was considered more mature and reliable. Shannon said, "*Facebook* is technically better set up than *MySpace*. With *MySpace*, you're always fighting with technical errors…and *Facebook* has a place where you can list your political beliefs and religious beliefs, so that helps give a more serious attitude to it. *MySpace* is more lighthearted and fun."

The students responded to these differences in genre by constructing distinct identities on the two social networking sites. Ashley said she saw *MySpace* as a place to have fun with what she posted and she said, "I put up some things on *Facebook* because I think they are ideas I want people to think about. Though I have fun there too. But sometimes I think you have to let the world know what you believe in." It is important to note that all student pages on social networking sites relied a great deal on popular culture content. *Facebook* pages may not have as many images, but identities are still constructed through lists of favorite movies or songs, favorite quotations and catchphrases, and group memberships focused on popular culture. Students also accepted without questioning the kinds of information that was asked for on social networking templates. They did not question why popular culture content might be emphasized over other ways of constructing identity, seeming to take for granted that such information was the bedrock of social interactions, as I discussed in chapter 4. Just as we used to ask people on their first dates about their music and movie preferences, students now get that information from *Facebook* and *MySpace*.

Students' familiarity with reading and writing through the templates on social networking sites also influences their ideas about speed and attention online. As I noted in chapter 3, speed is a vital element of online literacy practices, including conceptions of genre. Any webpage, including those on social networking sites, has just moments to grab the attention of potential readers. Templates play into this desire for speed by reproducing predictable texts, and students work within the conventions of these templates to try to walk the fine line between predictability and novelty.

The students I spoke with feel they understand how the author of a page is using the genre expectations to communicate affinities through the textual and hypertextual moves (Davies and Merchant 2007). Not only do they feel they understand more about the person who wrote the page, including taste and personality, but they feel the lists, images, videos, and songs allow them to read the identity of the page writer quickly and accurately. Shannon said:

> On *MySpace* there's more on the page so people can have different backgrounds, different songs, different layouts, so I think you can tell more automatically just by looking at their page than by necessarily reading and that helps you figure out who someone is pretty fast, what you might have in common with them, what kind of sense of humor or musical taste they have. And you can do that sort of all at the same time.

The speed with which images allow for comprehension, and the preference for this speed over the pace of reading print, has been reflected in other research about student reading and popular culture (Williams 2002; Keller 2007). Yet scholars have noted that images are not in fact read simultaneously and that arrangement in space emphasizes particular elements on a page or screen and draws readers' attention to those images (Kress 2003). Different people will be drawn to different images based on their interests before they open the page. In addition, the templates that make social networking pages so easy to set up also directs the reading of them. A template, whether on a *MySpace* page or a blog or a newspaper or a television news program, creates genre expectations that individuals use to guide their reading and to make decisions about what is worth paying attention to. Just as television viewers with a remote control in hand can quickly zap through channels, recognizing instantly whether a program is news, sports, sitcom, and so on, visitors to social networking sites say they make similar rapid judgments.

Conclusion

A consideration of the genre conventions that students are learning through online popular culture, and the ways in which they are learning them, offers several intriguing insights into current literacy practices. First, while students learn about genre through reading and composing texts, the social aspects of genre construction and reproduction are more explicit online. Whether it is a veteran game player instructing a novice or a beta reader on a fan fiction site offering advice, there is often much more direct instruction in genre conventions and direct criticism when the conventions are violated. Students reading and writing online expect response in general and have also come to expect response about the genre conventions about different media and texts, even if they don't talk about it in terms of genre. As with so much of online popular culture, participation is not only an option, it is an expectation.

Also, students increasingly expect popular culture texts to cross media and genres. They are reading and writing about the same characters and narratives in different ways for different purposes. Transmedia storytelling is not only changing the way they expect to find popular culture content, but it is changing how they read the content they find. Students may watch *The Matrix* movies and play *The Matrix* computer games, encountering the same characters and setting but having very different expectations about the nature of the text and the genre expectations they should hold. They are less likely to create hierarchies of media or genres—to hold movies over television or print novels over graphic novels—and yet are more likely to move back and forth between genres and their conventions with ease.

Finally, students are more comfortable with fragmented, unstable texts. From massive multi-player online games that have no set narrative to television programs such as *Heroes* and *Lost* that routinely play with time and linear narratives and on to graphic novels such as the *Watchmen* series that challenge narrative and character conventions, students are able to deal with texts that are not linear and do not result in tidy conclusions. Instead, they are willing to engage with unstable, fragmented texts and expect that part of the meaning-making process will come from their own participation, perhaps as players or perhaps through online or face-to-face discussions with other audience members. Certainly, it would be wrong to overstate students' interest in such postmodern texts, as is indicated by the continued popularity of linear, straightforward narratives in summer blockbuster movies. At the same time, however, those blockbusters have included films such as *The Matrix* or *The Dark Knight*, with their morally ambiguous characters and open-ended narratives.

The development of new media technologies has increased the capability of individuals to read and write in multiple media and multiple genres. Understanding how students learn about and learn to read and write within new and changing genres is essential to thinking about how we can talk about and teach genre in convergence culture.

CHAPTER 6

The Pleasure of Irony

Emotion and Popular Culture Online

Everyone knows that this is the age of irony.

Mitchell belongs to a *Facebook* group called the "Church of Keanu Reaves" that has a digitally altered image of Jesus with the face replaced by a photo of the movie star. The description of the group is "Hail Keanu Reeves as 'THE ONE' and knows kung fu." Mitchell also likes online videos where people "make fun of things that are too serious." He shows me one of his recent favorites, the video satire of the 2008 U.S. presidential race on *JibJab.com* called "Time for Some Campaignin'," in which animated caricatures of Barack Obama, John McCain, and others sing a parody of "The Times They Are a Changin'."

Everyone knows that popular culture breeds sentimentality.

Francesca said that when a friend died the surviving friends on *Facebook* created a group to his memory. The content that was posted to the page was printed out and given to the parents of the friend. "People posted all kinds of things, stories about him, pictures, lyrics from songs that helped them. Lots of lyrics from songs that helped people deal with it. It's just like a way to tell them goodbye and there's always that date on and list of friends. His mom just bawled when we gave it to her."

In fact, irony and sentimentality permeate popular culture, both online and off. It is no surprise then that irony and sentimentality are rhetorical strategies that permeate the online literacy practices of our students, often in quick succession or close juxtaposition on their personal pages, blogs, and other sites. Further, it should be little surprise that students are drawn to irony and sentimentality in popular culture, in the texts they read and watch, in the content they appropriate and employ, and in the rhetorical moves they learn. While the emo-

tional appeal of popular culture has been the subject of much scholarly discussion, the advent of online technologies has changed the
way individuals read and respond to such emotions. The online literacy practices of students highlight the dual-sided and mercurial nature of emotion in contemporary popular culture as they read and
create texts that switch rapidly between the poles of irony and sentimentality.

Conventional wisdom holds that the allure of popular culture
rests in large part in its emotional power. Popular culture texts tap
into our emotions in cheap and easy ways and that provides us with
cheap and easy pleasures. Sven Birkerts's (1994) comment is emblem-
atic of the positions of so many cultural critics. "With visual media...impression and image take precedence over logic and concept,
and detail and linear sequentiality are sacrificed" (122). These kinds
of laments from cultural critics on both the right and the left are
grounded in concerns about the connections between emotion and
pleasure, and the implication that they supersede rationality and critique. The same wariness of emotion concerns many educators, according to David Buckingham (2003), who:

> Continue to distrust students' pleasures in the media. We are wary of
> sensuality, emotion, and irrationality, and we find it hard to deal with them
> when they inevitably arise. We are led by a political drive to fix and define
> meanings and pleasures that can be rationally evaluated and contested.
> While we are beginning to acknowledge the educational potential of media
> production, we are often suspicious of the creative play with meaning that it
> seems to afford (314).

Yet, in conversations with students, it becomes clear that the
pleasures in their online popular culture practices are not necessarily
rooted in easy sentiments but are a complex mixture of control, participation, and emotion. Such mixtures have a powerful effect on students' motivations for engaging in online literacy practices. In this
chapter, I examine how emotion plays out in students' online reading
and writing with popular culture. I focus on students' uses of irony
and sentimentality, both in the texts they find appealing and the references deployed in the performance of identity. I also explore the
role of students' perception of pleasure in the manipulation of popular culture texts and how that motivates students' literacy practices.

Popular Culture's Power of Emotion

Emotion and popular culture have always been linked. Popular culture lets us feel things, experience emotions familiar and strange. As Lawrence Grossberg (1997) has argued, popular culture appeals in many ways, but among its most important qualities is the way programs and advertisements are often structured around extreme highs and lows of emotion. Dramas are meant to tug at our hearts, comedies to surprise us with laughter, advertisements to arouse anxiety or desire. Even television and web news are often focused on stories or discourse that will provoke anger at injustice or anxiety about danger or pity about tragedy. There are many elements popular culture producers use to evoke emotional responses. Images and icons provide shortcuts to cultural concepts and values (Hill 2004). Familiar narratives and tropes tap into common myths, prejudices, and ideologies. Stories, synecdoche, and metaphor often target our emotional responses rather than our analytical processes.

If the goal of mass popular culture is to reach as many consumers as possible and to keep them consuming, then emotion is a powerful tool. If a movie or television program or song can touch our desires or insecurities, then we will be less likely to turn from it. Psychological research has demonstrated that it is easier to retain material or events that incite emotional responses. If the text connects in some way to us, by allowing us to identify with the characters or emotions, then we feel fulfilled. Consequently, it is often more important for a television program or movie to reflect an emotion or attitude than it is to make a particular point or take a particular position. Ron Lembo (2000) says that television viewers often evaluate a program on its "plausibility" or whether it in some way connects to viewers' experiences. Mass popular culture producers, in search of mass audiences, adapt and reuse familiar narratives that will evoke a common set of emotions in the widest audience possible. In doing so, they often smooth off any sharp emotional and intellectual edges that could alienate potential audiences (Bourdieu 1996). Consequently, many television programs and movies resolve their narratives with widely held emotional commonplaces that dominate the culture. We all know the morals to these popular narratives and can easily think of movies and programs that have used them: stand up against injustice, family matters most, love conquers all, be true to yourself. The fact that academics often dismiss such commonplaces as naïve and simplistic acceptances of dominant consumer culture does not lessen their power among the culture at large, including our students (Newkirk 1997).

At the same time, the emotional appeal of popular culture can come through its challenges to dominant cultural attitudes and values. There is no denying the subversive and unsettling effect of rock music at any number of points in its history from Elvis to the Sex Pistols to Marilyn Manson. Even as those performers were making money for corporate recording labels, they were also genuinely disrupting certain dominant cultural positions, particularly in terms of authority and sexuality. The recent debate about violence in computer games and content on *MySpace* pages also indicates how popular culture can challenge dominant cultural assumptions. Such challenges are especially appealing to adolescents and young adults, who often feel they are chafing under the stifling constraints of adults. Yet the emotional appeal of subversive popular culture also stems from the reality that while the new music or computer games may irritate and baffle the older generation and provide some pleasure in constructing independent identities, it also does not require a genuine—and genuinely frightening—act of rebellion. You can listen to Eminem, drive your parents to distraction, and yet still go to college, get married, and carry out your part in reproducing the dominant ideology.

Regardless of whether our emotional responses to popular culture arise from a fulfillment of desire or a challenge to authority, it is a mistake to imagine that such responses are either simple or passive. Instead, we respond as active readers of texts, connecting them to our own experiences, using them in our own contexts, in terms of emotions just as we do in other aspects. A movie depicting a baby can have a very different emotional impact on a new parent than it did on the same person a year before. In addition, our dissatisfaction with a popular culture text can drive our emotions as much as our satisfaction. Fans of programs or movies can feel a mixture of devotion and frustration. Fan forums and fan fictions are often driven as much by the failure of popular culture narratives to completely satisfy as they are by simplistic adoration (Jenkins 1992). Or, as Ashley described her motivation in writing *Harry Potter* fan fiction, "I don't like frustration (with particular plot turns in the series) and that's like others in the fan fiction community. OK, we like the series, but we like what we write better. We like how *we* end it better."

Emotional responses to popular culture texts change not only with the context of the reader but with the context in which the movie, program, song, or game is employed. Popular culture texts, in articulating our emotions, do connect us to the wider world. We can, in turn, use these same icons, images, songs, and narratives to re-create emotions for ourselves, or, if we deploy them correctly, for others. It is instructive to think about how a single text can be appropriated ironically or sentimentally and back again, yet the message is always clear to the audience. For example, consider the song "What a Wonderful World," recorded by Louis Armstrong. It was initially released in 1968 as a plea for understanding during that turbulent year of U.S. history. It made its significant comeback in the public imagination in 1987 in the movie *Good Morning Vietnam*, when it was used with poignant irony in a montage of images of warfare and violence. Yet, soon after the film, the song was adopted sentimentally into wedding reception dances by the thousands and into other movie soundtracks, such as the 1998 film *Meet Joe Black*. The song was then given another ironic, and this time cynical, turn in 2002 by director Michael Moore in his documentary *Bowling for Columbine*, when he used it with a montage of images of violence around the world supported by the U.S. government.

While there are many ways popular culture producers and students use to evoke emotion, irony and sentimentality are rhetorical devices that dominate emotions in convergence culture. These seemingly disparate approaches—irony with its emphasis on detachment and subverted meanings and sentimentality with its emphasis on evoking powerful and uncritical emotions—are actually used in rapid succession or close juxtaposition in participatory popular culture. Students move quickly from the skepticism and superiority to the poignancy and longing of sentimentality in both the ways they read and write with participatory popular culture. Both approaches, then, merit consideration. I will begin with irony.

Irony and Double Meanings

It is probably harder to avoid irony in popular culture than it is to find it. Irony (and its various forms: sarcasm, satire, parody) is all over the place including *The Daily Show*, *The Colbert Report*, *Robot Chicken*, *The Onion*, *David Letterman*, *South Park*, *The Family Guy*, *Saturday Night Live*, *Airplane*, the *Scary Movie* series, and advertisement after advertisement, just to name a very few. What's more, convergence culture has opened up the opportunities for everyone to be part of irony-fest, from "sweded" movie re-creations of *Star Wars* and *Die Hard* to mashups like "Why is the Rum Gone?" to machinima such as "Red vs. Blue." In terms of reading and writing, irony is a rhetorical or literary strategy that creates discord between what you say or do and how people interpret the meaning. In terms of the rest of our lives, irony can also be a situation that is deliberately opposite of what you expect. So if you drop a plate and it shatters and I say, "Nice move," I am being ironic. If I tell you that I am becoming vegetarian to improve my health while lighting up a cigarette, my actions are ironic. If, in a movie, a character says, "Surely, you must be joking," and another replies, "I'm not joking. And don't call me 'Shirley'," that is ironic. (On the other hand, irony is not simple bad luck or things just not turning out the way you want them too. As comic Ed Byrne put it, rain on your wedding day is ironic "only if you're getting married to a weatherman and he set the date.")

There are many reasons why irony is particularly powerful in popular culture. For one thing, it's easy to do. As with the example from *Bowling for Columbine*, where "What a Wonderful World" is played over images of violence, it is easy in a multimodal text to have one of the modes undercut another. The music can run counter to the images or images run counter to print and so on. Stephen Colbert, on *The Colbert Report*, uses such an approach when, as he gives a commentary, captions appear on the screen that run counter to his spoken words. Such juxtapositions are the rhetorical device at the heart of many online video mashups that remix video and audio to create an ironic version of both texts. The numerous online videos that parody the film *300* by remixing its dialogue and music with clips from everything from *Star Wars* to *Masters of the Universe* to *The Teletubbies* are just one example of this.

Students talked about how much they liked these texts that used multimodal juxtapositions to create irony. Mitchell talked about a machinima that used characters from the *Final Fantasy* computer game in a parody of the Michael Jackson *Thriller* music video: "It's just funny to see them dancing like that. It like totally makes it hard to take the song seriously. Or the game too. And then there's a *Thriller* with Legos that cracks me up." Amy showed me a video called *A Hard Day's Night of the Living Dead* that cuts together clips of the Beatles' movie *A Hard Day's Night* with clips from zombie films to make the band's comic flight from screaming fans seem more like an extended chase seen in a horror film. "That's good, huh? I love the way they kept the sound of all the screaming girls and now it sounds like they're not fans but that they're being eaten," she said. Students also drew on multimodal approaches to irony when appropriating popular culture for their social networking site pages. *Facebook* has a popular application called bumper stickers in which images, very often from popular culture, are paired with ironic labels. An image of a pint of Ben and Jerry's ice cream is captioned "I spent Saturday night with my boyfriends...Ben and Jerry," or a drawing of two Victorian-era people sitting on a sofa has the caption, "Until you see *The Dark Knight*, our friendship is put on hold." An image of Darth Vader is labeled "Join Me Now! And Receive a Free Toaster Oven." As Mitchell rather succinctly put it, "You can make pretty much anything a joke if you put the right music with it."

Irony also works by creating detachment and distance from the original text. In order for irony to work it is necessary to be able to step back from a text and understand how it could be interpreted in a manner opposite of its surface content. Consequently, irony necessitates a disengagement from intense emotions and instead engages cynicism, skepticism, and even a certain sense of superiority at being in on the double meaning. This kind of skepticism and detachment can be appealing to adolescents who are looking for ways to establish their independence and subvert the authority of the adults in their lives. The postmodern construction of many popular culture texts that copy or sample from serious texts and then mock them, is the culture which young people have grown up with since they saw parodies on *Sesame Street* of everything from *Oklahoma* to *Masterpiece Theatre*. The irony in popular culture, from *Bugs Bunny* to *Monty Python* to *Robot Chicken*, has always had a particular appeal to young people eager to detach themselves from, and also mock, adult culture that was deemed "acceptable and mature." Online literacy practices, with their accessibility for adolescents and their capabilities of creating ironic remixes of serious cultural texts, have proved to be attractive and natural venues for young people seeking to challenge authority. Boyd (2008) notes that students, in evaluating *MySpace* pages, struggle with creating "cool" pages that would appeal to their peers and the "lame" pages that would be acceptable to their parents.

Irony also matches adolescent students' frequent desire to minimize the risks of emotional investment. Baudrillard (1994) and others have argued that the more we encounter events through mass-mediated representations, the easier it becomes to detach ourselves from their reality, their emotional and embodied impact. Watching videos on *YouTube* of plane crashes or people taking terrible tumbles from bicycles becomes just another two minutes of entertainment to be watched in between music videos. Such an over-represented world is our students' world. Adolescents, then, are wary of looking foolish, wary of looking naïve, and, above all, wary of not looking "cool." The use of irony reduces the risk of seeming to care too much, of looking as if one is buying in to adult culture.

When I asked students about popular culture content they had employed ironically on their pages, a number of them said that their motivation was both to entertain and to keep people from taking their pages too seriously. As Natalie, in discussing a clip from *The Family Guy* she had on her *MySpace* page, put it rather succinctly, "Would I put a clip of two guys having a farting contest on my page if I wanted people to take it too seriously?" Other students talked about putting items on their page in order to provide some distance from the more serious information. A number of the students had filled out questionnaires that they had placed on *MySpace* pages. They would alternate what one could assume were sincere answers with more ironic answers. Tony's questionnaire, titled "Tell Me About Yourself," had honest answers such as "Your Heritage: Italian and some Irish and German," and more ironic answers like "Favorite Drink: Vodka Martini. Shaken, not stirred." The questionnaire reflected a mix of serious and ironic material on both his *MySpace* and *Facebook* pages. "I want people to know who I am. If you can't get a picture of me from my page then what's the point. But I don't want to look so super serious that it's too intense. I want people to know I'm not taking myself too seriously. People hate that." Mitchell said that he belonged to the "Church of Keanu Reaves" group because it was funny and it was funny to have it listed on his page. But he said he would not fill out the part of the *Facebook* page that listed his actual religion because he wanted to keep that more serious information private.

Angela's *Facebook* page also had a mixture of serious and more ironic content. She said that her political and religious views were sincere, as were some of her quotes, such as one from Charlotte Bronte: "Life seems to me to be too short to be spent nursing animosity or registering wrongs." But she also pointed to material she had displayed more ironically, such as the results to a quiz titled "Who is Your Celebrity Love Match?" which in her case was Mr. T. "I totally made the quiz come out this way. I took it about five times until I got the answer I wanted because I wouldn't want to put anything real down for something like that. I don't want people to know that about me." Angela, like other students, spoke of the need to protect herself on her pages. She said to be too honest would increase the risk of being hurt.

This is the position we see many students take in classes where they are reluctant to participate, to try too hard, lest they be accused of being a "teacher's pet." In addition, the ironic stance minimizes the risk of being hurt. If you can detach yourself from a situation, pretend not to care, say you were only joking when you said "I love you," then you lessen the possibility of being hurt or at least letting others know how much you have been hurt. The extreme of this position can be trolling, where individuals invade forums or websites, mocking the often-serious discourse in the hopes of eliciting outraged responses.

Out-Mocking Critique

Popular culture producers, of course, understand the allure of irony among their audiences and how large the audiences for irony can be. Indeed, television, movies, and online popular culture texts often assume a self-referential, ironic stance that out-positions any attempts at critique. Television programs such as *Monty Python*, *Saturday Night Live*, *Seinfeld*, *The Simpsons*, and *The Colbert Report*, as well as film parodies, mock not just other television programs but themselves. On an episode of *South Park*, for example, Cartman turns to Towelie and says, "Towelie, you're the worse character ever," to which Towelie replies, "I know." *South Park* often sets up episodes so that they seem to be ending with the kind of heart-warming conclusion that marks many sitcoms, where the central character learns an important truth, only to undercut the message with a final ironic joke. Such ironic self-referentiality makes external critiques of popular culture all the more difficult. If even the people who make television programs and movies understand that their products are mindless ways of wasting time, then there is little power in making the case again. As Bill McKibben (1992) says about television, "You can hardly deconstruct it—it's deconstructing itself. There's nothing on TV to push against; even if you're inclined to push, after a while you stop and are carried along for the ride. On a medium that mocks itself, seriousness does not play" (241). If we already know not to take popular culture seriously, then why pay attention to any critique?

Again, it is not surprising to see that the programs that are often the most relentlessly ironic are among the most popular with our students. The students I talked with invariably listed the most ironic programs on television as among their favorites. "I love *South Park*. I know it's been on forever but they will make fun of anything," Ted said. "*Family Guy* is like that too. Nothing is sacred on those shows and I like that. When things get taken too seriously in the world, it's important to take them down a notch. That helps me keep perspective." Students find pleasure and control in playing the "game" of television, in which they mock the conventions of serious programs and gravitate to shows that mock themselves (Lembo 2000). Such readings provide students ways to "continually recreate an awareness that they were not taken in, or duped, by the unreality of television" (191). Similar stances are reflected in some computer games. An online game on the *Cartoon Network* website titled "Five Minutes to Kill (Yourself)" involves controlling an office worker as he wanders a corporate office trying to kill himself with staplers, photocopiers, and other equipment. Ted liked the way the game mocked both office workers and the genre of computer games. He showed me that it was listed under the categories of "Adventure Games." "Usually you think of 'Adventure Games' like war or fantasy games that are in exotic places, where the point is to kill other people or creatures and not get killed. But this is just the opposite. You're in an office and the point is offing yourself. So it's a satire of the other."

At the same time, the ironic remixes created with popular culture texts are also attractive because the challenges to authority are actually quite minimal. Mocking a movie or television program may make one feel subversive or rebellious but won't require anything as drastic as rejecting parents' financial support or dropping out of school. Amy said she frequented sites that mocked the news. "I like *The Onion* or websites like that and then different blog websites like *Mental Floss* or like *Neat-O-Rama*, just really random pages. Nothing that takes itself too seriously." But she said that such sites did not have a significant impact on her commitment to politics or political news. She said she drew distinctions between ironic sites she read for fun and serious work she did for school or work. "There are the things you go to for pleasure. But that's not like what I care about. Some things you don't joke about."

Some students did discuss their awareness that irony can offer a superficial sense of subversiveness. They understood that, while programs such as *South Park* and *Family Guy* may be irreverent and critical, the programs were still products of large corporations that were broadcast to make money. Brianna talked about the reality television programs she both watched and visited the websites for:

> I used to watch The Real World, but after Las Vegas I really stopped watching it, it got boring, so like all these shows now really just got out of control to me like I Love New York II, The Flavor of Love III. Who does that? I'm like, "Why do you keep going through that you haven't found love by now then you just need to give it up, quit having a TV show." But hey, it's all about making money, it's all about ratings and people watch it.

This critique may be a result of effective media education programs in their previous schools, a result of having grown up in a more cynical and media-saturated world, or a combination of both. For example, Genevieve said that though she enjoyed movies and music, she was also wary of ways in which popular culture texts were influencing her or her friends. "People my age, they're interested in stars. And what do stars look like and what do they wear and what, what kind of image do we have to fill as teenagers or as young adults to be accepted by society," she said. But that awareness did not stop her from enjoying popular culture as well. "I think you can know the truth about what they're trying to get us to buy and still enjoy a magazine," she said.

Rhetorically, irony requires both an ability to step back from a text and an understanding of the conventions of text. Watching *The Daily Show*, for example, only works if you understand the conventions of cable television news programs. As I have argued before (Williams 2002), stepping back from a text to comment on its conventions is the first step necessary for analysis. Gray (2005) notes that fan forums that are focused on "antifan" discourses connect irony and critique for their participants. Detachment from a text is the position that carries with it substantial cultural capital (Bourdieu 1984). Such a rhetorical move is not by itself analysis. Irony often ends with a glib comment rather than a sustained analysis. In fact, it is important not to read too much critique into the ironic displays of students. As Buckingham and Sefton-Green (1994) point out about adolescent uses of irony, "The desire to validate subcultural forms often lapses into a kind of romantic celebration, which discovers elements of 'resistance' which users of those forms would not themselves recognize" (158).

Even so, when students understand textual conventions enough to make detached, ironic rhetorical moves, it does indicate an understanding of conventions and an ability to apprehend and comment on texts that should interest teachers.

At the same time, if you are unable to understand the conventions and how the irony is working against the conventional interpretation, then you read the text either *with* the conventional interpretation or cannot interpret it at all. The danger of irony is always that, without the contextual knowledge to understand the potential multiple readings, an ironic text is read sincerely. I observed a class where students had been given a satirical article from *The Onion* about a government program to fund the construction of a $1.3 billion national poem. The instructor and I understood the use of irony to mock government budgeting processes, as well as the funding of arts programs. Many of the students, however, who were not avid newspaper readers or followers of either the government budget process or arts funding, were puzzled by the story. It seemed as if it was real to them, though somehow not quite right. When I asked the students I interviewed if they worried that ironic material on their personal pages might be misread they dismissed the concern and spoke of feeling confident that others would get the jokes, as I discussed in chapter 4. On the other hand, when I asked them if they always knew whether material on other people's pages was ironic, several echoed Amy's response, "I think so. I think I get the jokes. But sometimes I do look at a picture on someone's page and I'm not sure. Do they really mean that?"

The ability to know whether a text should be read ironically is part of its allure. Not only is there the pleasure of understanding the multiple readings but that very understanding is the mark of a certain kind of knowledge and competence as a reader (Gibbs and Izzett 2005). If you understand how to read a text against itself, you collude in the subversive reading of the original text. "Irony works to create ad hoc intellectual communities that lead audiences to view themselves, even temporarily as 'conspirators' in accepting the values to which irony indirectly alludes" (Gibbs and Izzet 2005, 132). Ironic online texts, from fake web pages to video remixes to memes, appeal to people in part because they get to be in on the joke. The insider status that drives a great deal of online popular culture content and communication (Knobel and Lankshear 2008) also appeals to students. Jenny said, "I enjoy lots of inside jokes. Like one of my (*Facebook*) groups is 'People for The Ethical Treatment of Staplers' and only my friends and I know what that means." Ashley had a similar perspective on the appeal of *Facebook* quotes, "A certain group of friends might say one thing to me, like a line from a movie we've been quoting, because it's an inside joke, but my other friends will be like 'What are they saying?' and I'm like, 'This is an inside joke and you don't need to know it.'"

Several of the students did worry about the limits of irony, however. Even as contemporary popular culture on programs such as *South Park* and in movies such as *Borat* have pushed the limits of what can be made fun of, there remain texts that stir debate when they are treated ironically. A scene from the film *Downfall*, about the last days of Adolph Hitler, has been remixed multiple times to create parodies of everything from Microsoft marketing tactics to Hillary Clinton's campaign. These videos have been very popular but also controversial in their use of the images of Hitler and his followers for ironic purposes (Heffernan 2008). Amy said that if there was one thing that worried her about how others would read her *Facebook* page, it would be the ironic attempts at humor on the graffiti part of her page that mixed popular culture references and macabre humor. "I have like a really horrible sense of humor actually. So do some of my friends," she said. "Horrible like dead babies or Helen Keller jokes or just like things that really shouldn't be funny at all and they are funny to me. But some people say I like really offensive things."

In general, however, the students I interviewed regarded irony as an attempt to create a text that mocked its own pretensions. They understood that the irony could be used as a way to pre-empt critique and protect themselves from judgment. There is, in their comments and their uses of irony, an understanding and awareness of language use and its effect on audience. They may not talk about these moves in the discourse of language and rhetoric that is familiar to us, but they do not engage is such moves without thought or reflection. It offers a place for writing teachers to begin engaging students in further discussions of the same issues.

Sentimentality and Attachment

If it sounds as if all these literacy practices represent a relentless flow of irony, that would be ignoring much of what is happening online with popular culture. Just as striking as the skeptical detachment of irony is the emotional commitment of sentimentality. It is no surprise to see sentimentality as a rhetorical move, often cheek by jowl with ironic content. Students display the ability to move from the ironic to the sentimental in their online popular culture practices with ease and whiplash speed. But instead of stepping back from a text and commenting on or subverting it in some way, the sentimental material embraces the emotions evoked by popular culture content without question or criticism.

Like irony, sentimentality is a long-standing and pervasive strategy in popular culture. From the fantasies of romantic comedies to the strong pull of tragedies, sentimentality has made popular everything from *When Harry Met Sally* to *Titanic*, from *Sex and the City* to *Grey's Anatomy*. Even the most frivolous sitcoms have often felt the need to have the occasional "very special episode" in which a character must learn to deal with death or abandonment or drug abuse. Even films steeped in irony, such as *Juno* or *Napoleon Dynamite*, both very popular with students, have sentimental moments designed to immerse audiences in sweet, affirming emotions. And love songs— well love songs certainly haven't gone out of style.

The reasons sentimentality is so common in popular culture seem simple but have more nuanced implications. First, strong emotions allow us to form strong attachments. While it may not be catharsis in the classical sense, if we feel happy or sad at a song or the ending of a movie, it offers us a kind of satisfaction that rational consideration by itself does not match. Briana said that she and a friend like to play a particular computer game for the emotional release it gave them. "We're like *Devil's Advocate* junkies. She gets angry and she's like 'I'm just going to play *Devil's Advocate*, OK? It's a stress reliever.' And I was like, 'Yeah, Let's play that.'" Popular culture audiences like to feel involved in a text, to be moved to tears or left with a smile. Alison's comment was typical of many students: "Sometimes I just want to not have to think about a movie. I just want to feel happy when it's over." When we approach popular culture for our entertainment we are often seeing the sensual pleasure that comes from such emotions. Time and again students referred to engaging with popular culture as pleasurable, mindless, and something that would help them escape from stress. This was true even when they discussed computer games and other texts such as horror films that required skill or engaged darker emotions.

Popular culture producers know that when we feel emotionally satisfied we are more likely to keep watching or buy more music or movie tickets. There are many stories of early cuts of movies, such as *Fatal Attraction*, that had dark endings, not being reviewed favorably by test audiences and being reshot and recut to make the endings happier. It is not difficult to see why "feel-good movie" is such a popular advertising slogan for so many movies. It is also the case, according to psychological research, that events and material that evoke strong emotions evoke strong memories. All of us, including students, remember the emotions a popular culture text evokes and then want to be able to return for more.

Students often draw on popular culture content and references as ways of expressing their own emotions. On social networking webpages, students often use quotes or lyrics from songs to express their emotions. Sandy, on her *Facebook* page, posted lyrics from the Sara Bareilles' song "Many the Miles" because "It was just where I was right then. And the song kept going through my head and it said how I felt better than I could." Posting song lyrics or quotes on personal pages often leads to comments from friends—along the lines of "That's so true" or "That song is perfect. That's just how I feel"—affirming the emotional affect of the song and their bond with the person who posted it. In a similar way Stern (2008) notes that students find online blogs, webpages, and forums often are vehicles for expressing intense emotions and describe the experience as therapeutic. "When they have a lot on their minds, many say, it is helpful to express themselves, whether through writing or adding music, art, or images. 'Getting it all out,' as one author put it, restores a sense of calm and often helps put a problem or emotion in context" (102). More often than not the music, art, or images are drawn from popular culture. Ashley said she changed the song that plays when her *MySpace* page opens to match her mood. "Some people just pick the song they like right then, but for me it has to show how I'm feeling. My friends all know this and if I leave a sad song on there too long their like 'What's with you? Are you OK?' because they know it's serious." Expressing emotions through songs or other popular culture content is not new. We've all put on sad music when down or more raucous songs when feeling celebratory or marked a romantic relationship by having a shared song with another person. What online literacy practices do, however, is to allow this expression to be published for others and allow them to respond with sympathy or congratulations. What's more, other people who might not know our mood, or know us well enough to know our mood, can now read that mood through the emotions signified in a ballad or a love song or a rebellious punk song.

Shared cultural images or songs or writing that evoke powerful emotional and sentimental responses are regularly dismissed by academics as formulaic, simplistic, and conservative. But Thomas Newkirk (2002b) argues that, for the general population including our students, the sentimental tropes and commonplaces in popular culture often carry substantial communicative and cultural power. The sentimental discourse that so often drives popular culture "seeks to activate compassion, to extend sympathy, to create conviction, to inspire courage—in effect to work against moral and emotional sluggishness" (24). In education, such goals and strategies are dismissed and disdained because they set themselves "against irony, doubt, displacement of emotion, ambivalence, critique" (24). By taking this stance, however, we risk missing the powerful motivations and appeals of such texts and the uses students make of them.

People are drawn to the sentimental in popular culture not because they are ignorant but because there is power in the emotions, and often power in the affirmations of such texts. When we are faced with those moments in life that are only beyond rational comprehension—love, loss, fear—sometimes the sentimental commonplaces are comforting and powerful. A friend of mine who recently lost her father in an automobile accident told me, "I'm just taking it a day at a time and counting on my friends to hold me up." Commonplaces? Yes. Clichés? Perhaps. But the emotional truths those words held for my friend were real. In terms of popular culture, the sentimental may also contain values that resonate powerfully for us. I have seen the film *It's a Wonderful Life* many times. I've read critiques of the film and can step back and analyze it through the lenses of film theory and cultural studies. Even so, when the final sentimental scene of the movie rolls around and the townspeople rally to George Bailey and Mary, his wife, gives him a look of love and relief and everyone in the house sings "Auld Lang Syne," I tear up. In that moment of film, there are values of friendship, community, love—"remember no man is a failure who has friends"—that move me and connect me with my experiences and values. As academics, we may hide or apologize for our susceptibility to the sentimental, but we all feel its power now and again, just as our students do.

Another reason that popular culture often employs sentimental approaches can be found in the use of sound and image. Certainly words in print can evoke emotions in us, and certainly much popular culture involves print. There is no doubt, however, that we can process images and sound much more quickly in most cases than we can process words. In addition, images and sound in popular culture, while representations of real things, do not have the extra distance that the abstraction of a printed word has from the event or object it represents. Consequently, images and sound communicate ideas and emotions more rapidly than printed words. Analysis takes time and reflection, reading only processes a word at a time, but images evoke a response before analysis. Hill argues that:

> Because our minds prefer to take the fastest and easiest route to making a decision, and because images or imagistic texts offer shortcuts toward the endpoint of making a decision, then images (or, to lesser extent, imagistic concrete language) will prompt the viewer to make a relatively quick decision, largely ignoring the more analytical, abstract information available in verbal form (Hill 2004, 33).

This does not necessarily mean that images are by themselves more or less emotional or useful as a sentimental strategy, just that they move us more quickly to our emotions with less chance for reflection and less distance from what we see represented. It is easier to put down a book, both physically and emotionally, than it is to turn from a movie or television screen.

The immediate emotional payoff of images and sound in popular culture can be important for students. A number of the students said that, if there were images or video on a page, as well as a lot of print, they would turn to the images and video first. "It's not that I won't read what's written. I can read, you know. But I'm always going to look at the pictures first," Natalie said. Tony was more specific in connecting images to emotions. "Words are going to give me information. That's what I read for, like textbooks in school and they're not going to make me laugh like a video will. Seeing something for yourself is going to make you feel like it's funny or sad or something." Students look for texts, then, that can provide them with that kind of emotional speed and connection. In a similar way, they think about keeping people connected to their pages and blogs by using popular culture content that will have an emotional impact. Natalie, as I noted in chapter 3, put a photo of a bloody tongue piercing on top of her *MySpace* page in order to shock people who visited the page and either drive them away or draw them in. Tony, on the other hand, put college sports logos on his *MySpace* page, including the background, because he wanted to be identified as a fan but also because "anyone else who's a fan is going to want to stay here. Well maybe they will. But they can know right away that it's OK to be a fan here, enthusiastic."

The groups that students list belonging to on *MySpace* and *Facebook* pages also work as quick emotional references. Just listing membership in a group, such as Brianna's listing of "Help Free the Jena Six" about the controversial civil rights case in Jena, Louisiana, has an emotional impact. Other less serious groups use popular culture references and content as sentimental strategies. Angela said she liked groups such as "Born in the 80s, Raised in the 90s" and "If you remember this you grew up in the 90s." She said, "In the group profile there are things from the '90s like Pogs and Power Rangers and all that stuff. People remember things you forget and it's funny going there. It also makes you nostalgic for your childhood, for all the things you miss now."

Nostalgia as a Rhetorical Strategy

Looking back at popular culture of the 1990s, or any decade, is just one example of the powerful hold nostalgia has as a form of sentimental appeal. Popular culture is such an integral part of all our childhoods, through toys, television, music, and movies, that we connect many of our warm memories of growing up with mass popular culture items and texts. How many of us have, on hearing a familiar theme song or spotting a toy at a yard sale like one we used to own, have feelings that go beyond simple recognition to the sweet melancholy of nostalgia? Not only is the recognition of popular culture texts and their roles in our past often important for our nostalgia but popular culture texts, through their contact with mass audiences, often help us connect our nostalgia with the nostalgia of others. We end up creating community in conversations about where we were when a song was popular or share memories of similar toys we owned. Popular culture producers often count on the power of individual and shared nostalgia as a marketing device or as a way of recycling texts, such oldies stations on the radio or the decades-old sitcoms that play on the cable channel TVLand.

Even as popular culture has been used in the past to evoke nostalgia, once again online media technologies have made it easy for everyone to access and deploy popular culture content to evoke nostalgic feelings in others. Popular culture may be talked about as ephemeral but in fact has always lasted from one generation to the next, as seen in the undying popularity of toys such as Barbie dolls and Hot Wheels cars, movies such as *The Wizard of Oz*, or popular music of groups such as the Beatles (Mitchell and Reid-Walsh 2002). The online capabilities of new media technologies now make it possible for even the most obscure and marginal popular culture texts and content to be preserved and distributed. On websites such as *Hulu.com*, it is possible to watch television programs from decades ago. There are hundreds of videos uploaded on *YouTube* that use the toys from McDonald's Happy Meals. And on countless other websites it is possible to find material from everything from comic books to music videos to fashion fads. If material is available online, then it is available for students to access and read and it is available for them to sample from and reuse. Students draw on this content to express or fulfill their feelings of nostalgia and often to connect to similar experiences from others.

Francesca showed me some of the remixed music videos she liked to watch on *YouTube*. One, for example, sets clips from the film *Titanic* to a melancholy instrumental tune Christopher Beck titled "Close Your Eyes" that was originally written for the television series *Buffy, the Vampire Slayer*. She said *Titanic* was one of her favorite movies, both for its story, "and because I watched it with my mother and sister when I was little and so it brings back good memories. I know it's (the video) sort of sappy. But when I'm feeling down or have a lot of things to think about, I can lose myself in these videos and it makes me more peaceful." And Sandy, whose *MySpace* page says, "I like mostly fantasy stories about love and adventure. I'm a woman, what do you expect?" also includes images of Winnie the Pooh and heroines from Disney films such as Belle and Jasmine. She said she included these images on her page because they reminded her of her childhood and made her smile. When I asked her what effect she wanted the images to have on people reading her page, she said, "I think it will make them smile because all of the pictures come from the movies we liked as little kids. I'm still pretty much a kid at heart and I don't want to lose that. And I want other people to know something about my heart." Female students tended to be more likely to display popular culture as nostalgia on their personal pages, and certainly were more open in talking about the material in nostalgic and sentimental terms. This is perhaps indicative of the tendency of some girls and young women to treat the more public space of the web as a more private space where they could express their emotions more fully (Mitchell and Reid-Walsh 2002). Even so, both male and female students talked of feeling nostalgic when reading some kinds of popular culture texts. While male students were less descriptive in their emotions, it was not difficult to hear a note of wistfulness in Peter's voice when he came across a video clip from a television program he used to watch and said, "*Pokemon!* Oh man, you've no idea how much time I used to spend on that. It was my whole life."

The Appeal of Emotion

The use of sentimentality in popular culture and by students also helps illuminate how pathos works in online literacy practices. In popular culture, certainly pathos is privileged over logos. The central concern for popular culture producers is to appeal to the largest audience possible, and the road to this goal is more often through emotional appeals than through extended, deliberate, logical argument. What passes for debate on television cable news programs is more of a set of ritualized exchanges that focus on hitting emotional hot buttons with loaded words and hysterical rhetoric. Such programs offer the appearance of disagreement but are as predictable and seemingly scripted as church liturgy. Advertisements, songs, movies, even television news programs play to emotions of one kind or another. Considerable research (Buckingham and Sefton-Green 1994; Alvermann, Moon, and Hagood 1999; Williams 2002) demonstrates that such emotional appeals are not wasted on students; still they do understand that emotion is being used as an appeal. Lisa said, "I like deep movies, movies that make you think, you know? But I also like romantic movies when I just want to feel happy. Everyone knows how the movie is going to end, but it still makes you happy. Everyone needs guilty pleasures." Most of the students echoed Lisa's idea that popular culture could be emotionally fulfilling. As often happens in discussions of popular culture, however, a number of them said that others were more susceptible to emotional appeals than they were.

Yet those who critique popular culture, particularly in the academy, not only disparage emotion but warn against its nefarious influences. Critics from both the left and the right—with differing rationales—argue that emotional appeals play easily upon the passions of an ignorant and vulnerable population. Such "culture jammers" as Jenkins (2006a) calls them, advocate for attacking and forming popular culture with a "melodramatic discourse about victimization and vulnerability, seduction and manipulation, 'propaganda machines' and 'weapons of mass deception'" (247). The answer, according to these critics, is to teach students and the general populace to critique popular culture texts with an emphasis on viewing emotional appeals with deep suspicion. Implicit in this position is an assumption of social class in which affluence and higher class status is marked by the ability to step back from a text and apprehend and analyze its form rather than simply use its function (Bourdieu 1984). In digital media, this class divide is often marked by machines and software and education for affluent people that teaches them how to create and analyze with new media, while the less affluent are taught clerical and service skills and have access to less expensive technology. Within those different models of education, affluent students are urged to analyze and critique new media while the assumption is made that less affluent students will simply play with the machines if left on their own (Seiter 2008).

Even in the academy, however, we know that pathos can be an important part of rhetoric. Some academics may tell themselves that all of their work and thought is detached and analytical, but in fact we all often find emotional appeals productive and useful. To listen to researchers talk about the importance of their work, to read the conclusions of research studies, is often to encounter emotional appeals. In terms of popular culture, emotional appeals often provide an important rhetorical strategy, even for the most serious-minded works. Television documentaries, such as the famous *Harvest of Shame*, make powerful emotional appeals. Dramas such as *Schindler's List* or *Hotel Rwanda* have political and social messages but use emotion to convey their messages.

When I talked with students about emotion and popular culture, their responses indicated that it was a subject they had thought about but not in the rhetorical terms we would recognize. Students talked about the texts they read as containing emotions or of having an emotional effect on them. Movies or songs or programs were "sad" or "happy" or "ridiculous" or the texts "outraged" or "depressed" or "inspired" them. Or, when it came to their blogs or personal pages, they talked about wanting to be taken seriously—or not taken seriously. But the students did not talk specifically about how the text worked in terms of its rhetorical appeals. On the other hand, if I asked students why a particular movie might make them sad or a particular piece of content on their pages or blogs might make people take them more seriously, they were able to describe in more detail how the content would work on the audience. Brianna, for example, is an enthusiastic fan of horror movies—"I really don't like chick flicks"—and when asked could explain the emotional appeals of horror films in ways that echo many film theorists:

> I sit in the very front (of the theater). I get more reaction than the people who sit in the damn front than in the back up at the top, because they are kind of distant. So they are like, "OK, it's real but it's not." But if you sit in the front dead center it's like you're almost there and in it, so fun. It's like a rush and that rush is what it is about. It's about the way the surprises make you feel. There is the most normal moment, and you've got to have everything normal or it won't work even if you know the other is coming, and then all of a sudden the most unbelievable thing happens and you are alive and charged up. I tell people that all the time. I get to get a charge, to feel surprised, but I'm not really going to be in danger. I'm like "It's not real, it's so fake, nothing like that can happen." And that really, when it's over, makes you feel relieved, like you're safe in the real world.

Although Brianna is not discussing the films in terms of specific rhetorical appeals, she does understand that horror films are constructed to evoke particular emotional responses to her both during her viewing and after. She sees that the scene of normality disrupted by the horrific is designed to create a specific, adrenaline-filled response of shock and horror, that, when finished, is cathartic. Ted focused more specifically on how he understood emotional appeals in popular culture texts. His comments about one of his favorite movies shows his understanding not only of the role of emotion but also how a particular scene changes the emotional context of the film:

> I think Saving Private Ryan is a great movie, one of my favorites. The battle scenes are amazing and the acting is great, and I usually think Tom Hanks is sort of irritating. But the movie is set up to hit you in the heart. That's what that final scene is for. You see the old Ryan in the cemetery and he's asking if he's been a good man and that is all there to make you feel all the sadness. If they'd just stopped the movie with the battle it would have been sad but it wouldn't have had the impact of seeing him, the one guy who survived, saluting the dead.

Students like Brianna and Ted can identify which emotions popular culture texts evoke in them, as well as how the texts are created to produce specific emotions. When I talked with students and they told me that a television show or movie or song or computer game made them feel a particular way, I would try to follow up by asking them why. Most students would propose some kind of reason, even if it took them a moment to get beyond an initial moment of surprise at the question. Even students who couldn't explain why a text evoked an emotion seemed intrigued at the question, at wanting to understand how popular culture texts worked through emotional appeals.

When it came to constructing their own online texts, many of the students also talked about how they considered the emotions their work would evoke in others. Ashley said she had to be cautious when posting to fan forums not to be too strident in her tone. "I know when I feel strongly about something I can be pretty harsh and past experience has taught me that all that does is stir people up. If I want people to focus on what I have to say, then I can't be 'This is the only way to think about this character.'" Genevieve, as noted in chapter 2, said that she avoided forum posts that came on too strong: "If somebody makes a really, really strong comment about a video, I don't trust them at all. If they say 'This is the worst video ever, I hate this, I hate that about it,' I'm like 'Maybe you're not to be trusted because of your personality.'" And Megan said that she had found that often starting a post with an apology was an effective rhetorical strategy. "If I say I'm sorry for not being sure of my comment people tend to listen more to what I have to say."

The effect of emotional appeals on performances of identity on personal pages was also a concern to many students. As noted in chapter 4, students worried about seeming too dark or frivolous or to be otherwise misread on their pages. As a result, some students talked about what emotions they wanted readers to feel when reading their pages. Natalie, with her image of the pierced tongue, wanted to shock her audience. Catherine said that she knew that listing television programs such as *The L Word* and *Project Runway* and films such as *Priscilla, Queen of the Desert* would "pretty much tell people I'm a lesbian. They're either going to love me or hate me then, you know?" Jenny said she tried to compensate for the fact that some people reading her *Facebook* page might think her musical choices were too dark through her choice of quotes:

> I have quote from South Park ("Well, ya ain't Fionna Apple. And if ya ain't Fionna Apple then I don't give a rat's ass.") and from Stephen Colbert ("It's like boxing a glacier...enjoy that metaphor while you can because your grandchildren won't have any idea what a glacier is."), and Futurama ("I am having one of those things, umm, a headache with pictures." "Do you mean

an idea?" "Oh yeah!") to show people that I can lighten up. I've got a sense
of humor. And they make me laugh too.

The ability of students to recognize how emotion works on audiences in the popular culture texts they read and the texts they compose is more complex than dismissing emotions as easy responses. As
these students' comments make clear, their considerations of emotion
are not necessarily an antithesis to rationality and critique but work
along with it in complicated and nuanced literacy practices. As Jenkins (1992) argues, fans read popular culture texts "with a mixture of
emotional proximity and critical distance" (278). That fans love shows
or movies or bands is expected, but it is important to realize that this
love is not unconditional. "Fandom involves a particular set of critical
and interpretive practices" including critiques of internal consistency,
narrative gaps, character behavior, and production techniques (278).
Such critique and analysis of popular culture texts often is, in fact, inextricable from emotion. Whether driven by love or hate for a text, the
parodies, debates, fictions, and conversations about popular culture
texts are often both playful and critical (Jenkins 1992; Buckingham
and Sefton-Green 1994). It is the power and ability to be both playful
and critical that creates for students one form of pleasure and motivation they find in popular culture.

The Pleasure of Accomplishment

Pleasure, in terms of popular culture, is often mistakenly regarded as
only the result of relaxing and sensual experiences. If the colors are
pretty and the sounds soothing, then the audience, as passive spectators, will find pleasure in the spectacle. To be sure, the pleasures we
receive from popular culture are often quite sensual. The ease with
which electronic media can provide sensual pleasures, particularly for
our eyes and ears, is remarkable and certainly part of its allure. The
vivid and inventive detail of a computer game such as *Spore* or the
stunning landscapes and swelling soundtracks of *The Lord of the Rings*
films are thrilling to our senses. We do find such popular culture material pleasurable, sometimes relaxing, and often fun. The narrative
that often surrounds such popular culture pleasures is that, because
they are sensual and fun, they are also frivolous and a waste of time.
Even students, when talking to me—a researcher and teacher—will
talk with enthusiasm about the pleasure they find in popular culture

but then feel the need to apologize and explain that they know they have been wasting their time on guilty pleasures.

Yet all pleasure found in participatory popular culture cannot be dismissed as sensual and easy. What do we make of the student who spends hours upon hours at a computer game, trying and failing time and again to advance to the next level? Games that are long and quite challenging, that take hours or days to complete, are among the most popular games on the market (Gee 2003). It is hard to think of such activities as easy or passive, but for many people playing the games is certainly pleasurable. When Jenkins (2006a) argues that popular culture dominates much of convergence culture "because playing with popular culture is a lot more fun than playing with more serious matters" (246) he is talking about "fun" as non-serious activities but is understanding it as a sense of engagement that provides pleasure. The participatory popular culture activities that take place online, such as playing a computer game or composing and constantly revising a website, is not always "especially fun at the moment. It can be a grind, not unlike homework. The effort allows the person to master skills, collect materials or put things in their proper place in anticipation of a payoff down the line. The key is that this activity is deeply motivated" (Jenkins et al. 2006, 23). The motivation of meeting a challenge or creating new texts or composing an identity and creating community is not new but is now exploding online.

It is clear in conversations with the students who have created *MySpace* and *Facebook* pages, for example, that the allure of play and irony that shapes much of the popular culture they use on their pages exists in combination with their desires to have their profiles reflect a particular sense of their identity. Within the same sentence, students may dismiss the serious intentions of the pages they create and worry over how others will read the pages. Even when they discuss the construction of their pages in terms of play and fun, they also reveal their hard work and sense of engagement in their descriptions of the substantial amounts of time they spend revising and re-revising their pages. Certainly they spend more time revising these texts than they do with any school-based text they compose. A tremendous amount of work and attention goes into the "play" of creating *MySpace* and *Facebook* pages.

We all know that many of the pleasures we find in life are not products of easy sensuality but the result of hard work, learning, and accomplishment. Just as a person learning to ice skate or play the piano or cook fine cuisine must try, fail, reflect, and learn in order to find the pleasure of accomplishment, so do students find pleasure through the learning and accomplishments they find in participatory popular culture. Pleasure that comes through acquiring advanced skills and accomplishing tasks is often highest when several factors are present: clear goals, control over the nature of the endeavor, meaningful feedback, and intrinsic rewards (Csíkszentmihályi 1990). Similarly, Gee (2003) argues that having to put forth effort for meaningful and intrinsically rewarding results are essential principles of effective learning. Studies of adolescent literacy practices illustrate that reading and writing tasks that have these qualities—particularly the sense of control and the meaningful feedback—are the ones that young people are most committed to and excited about (Smith and Wilhelm 2002). Other research has argued that students respond to participatory popular culture that emphasizes the participatory aspect, allows them to share their passions and get feedback from others, and allows them to find challenges that connect to their skills and knowledge (Knobel and Lankshear 2007). It is easy to see these qualities in the participatory popular culture literacy practices in which so many students engage. They choose the texts they want to read and write and that are a good match for their skills, knowledge, and identities. They have clear goals for what they want to accomplish, get meaningful feedback about their efforts, and feel intrinsic rewards when they are finished.

Students' sense of pleasure through challenge and accomplishment was evident in tasks of varying size and scope. On the one hand, there were student projects that spanned years and had required long periods of learning, such as online games or fan fiction. Natalie had been playing *Furcadia* for six years and said she was still "addicted to the game. If I'm not doing homework, I'm on the game." Initially, she said she had struggled with the game, but "as I kept playing I started to get better. And then, when you can do a couple of things and you see other people doing other things, that makes you want to figure out how to do that too. You want to keep getting better." Even now, she said there were controls she had yet to figure out that she hoped to learn from friends or from reading advice on forums.

Ashley had a similar narrative about writing fan fiction, which she had been doing for five years. She said she wrote initially "for my own pure enjoyment," but as she began to read other stories, she decided she wanted to improve as a writer. "You start reading other writing and you begin to think 'That's better than mine. I'm really sort of embarrassed about what I wrote.' And that's what makes you want to figure out how to be a better writer." Once she had decided she wanted to improve her writing, she said it was feedback from readers that helped her improve the most. "The only way you're going to get better is to listen to what people have to say about your stories. When you get responses from readers, you can figure out what's working and what they didn't understand or thought took too long or that maybe you left out." Figuring out how to use the responses to revise and improve her writing was the key to improving her writing, Ashley said. She also said that she was still trying to improve her writing with the feedback she received.

Yet students talked about ways in which even smaller challenges could, once surmounted, provide them with pleasure. Mitchell said the first time he composed his *MySpace* and *Facebook* pages took some time and effort. "You can get online pretty fast, but to get it to look good takes some time. You spend a lot of time at first getting it right, but when you do it's like, 'Yeah, that's good,' and you want people to take a look at it." Catherine spoke of similar experiences with her personal pages. "I took a long time to make it the way I wanted at first." She said her friends would help her. "I kept asking them what they thought of this and they'd tell me what they thought I should change. Or sometimes people would send you a message and tell you about a cool thing you could add to your page to make it better." And Peter said he had just tried putting together his first music video for his band and posting it on *YouTube*. He showed the video, with images of the heavy metal band juxtaposed with film images of the war in Iraq that he had sampled. "I know it's pretty crappy right now, but you have no idea how long it took me to finish this, so I'm proud of that anyway. But it's just a start. Now that I've done one, the next one will be better." Clearly, the participatory nature of these students' online literacy practices was important to their sense of pleasure that came through learning new skills and discourses. When students talked about the pleasure of accomplishment, it was often, as with these examples, linked not only to the achievement itself but to the feedback they received online.

The other pleasure of accomplishment that students talked about was the pleasure that came through being able to respond to texts, whether from popular culture producers or from other individuals.

Sometimes this response was as simple as sending a message to a friend's social networking page or posting on a fan forum. Other times it was as complex as writing fan fiction that writers such as Ashley hoped would provide new perspectives on a popular culture text. Posts to fan forums, fan fiction, or video remixes indicate the desire of individuals, of members of the audience, to respond to those elements of popular culture texts they find somehow unsatisfying. There is often a productive tension for fans between their affection and appreciation for a movie or program or game or song and their dissatisfaction with some of its elements (Jenkins 1992). Participatory popular culture allows audience members to become part of the narrative through games, fan fiction, and fan films. Others choose to become part of the collective intelligence and meaning-making process through blogs, and fan forums. Whatever the approach, individuals are motivated to rewrite the story, argue about the ending, remix the film, to express their own ideas, and in doing so find the pleasure in completion. Buckingham and Sefton-Green (2004) argue that such participatory practices don't just happen after students have read a text but that the appropriating and remixing happens as they read and write simultaneously, making agency "an indispensable part of the process rather than something that is exercised post hoc" (19). In addition, they want to communicate to other fans the intertextual connections they make (Jenkins 1992). Sandy said that she posted comments to fan forums that often contained her thoughts about how different popular culture texts intersected. "A lot of the time I'm watching a movie and something in the story reminds me of another movie or even a book. So I point that out in what I post. I like to see those connections that maybe other people haven't and a lot of people respond by saying they hadn't thought of that, which I like," she said. The tensions that popular culture fans feel between the original text and their interpretations or adaptations sometimes frustrated the students I spoke with, but they always spoke of their ability to respond with an evident sense of excitement and accomplishment.

Motivation and Control

The pleasure in accomplishment that students describe from the often difficult and time-consuming work they put into online popular culture literacy practices stands in contrast to the way they often describe their work at school. When I asked students if they perceived connections between their online literacy practices and those they encountered in school, they all struggled to find connections. "It's all writing, I guess," Greg said with a shrug. "But what I do at home is for fun. School is work." The binary between work and play, between drudgery and pleasure, was a common theme of student comments. Sandy said, "What I have to read and write for school I need to do, but it's not like I want to do it. That's the difference. When I go online that is just my time to enjoy doing what I want to do." School-based literacy practices beginning in early adolescence with middle school are often perceived by students as work and an obligation. Such perceptions are reinforced by the often rigid literacy pedagogies teachers have been burdened with to satisfy standardized testing and assessment regimes that have been imposed on schools. While outside of school, they often do not even consider what they do as "reading" and "writing" according to the definitions of educational institutions. In addition, when new media technologies are introduced into classrooms, they are often positioned by the teachers as "play" to distinguish it from the work sanctioned by the school (King and O'Brien 2002).

Online and outside the classroom, however, students feel in control of their literacy practices and confident and clear about what they are doing and why. Not only do their literacy practices often help them draw and develop their own expertise, they are also often working directly against what they perceive as adult authority and control. In fact, as I noted earlier, participatory popular culture, while engaging students with corporate-produced texts, also allows them to subvert and resist those texts through irony, parody, and remixing. In school, students are always being assessed on learning the expertise of the teacher, on demonstrating their understanding of the sanctioned and approved interpretation of a text, and their ability to produce similarly appropriate texts. In such a system, as Gee (2004) notes, students feel "little motivation to study and become competent, when the learner has no real idea of what it feels like to act effectively in a domain or why anyone would want to become competent in the area" (111). Online, however, students are able to contribute to meaning making and the creation of texts that receive feedback from the audience but not assessment from an adult authority source, whether it be a teacher, parent, or popular culture producer. "No wonder that what excites young people about the internet is primarily the peer-to-peer opportunities it affords, in which they provide for each other the responsiveness, criticism, humor, feedback, openness, and network-ing that so often is absent from content designed for children by adults" (Livingstone 2008, 116). Indeed, a website's credibility with adolescents often increases if they believe it is the work of peers rather than adults (Lankes 2008).

Students were clear in how much control meant to them in the online activities. "You will probably never see my status on *Facebook* to say I'm offline. If I'm not in classes, I'm online because that's where my friends are and that's where I can do things that I want to do," Ashley said. Catherine said that she sometimes reads serious websites on her own, such as CNN or MSNBC, but that she liked to have a choice about doing so: "I have a huge addiction to the news so I'm always checking news sites all the time. But I do drift off to other things when I want to. I'll hit *The Onion*, just anything I can find. It's better than a newspaper because I can go where I want when I want to." And Ted said he would read a novel if he chose to do so but was more resistant to assigned readings. "I can be stubborn, not always one of my best traits," he said. What he said he liked about reading and writing online was his level of control of what he read and wrote. "It's up to me what I want to watch or read. If I want to have a couple of windows open at the same time I can. Or if I want to I can play a game or write to someone or tweak my (*Facebook*) page. The point is I do it when I want to do it and the way I want to do it," he said.

Students, then, feel empowered in their uses of popular culture literacy practices, not by being passive readers and cultural dupes but by taking control of a text and making their own uses of it. This sense of control is essential not only to the pleasure students feel in their online literacy practices but to their motivation for engaging in the activities in the first place. The same qualities that provide pleasure through accomplishment—control of the task, clear goals, meaningful feedback, intrinsic rewards—are the keys to motivating individuals to undertake literacy practices in the first place. Other research on liter-acy practices outside the classroom reinforce the powerful motivating force of reading and writing activities that contain these qualities (Newkirk 2002a; Smith and Wilhelm 2002; Gee 2004; Vasudevan 2008). If we truly want students to do the difficult work required to learn sophisticated, creative, and critical ways of reading and writing, then we need to take seriously the hard work and hard-won pleasures they find in their online literacy practices with popular culture

Conclusion

The force of emotion in popular culture is appealing to students. The force of emotion as appeal in popular culture is understood by students. Emotion is central to how students read popular culture texts across media. It is equally important to how they approach participating in convergence culture. They find both emotional satisfaction and motivation in the actions of reading and writing with popular culture online. This does not mean, however, that what emotions provide for students, and others, when they are reading and writing online should be viewed as negative by literacy scholars and educators. Yet emotion is not simply what we feel at a given moment; emotion is also what makes us act. As Jonathan Gray (2007) notes, "Emotion, after all, is what makes us care to think rationally in the first place, and it is emotion that drives us to work for change or for conservation. Emotion lets us deliberate, and then encourages us to act on that deliberation" (79). When we emphasize detachment and critique to the exclusion of everything else, we both deny our students powerful rhetorical tools as well as miss what students are learning when they read and write with popular culture texts. Of course I'm not arguing that we give up critique and analysis, only that when we ignore emotion "we can lose touch with the way discourse operates in the wider culture, and, most tellingly, fail to recognize how it operates in our own lives once we leave the office and listen to the radio or attend the graduations of our children" (Newkirk 2002b, 25). Rather than dismissing how students understand emotion in popular culture and how they employ rhetorical strategy such as irony and sentimentality in complex and thoughtful ways, we should listen to what students have to say about how they read and write with popular culture online. The pleasures and motivations that students find in reading and writing online are powerful forces we need to consider if we want students to act with passion and commitment in other parts of their lives as well.

CHAPTER 7

What's on Next?

Conclusion and Implications

A student spends hours rewriting a fan fiction narrative online. Another student updates a social networking page with more than seventy popular culture elements and references on it. Still another visits fan forums to catch up, and join in, on the discussions of her favorite television program. And another updates his blog and then watches a remixed video on *YouTube*, where a clip from a Bollywood movie has been given comic subtitles. At every moment, the students show me what they are doing with pride and pleasure.

Later, I stand in a school hallway and talk to two fellow teachers. I describe the research for this book and how exciting I find the range and sophistication of students' online literacy practices. "That's the problem," says one of the teachers. "They're spending all their time on popular culture." To which the second teacher adds, "And that's why they can't handle the work in our classes. It's ruining them for serious reading and writing."

These two scenes, which starkly contrast confidence and pleasure with fear and dismay, have grown quite familiar to me. When I talk with students and observe their online literacy practices involving popular culture, I see confidence, pleasure, curiosity, and creative and critical thinking. When I mention what I have seen to teachers, the response is disdain, alarm, or at best, discouragement. Even as educators are increasingly embracing new media technologies for teaching reading and writing—though often as a deterministic panacea for engaging students—the reality that popular culture is central to students' online literacy practices is either ignored or seen as being deeply problematic. Popular culture, in the eyes of many teachers, does not involve thinking and learning, is not real reading and writing, and should not be part of literacy education.

I don't approach my research with the expectation that everything I learn can have immediate classroom applications. It is valuable to explore literacy practices outside of the classroom as important activities by themselves without necessarily somehow squeezing them into our curriculum. Yet, my identity as a teacher is inextricable from my identity as a researcher or as a writer. When I find out how and why students are reading and writing outside of school, I find myself wondering how they are learning, how they are being motivated, and what I can learn from these practices to make my teaching more effective, relevant, and engaging. In this final chapter, then, I discuss some of the implications of what students are learning when they read and write with and about popular culture and how—or whether—we can connect their expertise and their passions with our pedagogies. The answers to these questions, both ethically and practically, are not simple but are important to consider as we teach students for whom such literacy practices are an integral part of their daily lives.

Panic Over Popular Culture

There is nothing new in the panics over the influence of popular culture on young people. From the rise of mass popular culture a century and a half ago, the effects on young people of the most popular form of the day have led to laments and grumbling from those with political and social power. Educators, and literacy educators in particular, have often joined in such choruses of concern. In the pre-online era, Mark Rocha's (1988) comment was typical. He wrote that if a student "is to become a successful *adult* writer (Rocha's emphasis), he will need to overcome the television-ization of his critical capacity to examine received values" (27). Neil Postman (1985) regarded his bestselling book, *Amusing Ourselves to Death*, as a "lamentation about the most significant American cultural fact of the second half of the twentieth century: the decline of the Age of Typography and the ascendancy of the Age of Television" (8). Criticisms of popular culture have not been limited to more conservative commentators. Critics from cultural studies and critical pedagogy have been equally concerned about the power of popular culture, if for different reasons. James Berlin (1996), for example, regarded the study of popular culture as an unfortunate necessity to teach students to "negotiate and resist the cultural codes championed in the programs they watch" (123). While Kay Ellen Rutledge (1994) denounced the ways that "Music videos, televised bombings, glib advertisements for liquor, tobacco, cars, clothes, cosmetics, or cereals proclaim the decline of the word and the power of the image in our rhetorical environment" (204). Teachers often buy into cultural narratives that popular culture is, by its very nature, harmful to students as people and as readers and writers. These perceptions exist despite a substantial lack of evidence that engagement with popular culture is harmful to literacy learning and academic achievement (Beach and O'Brien 2008).

New media technologies have, if anything, intensified the concerns of many critics about the effects of participatory popular culture. Andrew Keen's (2008) comment is typical: "Instead of more community, knowledge, or culture, all that Web 2.0 really delivers is more dubious content from anonymous sources, hijacking our time and playing to our gullibility" (12). As with so many developments of new media and accompanying new genres, the resistance and pessimism are often expressed as concerns about information—and potentially dangerous ideas—and less intellectually rigorous diversions becoming too rapidly accessible to a potentially gullible public.

Clearly, such pessimism is not shared by the students I interviewed and observed. Although they may sometimes question the utility of some of what they do with popular culture online—as Pat said, "Let's face it, you can spend a lot of time online and not be sure what you've been doing that means anything"—in general, the students I interviewed spoke with enthusiasm about their activities. Brianna's comment, while particularly enthusiastic, captured the sense of engagement that students described: "I'm on the web all the time. I don't know many people my age who could live without it. My granny doesn't get it; she's saying things about how much time I'm on the web. But that's where the music and games and people are, so that's where I am." At the same time, Brianna, like other students, expressed a savvy skepticism about her online popular culture practices. "Everyone knows it's fun, but everyone also knows it can be trouble. You've got to know your limits and you only know your limits if you do enough to figure them out," she said. Brianna's comment echoes what many literacy teachers and scholars know, that the only way to acquire more sophistication and skill with reading and writing is through practice, feedback, and reflection.

Yet, as I have argued previously (2002; 2003), the response of teachers and scholars to the popular culture practices of students has too often been to regard literacy education as, in part, a social inoculation against the deleterious influences of popular culture. From this perspective, students are regarded as unthinking, uncritical consumers of media texts. Their teachers, drawing on a traditional liberal humanist position, feel obliged to demonstrate to them that only school-sanctioned critical literacy assignments will allow the students to resist and evade the anti-intellectual and seductive world of popular culture and bring them back to the one true faith of print literacy. At its most extreme, "The debate keeps getting framed as if the only true alternative were to opt out of media altogether and live in the woods, eating acorns and lizards and reading only books published on recycled paper by small alternative presses" (Jenkins 2006a, 248–249). At best, such a position grudgingly regards popular culture as a possible bridge to move students from easy, frivolous texts to serious and important ones. But it's just a ploy, a gimmick to lower student resistance and make the teacher appear relevant.

Students, however, are not buying the curriculum and message of culture-jamming pedagogies. "Personally, I hate it when we have to watch movies in class because it usually means we then have to start taking them apart over and over until all the pleasure is gone," Mitchell said. He added that "when something becomes part of school," it becomes dominated by the pressure of assessment and grading. "You can't do anything in school just for fun. You know there is a grade lurking." And Amy said that studying popular culture in school was no different from studying other subjects. "You figure out what the teacher wants to hear and you give it to them. If they want to hear that popular culture is rotting my mind then that's what they get." As David Buckingham (2003) points out, however, rather than appear relevant, such approaches to popular culture make students wary and resistant:

> Teachers' attempts to impose cultural, moral, or political authority over the media that children experience in their daily lives are unlikely to be taken seriously. They are often based on a paternalistic contempt for children's tastes and pleasures and are bound to be rejected. The notion that students might be somehow weaned off what they perceive as their own popular culture in favor of the teacher's cultural or political values would seem to be increasingly impossible (314).

Instead, as literacy teachers, we need to understand what students are reading and writing without immediately hoping to "fix" their literacy practices.

First, we need to realize that the binaries of online/offline behavior may seem meaningful to us but are not the way many young people view their lives (Thomas 2007). Although I agree that too much can be made of generational differences when it comes to literacy practices with new media, that does not mean that there are not some distinctions worth paying attention to. If it is going too far to buy into the rhetoric of "digital natives," it is still useful to realize that growing up online, in a digital, networked world, creates some different perspectives about communication and technology for students than for those of us who have adapted to the digital world as adults (Heverly 2008). The expectations of an interactive popular culture are part of those differences. The young person seated in front of multiple screens, or watching remixed videos on *YouTube*, or discussing bands on a fan forum, or playing *World of Warcraft* with people in other countries does so from a position of confidence and control that puzzles and even unnerves many of the teachers with whom I talk. Not only were they concerned about the influence of popular culture to begin with, now they must contend with a participatory popular culture consisting of genres and media with which their students are much more familiar and facile. To respond to the rapid changes brought to reading and writing by online popular culture by advocating a more conservative, and familiar, pedagogy of print literacy and the exclusion of popular culture texts is perhaps understandable but in the end not productive.

Instead, if we allow ourselves to observe what students are doing with online popular culture, and to defer judgment until we consider the practices carefully, we can understand the complexity of their reading and writing activities. What Gunther Kress (1997) said about multimodal literacy practices in general is equally true about their practices with online popular culture: "We know that tomorrow will not be like today. That is one of the few certainties of the present period. We can perceive only dimly what the day after that tomorrow is likely to be like" (157). The rapid changes of participatory popular culture are in many ways encouraging; new media have students writing and reading far more than they were even ten years ago. Print, along with sound, video, and images, are integral parts of the texts young people compose and read. For the students I interviewed, and the students I teach, "life on the screen is an everyday, natural practice—they know no other way of being" (167). In addition, participatory popular culture puts them in contact with people and texts around the world. This cross-cultural reading and writing of texts has fascinating and profound implications, not only for literacy practices but for daily life in a complex, interconnected world (Thomas 2007; Black 2008). Unfortunately, the issues of participatory popular culture on a global scale proved beyond the scope of this book, but are important for continued research and reflection.

Learning Through Cultural Practices

I would argue that it is clear that students are reading and writing a great deal online and with and about popular culture. I would also argue that students' discussion of their online reading and writing, as illustrated in these chapters, reflects a thoughtful, complex, and critical set of practices. Also, I would argue that through these practices, which include responses from other readers as well as a great deal of practice in using language and sound and images, they are learning a great deal about literacy. David Barton's (2003) cycle of learning and literacy is useful to keep in mind here. Barton envisions a cycle with three points—ways of participating, identity, and skills located in practices. He regards these three elements as mutually reinforcing. We can see the learning that students do in their online reading and writing represented in this cycle. Online technologies and students' sense of mastery and confidence over popular culture texts offers them ways of participating in literacy practices, as well as the motivations for doing so. As they participate, learn genres and conventions, post texts and receive responses from their audiences, and interpret and evaluate texts, they hone the skills located in specific practices. With increased confidence and the pleasure of accomplishment, students construct their identities as competent participants in these online literacy contexts, which leads them to seek increased participation, and so the cycle continues.

As Gee (2004) points out, direct instruction in reading and writing only takes a person so far. Acquiring complex and creative literacy abilities requires a lengthy immersion in cultural practices, where a novice can observe and collaborate with those with more sophisticated abilities, be provided with and shown how to use appropriate texts and tools, and be given continual and relevant feedback, particularly when the novice has a problem or question to be solved. "Finally, learners are aware that masters have a certain socially significant identity...that they wish to acquire as part and parcel of membership in the larger cultural group" (12). The principles of learning the cultural practices of literacy that Barton and Gee outline are demonstrated time and again in students' engagement with participatory popular culture. Motivated by their own interests and desires to construct an identity that connects them to a particular cultural group, they are able to observe more complex and sophisticated literacy practices, make their own attempts at similar kinds of interpreting and composing texts, and receive meaningful direct and indirect feedback.

Certainly new media technologies are vital to this process for many students. If they did not have the ease of access to a variety of texts that are important to them and the ease of sampling, publishing, and responding to texts that come with online technologies, this kind of engaged learning would not take place. New media technologies have fundamentally altered students' ideas about audience, authorship, and the nature of texts. They make rhetorical choices and intertextual connections in active, meaningful ways that offer substantive accomplishments and real consequences. If they misjudge their audience or the rhetorical context, they can see the results and often find out exactly what their audience is thinking. But, as students have shown me time and again, their online literacy practices are deeply involved with participatory popular culture. Their engagement with popular culture influences how they read and write online in significant ways. The proclivity of popular culture for parody and pastiche, for example, influences how students learn and respond to genre and the stability of texts. The perception of popular culture texts as unauthored and low-culture encourages students to sample and reuse textual material. The perception of popular culture as common culture shapes students' willingness to compose with it for its intertextual connections. If we want to understand how students are learning about audience, genre, emotion, authorial position, evidence, narrative, and other critical rhetorical concepts, then we must pay attention to their practices with participatory popular culture.

As a teacher, then, I find myself asking the same question I am asked by other teachers when I talk about this research. If students' engagement with participatory popular culture influences their rhetorical knowledge and literacy practices, what does it mean for our classroom practices? Clearly, attempting to build a wall between out-of-school popular culture literacy practices and school-sanctioned reading and writing is both futile and foolish. If students are learning how to read and write one way outside the classroom—collaboratively, multimodally, intertextually—they will not simply leave those skills and perceptions behind when they enter the class-room. Instead, they will try to integrate their various approaches to literacy, whether we ask them to or not, with varying degrees of success. In addition, as Alvermann (2008) points out:

> When teachers, teacher educators, and researchers tap into young people's interests in producing online content, they open themselves to appreciating a wide range of competencies that might otherwise go unremarked in the everyday routines of examined classroom and research practices (17).

It seems both impractical and unethical, then, to ignore students' participatory popular culture literacy practices or to ban them from the classroom.

On the other hand, adopting popular culture as part of the sanctioned school curriculum runs its own risks. "As soon as popular-culture texts are imported into the classroom, they no longer retain their original meanings constituted by how they serve to resist school and authority" (Beach and O'Brien 2008, 797). Once teachers make popular culture texts and literacy practices part of the classroom, it takes such texts and activities out of the control of students and invests them with adult, institutionalized meanings. Popular culture in the classroom is no longer something over which students have power and is certainly no longer subversive. What's more, popular culture in the classroom becomes material by which students will be assessed by adults. Students must now produce material or offer interpretations, not for their own uses, but to satisfy the teacher's concept of correct and acceptable material. If we think again about what elements create pleasure and motivation in acquiring literacy and other skills, control over the project and intrinsic rewards are vital. Students find these elements in the out-of-school popular culture activities, but resent having them taken away by school-sanctioned assignments. Anyone who has used popular culture in a class has encountered the resistance of students who complain that the assignment, analysis, and assessment constraints of school will rob them of the pleasures they find in popular culture. Teachers often regard such protests as indications that popular culture is superficial, easy, and incapable of engaging students' minds. Instead, however, such complaints may be directed more at the students' frustration and resentment of having material and experiences once under their control now co-opted by an institution that reminds them on a daily basis how powerless they are.

Indeed, when we pay attention to what students do online and what they tell us about how and why they do it, it is obvious that their work is not mindless or superficial but often reflects planning, analysis, and reflection. Just as we do not want to make students feel we are robbing them of their control and of their pleasures when it comes to popular culture texts, it is also important to understand what they know when they enter our classrooms. I certainly align myself with scholars and teachers (Freire 1972; Newkirk 1997; Knobel and Lankshear 2004; Beach and O'Brien 2008; Alvermann 2008) who have argued that it is pedagogically productive and ethically necessary to find out through dialogue what students know so we can help them develop that knowledge in ways that matter to them. We must help them value what they know and learn how they can empower themselves by thinking critically about that knowledge.

A Balancing Act in the Classroom

Engaging with participatory popular culture in the literacy classroom, then, requires a balancing act. We must find ways to engage students' knowledge while not engendering resentment and resistance. To achieve this goal, I would propose three approaches.

First, it is essential that we find out what students know, listen to them, learn from them, and connect our language with their knowledge. If this sounds simple, it is not and requires an ongoing and honest dialogue, where our listening is the most important first step. Too often, students' first encounters with popular culture in the classroom are lectures from teachers about why a novel is inherently better than a television program, computer game, or blog. Instead, we need to have an extended and respectful dialogue with them about what practices they engage in online, how they think about the work they do, what they find valuable, and what more they would like to learn. What do they do online and how do they make sense of those practices and learn from them? Such a conversation will teach us what they know, as well as help them think more explicitly about that knowledge and how they developed it. Of course, we should expect initial reluctance from students to such a conversation, given how often they have been told by adults that anything they have done with popular culture or even online has been a waste of time. It requires patience and time to convince students we are not out to scold or convert them.

Students may also not talk about their online literacy practices in the academic language we recognize. But if we listen closely, we will find that their literacy practices and resulting rhetorical knowledge can provide new opportunities for connecting our pedagogies with their lives. For students, engaging in such conversations inevitably brings them a more nuanced and sophisticated understanding of how they have been reading and writing with popular culture. Most of the students I interviewed and observed told me at some point how much they had learned about their literacy practices just through the conversations we had. I did not lecture them or instruct them directly. I simply asked questions, listened carefully, and let them show me what they knew and describe how they knew it. Their interest in what they were doing, and their desire to know more about how they were doing it, led to conversations in which their reflection led to greater knowledge.

Also, we should think about how the self-motivated, self-directed learning that students accomplish online takes place. As Gee (2003) points out about computer games, which are complex and take a great deal of time and effort to master, the online popular culture activities that students have learned could teach us a great deal about learning. Rather than worry first about whether we can use popular culture content to make our current pedagogies and literacy goals more relevant for students, we should pay more attention to how they engage with and learn reading and writing online in multiple modalities. Adapting ways of thinking and learning from the ways students approach participatory popular culture literacy practices is more important than the texts themselves (Knobel and Lankshear 2004). We can rethink our curriculum and pedagogies so that we create learning opportunities that offer students control, clear goals, and meaningful feedback that is not simply justification for assessment. Teachers have always sought ways for students to find intrinsic motivations and rewards for what they read and write. A greater understanding of the participatory popular culture practices will offer us greater insights into how they are finding these motivations and rewards by learning to read and write on their own. Of course, this requires getting beyond—or at least momentarily escaping—the

ideologies that drive rigid standardized assessment, a task more easily stated than accomplished in many schools. Still, if we can create
pedagogies and classroom atmospheres that allow students to engage
in work that draws on the playful, collaborative, intertextual, and
multimodal qualities of participatory popular culture—and allow
students to have some control of the nature and direction of their projects—we may very well find that they adapt their out-of-school expertise to our classrooms. We build on such knowledge to teach both
traditional practices of reading and writing as well as new literacy
practices such as appropriation of media content, networking, negotiation of social contexts, and working with multiple media (Jenkins
et al. 2006).

Finally, it is possible to connect what we know about rhetoric and
literacy with what they are learning through popular culture without
robbing them of their pleasure in the latter. Drawing on popular
forms of reading and writing, if done as authentic exploration rather
than an assessment-driven project, can be engaging and empowering
for students. If we do not lecture to them about popular culture but
allow students to use their knowledge to explore these literacy practices, it can help students discover how analysis and reflection can
enrich the pleasure and control they feel over their online reading and
writing and over rhetorical concepts in general. Teachers have found
productive ways to build on students' facility with irony, for example, by encouraging students to create parodies or take other ironic
positions toward texts (Buckingham and Sefton-Green 1994; Williams
2002; Jenkins et al. 2006; Seitz 2007). Such projects help students understand genre conventions and are also fun. Of course, popular culture has never been a panacea for teaching literacy. But if this is how
students are reading and writing most of the time, then we need to
pay attention to it.

It is true, of course, that some popular culture material is inappropriate for the classroom and that popular culture often reproduces
representations of identity that are deeply troubling. It is also possible
to engage students in conversations about these aspects of popular
culture, if again we do it by listening to what they have to say. Many
of the students I spoke with were also troubled by what they encountered online and were interested in talking about it to someone who
would listen and respond thoughtfully without scolding them for
what they knew or rushing to sweeping indictments of all popular
culture texts. The keys to such projects are to work with students to

understand what they want to achieve through their online literacy practices and what knowledge and expertise they already possess. We can then work collaboratively with them to bring our knowledge of rhetoric and literacy to help them achieve their goals, and to understand how the same rhetorical concepts and knowledge are the foundation for other reading and writing endeavors they encounter in school and in their daily lives.

For as important as it is to pay attention to what is changing, it is just as important to recognize what stays the same. When it comes to thinking about participatory popular culture, it is easy to focus on how quickly and substantially things are changing. Popular culture has always moved quickly from one new fad, star, show, or phenomenon to the next. In the past decade, the explosions of new media and online technologies have only increased the pace of those changes. Indeed, in the year between completing the interviews for this book and the moment at which I am now writing the final pages, *Facebook* has significantly changed its template structure—to a certain amount of controversy—and sites such as *Hulu.com* and *Internet Movie Database* now have entire television programs and films that can be watched online for free. Those are just two of the changes that have happened this year. What will happen between today and the time you read this book, none of us can predict. Yet my point in this book is not to create a comprehensive document of how students are engaged in these activities. It is instead to look for the principles and activities that students are learning when they read and write online, with popular culture. Participation, collaboration, sampling, multi-modality, response, and identity performance will continue to be central to how they read and write, regardless of the technology or content. Social and institutional contexts, and the power relations inherent in them, will continue to shape these literacy practices. And, underneath it all, rhetoric will be vital to how we all compose and interpret texts. Audience, authorial position, evidence, style, genre and other rhetorical concepts are no less important when writing online about popular culture than they were ten, twenty, or a hundred years ago. The question, then, is not whether rhetoric matters but is instead how these concepts influence and are shaped by the evolving literacy practices of participatory popular culture.

A Collaborative Exploration

Our ability, as literacy educators, to be significant to our students and our culture will depend on how well we pay attention and listen to our students. I am old enough that the rapid change of new technologies sometimes catches me off balance and leaves me momentarily baffled and even disoriented. After all, the first students I taught to write composed by hand or on typewriters. Now I see young people growing up reading and writing in collaborative, online environments, negotiating multiple media and screens, and I realize that there are unending opportunities to learn from my students and for all of us to rethink how we communicate in words, images, and sound. I find the collaborative enterprise of exploring this evolving world of literacy an exciting and refreshing challenge every day.

It is time to understand participatory popular culture as not incidental to the literacy practices in which young people are engaging but as having a central role into how their reading and writing takes place. We need to attend not only to how students employ online technologies to read and write with popular culture but also to consider what rhetorical patterns and genre expectations influence how they read and write. As Henry Jenkins (1992) points out, there are reasons students use popular culture as reading and writing content: "Fans have chosen these media products from the total range of available texts precisely because they seem to hold special potential as vehicles for expressing the fans' pre-existing social commitments and cultural interests" (34). If we want to understand the desires, anxieties, and aspirations of our students, then we must pay attention to what they find compelling in the popular culture texts they consume and create. As convergence culture extends throughout our society, many of our students will be the most involved and the most comfortable composers and readers of multimedia, multimodal texts. Instead of turning our back on how the discourses and rhetorics of popular culture have become essential influences on students' literacy practices, we must instead seize this exciting opportunity to join students in a genuinely collaborative exploration of this rapidly changing world, so we may all learn how best to communicate in ways both enriching and humane.

List of Participants

All names are pseudonyms chosen by the participants. The amount of time each student spent online each day was estimated by the students themselves.

Alison: 18, female, African American. Major: Chemical Engineering. First-generation university student. Mother works in civil service in large city. Spends an average of one hour online each day.

Amy: 18, female, European American. Majors: Communication and French. Mother and father are public school teachers in large city. Spends an average of four hours online each day.

Angela: 19, female, European American. Major: Communication. First-generation university student. Parents work for businesses in small rural town. Spends an average of five hours online each day.

Ashley: 18, female, European American. Major: Business. Father works in business; mother works at home in small town. Spends an average of eight hours online each day.

Brianna: 18, female, African American. Major: Psychology. Father works as computer technician; mother works in restaurant in small city. Spends an average of eight hours online each day.

Catherine: 21, female, European American. Majors: Biology and Political Science. Father is a chemical engineer; mother works at home in large city. Grew up in Singapore. Spends an average of three hours online each day.

Francesca: 18, female, European American—Latina. Major: Biomedical Engineering. First-generation university student. Parents own a restaurant in large city. Spends an average of two hours online each day.

Genevieve: 18, female, European American. Major: Sociology. Father is in business and mother is a substitute teacher in large city. Spends an average of three hours online each day.

Greg: 19, male, European American. Major: Undecided. Father is an accountant in large city. Spends an average of two hours a day online.

Jeff: 18, male, European American. Major: Economics. First-generation university student. Mother works for a clothing store; father is a car salesman in a large city. Spends an average of one hour online each day.

Jenny: 19, female, European American. Major: Civil Engineering. Father is an engineer; mother works as administrative assistant in small city. Spends an average of five hours online each day.

Kevin: 18, male, African American. Major: Communication. Father is a minister; mother works at home in large city. Spends an average of four hours online each day.

Lisa: 19, female, African American. Major: Nursing. Mother is a nurse; father is a mechanic. Spends an average of three hours online each day.

Mitchell: 18, male, European American. Major: English. Parents are university professors in small city. Spends and average of five hours online each day.

Natalie: 18, female, European American. Major: Undecided. First-generation university student. Father works in factory; mother works in bakery in large city. Spends an average of six hours online each day.

Pat: 18, male, European American. Major: Political Science. First-generation university student. Mother works for an insurance agency; father works for a small factory. Spends an average of four hours a day online.

Peter: 19, male, European American. Major: Political Science. Mother works for a corporation; father works for a corporation. Spends an average of four hours a day online.

Sandy: 18, female, Asian American. Major: Psychology. First-generation university student. Parents own small business in small town. Spends an average of two hours online each day.

Sarah: 18, female, European American. Major: Psychology. First-generation university student. Parents work as farmers. Spends an average of two hours a day online.

Ted: 19, male, European American. Major: Biology. Father is a physician; mother is a realtor in large city. Spends an average of three hours online each day.

Tony: 18, male, European American. Major: Industrial Engineering. Parents own a small business in suburb of major city. Spends an average of three hours online each day.

Interview Questions

The following questions framed the initial interview with each participant. Other questions were asked as follow-up questions in the course of each interview. Subsequent interviews and observations were shaped by the students' interests and what they chose to discuss.

1. Name/Age/Class Rank/Major
2. How would you define the term "popular culture"?
3. What kinds of popular culture do you watch or use regularly? Be as specific as possible.
4. How much time do you spend with each form of popular culture each week?
5. Do you visit online websites in connection with your popular culture activities?
6. Which sites do you visit?
7. What activities do you engage in on those sites?
8. How much time do you spend online each week?

9. Do you engage in any online activities in which you write about popular culture?
10. Do you engage in any online activities in which you use popular culture images, phrases, or music to create a website or document? How often?
11. Do you engage in online discussion forums about any form of popular culture? How often?
12. What do you need to know to be able to read and write on the sites you visit?
13. How do you envision the audience for what you post or write online?
14. What do you like most about your online activities? What do you like the least?
15. How have you learned to do the things you do when you are online?
16. What motivates you to engage in the activities you described above? What do you enjoy about reading and writing about popular culture online?
17. How would you describe your proficiency in using computers?
18. How would you define the term *literacy*?
19. What reading and writing activities do you engage in both in and out of school?
20. How much time do you spend reading and writing each week?
21. What motivates you to engage in the activities you described above? What do you enjoy about reading and writing? What do you not find pleasurable?
22. Do you see any connections between the writing you do online and the writing in school? Any conflicts?

REFERENCES

Alexander, Jonathan. 2006. *Digital youth: Emerging literacies on the World Wide Web*. Cresskill, NJ: Hampton Press.

Altman, Rick. 1999. Film/Genre. London: British Film Institute.

Alvermann, Donna E. 2008. Why bother theorizing adolescents' online literacies for classroom practice and research? Journal of Adolescent & Adult Literacy 52 (1):8–19.

Alvermann, Donna E., Jennifer S. Moon, and Margaret C. Hagood. 1999. Popular culture in the classroom: Teaching and researching critical media literacy. Chicago: National Reading Conference.

Anson, Chris M. 1999. Distant voices: Teaching writing in a culture of technology. College English 61 (3):261–280.

Bakhtin, M. M. 1981. The dialogic imagination. Trans. C. Emerson and M. Holquist. Austin, TX: University of Texas Press.

Barton, David. 2003. Literacy and learning. In The Tenth International Literacy and Education Research Network Conference on Learning. Institute of Education, University of London.

Barton, David, and Mary Hamilton. 1998. Local literacies: Reading and writing in one community. London: Routledge.

Baudrillard, Jean. 1994. Simulacra and simulation. Trans. S. F. Glaser. Ann Arbor, MI: University of Michigan Press.

Beach, Richard, and David G. O'Brien. 2008. Teaching popular-culture texts in the classroom. In Handbook of research on new literacies, ed. J. Coiro, M. Knobel, C. Lankshear and D. J. Leu. New York: Lawrence Erlbaum.

Beavis, Catherine. 2007. Writing, digital culture, and English curriculum. L1— Educational Studies in Language and Literature 7 (4):23–44.

Bennerstedt, Ulrika. 2008. What does it take to "be" a player? The skilled work of role-players in online game space. In International Conference on Multimodality and Learning. Institute of Education, University of London.

Berlin, James A. 1996. Rhetorics, poetics, and cultures: Refiguring college English studies. Urbana, IL: NCTE.

Birkerts, Sven. 1994. The Gutenberg elegies: The fate of reading in an electronic age. New York: Ballantine Books.

Black, Rebecca W. 2005. Access and affiliation: The literacy and composition practices of English-language learners in an online fanfiction community. Journal of Adolescent & Adult Literacy 49 (2):118–128.

———. 2006. Language, culture, and identity in online fanfiction. E-learning, 3 (2), 170-184.

— — —. 2007. Digital design: English language learners and reader reviews in online fiction. In A new literacies sampler, ed. M. Knobel and C. Lankshear. New York: Peter Lang.

— — —. 2008. Adolescents and online fan fiction. London: Peter Lang.

Bloom, Lynn Z. 1996. Freshman composition as a middle-class enterprise. College English 58 (6):654–675.

Borgmann, Albert. 1992. Crossing the postmodern divide. Chicago: University of Chicago Press.

Bourdieu, Pierre. 1984. Distinction: a social critique of the judgement of taste. Trans. by R. Nice. Cambridge, MA: Harvard University Press.

— — —. 1996. On television. Trans. P. Ferguson. New York: The New Press.

boyd, danah. 2007. Viewing American class divisions through Facebook and MySpace. Apophenia blog essay. http://www.danah.org/papers/essays/ClassDivisions.html (accessed January 26, 2009).

— — —. 2008. Why youth (heart) social network sites: The role of networked publics in teenage social life. In Youth, identity, and digital media. 119–142. Cambridge, MA: The MIT Press.

Brandt, Deborah. 2001. Literacy in American lives. Cambridge: Cambridge University Press.

Brooker, Will. 2001. Living on Dawson's Creek: Teen viewers, cultural convergence, and television overflow. International Journal of Cultural Studies 4 (4):456–473.

Brummett, Barry. 1991. Rhetorical dimensions of popular culture. Tuscaloosa, AL: University of Alabama Press.

Buckingham, David. 1993. Children talking television: The making of television literacy. London: Falmer Press.

— — —. 2000. After the death of childhood: Growing up in the age of electronic media. Cambridge: Polity.

— — —. 2003. Media education and the end of the critical consumer. Harvard Educational Review 73 (3):309–327.

— — —. 2008. Introducing identity. In Youth, identity, and digital media. 1–22. Cambridge, MA: The MIT Press.

Buckingham, David, and Andrew Burn. 2007. Game literacy in theory and practice. Journal of Educational Multimedia and Hypermedia 16 (3):323–349.

Buckingham, David, and Julian Sefton–Green. 1994. Cultural studies goes to school. London: Taylor and Francis.

— — —. 2004. Structure, agency, and pedagogy in children's media culture. In Pikachu's global adventure: The rise and fall of Pokemon, ed. J. Tobin. Durham, NC: Duke University Press.

Burn, Andrew. 2007. "Writing" computer games: Game literacy and new-old narratives. L1—Educational Studies in Language and Literature 7 (4):45–67.

Burn, Andrew, and Diane Carr. 2007. Defining game genres. In Computer games: Text, narrative, and play, ed. D. Carr, D. Buckingham, A. Burn, and G. Schott. Cambridge: Polity.

Burn, Andrew, and James Durran. 2006. Digital anatomies: Analysis as production in media education. In Digital generations: Children, young people, and new media, ed. D. Buckingham, and R. Willett. Mahwah, NJ: Lawrence Erlbaum.

Bury, Rhiannon. 2005. Cyberspaces of their own: Female fandoms online. New York: Peter Lang.

Carr, Diane. 2007. Games and narrative. In Computer games: Text, narrative, and play, ed. D. Carr, D. Buckingham, A. Burn, and G. Schott. Cambridge: Polity.

Carr, Diane, David Buckingham, Andrew Burn, and Gareth Schott, eds. 2007. Computer games: Text, narrative, and play. Cambridge: Polity.

Connor, Steven. 1997. Postmodernist culture. London: Blackwell.

Cope, Bill, and Mary Kalantzis. 2000. Multiliteracies: The beginnings of an idea. In multiliteracies: Literacy learning and the design of social futures, ed. B. Cope and M. Kalantzis. London: Routledge.

Cooper, Marilyn. 1998. Postmodern pedagogy in electronic conversations. In Passions, pedagogies, and 21st century technologies, ed. C. L. Selfe and G. E. Hawisher. Logan, UT: Utah State University Press.

Crawford, Garry, and Jason Rutter. 2007. Playing the game: Performance in digital game audiences. In Fandom: Identities and communities in a mediated world, ed. J. Gray, C. Sandvoss and C. L. Harrington. New York: New York University Press.

Csíkszentmihályi, Mihály. 1990. Flow: The psychology of optimal experience. New York: Harper and Row.

Davies, Julia. 2006. "Hello newbie! big welcome hugs, hope us like it here as much as i do": An exploration of teenagers' informal online learning. In Digital generations: Children, young people, and new media, ed. D. Buckingham and R. Willett. Mahwah, NJ: Lawrence Erlbaum.

Davies, Julia, and Guy Merchant. 2007. Looking from the inside out: Academic blogging as new literacy. In A new literacies sampler, ed. M. Knobel and C. Lankshear. London: Peter Lang.

de Certeau, Michel. 1984. The practice of everyday life. Trans. S. Rendall. Berkeley, CA: University of California Press.

Deery, June. 2003. TV.com: Participatory viewing on the web. The Journal of Popular Culture 37 (2):161–183.

de Pourbaix, Renata. 2001. Emergent literacy practices in an electronic community. In Situated literacies: Reading and writing in context, ed. D. Barton, M. Hamilton and R. Ivanic. London: Routledge.

Dyson, Anne Haas. 1997. Writing superheroes: Contemporary childhood, popular culture, and classroom literacy. New York: Teachers College Press.

Eldred, Janet M. 1991. Pedagogy in the computer-networked classroom. Computers and Composition 8 (2):47–62.

Everett, Anna, and S. Craig Watkins. 2008. The power of play: The portrayal and performance of race in video games. In Learning race and ethnicity, ed. A. Everett. Cambridge, MA: The MIT Press.

Fiske, John. 1996. Media matters: Everyday culture and political change. Minneapolis: University of Minnesota Press.

Frechette, Julie. 2006. Cyber-censorship or cyber-literacy? Envisioning cyber learning through media education. In Digital generations: Children, young people, and new media, ed. D. Buckingham and R. Willett. Mahwah, NJ: Lawrence Erlbaum.

Freire, Paulo. 1972. Pedagogy of the oppressed. Trans. M. B. Ramos. London: Continuum.

Garrelts, Nate, ed. 2005. Digital gameplay: Essays on the nexus of game and gamer. Jefferson, NC: McFarland.

Gee, James Paul. 1990. Social linguistics and literacies—Ideology in discourse. London: Falmer.

———. 2003. What video games have to teach us about learning literacy. New York: Palgrave MacMillan.

———. 2004. Situated language and learning: A critique of traditional schooling. London: Routledge.

———. 2005. Semiotic social spaces and affinity spaces: From the age of mythology to today's schools. In Beyond communities of practice: Language, power, and social context, ed. D. Barton and K. Tusting. Cambridge: Cambridge University Press.

———. 2007. Pleasure, learning, video games, and life: The projective stance. In A new literacies sampler, ed. M. Knobel and C. Lankshear. London: Peter Lang.

Gibbs, Raymond W., and Christin D. Izzett. 2005. Irony as persuasive communication. In Figurative language comprehension: Social and cultural influences, ed. H. L. Colston and A. N. Katz. Mahwah, NJ: Lawrence Erlbaum.

Gleick, James. 1999. Faster: The acceleration of just about everything. New York: Pantheon.

Goldhaber, Michael. 1997. The attention economy and the net. First Monday 2 (4).

Goldman, Shelley, Angela Booker, and Meghan McDermott. 2008. Mixing the digital, social, and cultural: Learning, identity, and agency in youth participation. In Youth, identity, and digital media, ed. D. Buckingham. Cambridge, MA: The MIT Press.

Gray, Jonathan. 2005. Antifandom and the moral text: Television Without Pity and textual dislike. American Behavioral Scientist 48 (7):840–858.

———. 2007. The news: You gotta love it. In Fandom: Identities and communities in a mediated world, ed. J. Gray, C. Sandvoss and C. L. Harrington. New York: New York University Press.

Gregory, Eve, and Ann Williams. 2000. City literacies: Learning to read across generations and cultures. London: Routledge.

Grossberg, Lawrence. 1992. Is there a fan in the house? The affective sensibility of fandom. In The adoring audience: Fan culture and popular media, ed. L. E. Lewis. London: Routledge.

———. 1997. Dancing in spite of myself: Essays on popular culture. Durham, NC: Duke University Press.

Hawisher, Gail E., and Cynthia L. Selfe. 2000. Global literacies and the world-wide web. London: Routledge.

Heath, Shirley Brice. 1983. Ways with words: Language, life, and work in communities and classrooms. Cambridge: Cambridge University Press.

Heffernan, Virginia. 2008. The Hitler meme. The New York Times, October 26, 2008.

Heroes evolutions. 2008. http://www.nbc.com/Heroes/evolutions/ (Accessed April 5, 2008).

Herring, Susan C. 2008. Questioning the generational divide: Technological exoticism and adult constructions of online youth identity. In Youth, identity, and digital media, ed. D. Buckingham. Cambridge, MA: The MIT Press.

Heverly, Robert A. 2008. Growing up digital: Control and the pieces of a digital life. In Digital youth, innovation, and the unexpected, ed. T. McPherson. Cambridge, MA: The MIT Press.

Hill, Charles A. 2004. The psychology of rhetorical images. In Defining visual rhetorics, ed. C. A. Hill and M. Helmers. Mahwah, NJ: Lawrence Erlbaum.

Howard, Rebecca Moore. 2008. Pluralizing plagiarism: Identities, contexts, pedagogies. Portsmouth, NH: Boynton/Cook.

Ito, Mizuko. 2006. Japanese media mixes and amateur cultural exchange. In Digital generations: Children, young people, and new media, ed. D. Buckingham and R. Willett. Mahwah, NJ: Lawrence Erlbaum.

———. 2008. Technologies of the childhood imagination: Yu-Gi-Oh!, media mixes, and everyday cultural production. In Structures of participation in digital culture, ed. J. Karaganis. New York: SSRC.

Jenkins, Henry. 1992. Textual poachers: Television fans and participatory culture. London: Routledge.

———. 2006a. Convergence culture: Where old and new media collide. New York: New York University Press.

———. 2006b. Fans, bloggers, and gamers: Exploring participatory culture. New York: New York University Press.

———. 2007. Afterword: The future of fandom. In Fandom: Identities and communities in a mediated world, ed. J. Gray, C. Sandvoss and C. L. Harrington. New York: New York University Press.

Jenkins, Henry, Katie Clinton, Ravi Purushotma, Alice J. Robison, and Margaret Weigel. 2006. Confronting the challenges of participatory culture: Media education for the 21st century. Chicago: The John D. and Catherine T. MacArthur Foundation.

Johnson-Eilola, Johndan. 2005. Datacloud: Toward a new theory of online work. Cresskill, NJ: Hampton Press.

Kammen, Michael. 1999. American culture, American tastes: Social change and the twentieth century. New York: Basic Books.

Keen, Andrew. 2008. The cult of the amateur. New York: Doubleday.

Keller, Daniel. 2007. Literacies in transition: The reading practices of entering college students. University of Louisville, Louisville, KY.

King, James R., and David G. O'Brien. 2002. Adolescents' multiliteracies and their teachers' needs to know: Toward a digital detente. In Adolescents and literacies in a digital world, ed. D. E. Alvermann. London: Peter Lang.

Knobel, Michele, and Colin Lankshear. 2004. Cut, paste, publish: The production and consumption of zines. In Adolescents and literacies in a digital world, ed. D. E. Alvermann. London: Peter Lang.

———. 2007. Online memes, affinities, and cultural production. In A new literacies sampler, ed. M. Knobel and C. Lankshear. London: Peter Lang.

———. 2008. Remix: The art and craft of endless hybridization. Journal of Adolescent & Adult Literacy 52 (1):22–33.

Kress, Gunther. 1997. Before writing: Rethinking paths to literacy. London: Routledge.

———. 2003. Literacy in the new media age. London: Routledge.

Lankes, R. David. 2008. Trusting the internet: New approaches to credibility tools. In Digital media, youth, and credibility, ed. M. J. Metzger and A. J. Flanagin. 101–121. Cambridge, MA: The MIT Press.

Lankshear, Colin, and Michele Knobel. 2003. New literacies: Changing knowledge and classroom learning. Buckingham, England: Open University Press.

———. 2007. Sampling the "new" in new literacies. In A new literacies sampler, ed. M. Knobel and C. Lankshear. London: Peter Lang.

Leavell, Jane. 2008. How to write marginally readable fan fiction 2008 [cited April 12, 2008. Available from http://littlecalamity.tripod.com/HowTo2.html

Lembo, Ron. 2000. Thinking through television. Cambridge: Cambridge University Press.

Levy, Pierre. 1997. Collective intelligence: Mankind's emerging world in cyberspace. Cambridge: Perseus.

Lewis, Cynthia. 2007. New Literacies. In The new literacies sampler, edited by M. Knobel and C. Lankshear. London: Peter Lang.

Livingstone, Sonia. 2008. Internet literacy: Young people's negotiation of new online opportunities. In Digital youth, innovation, and the unexpected, ed. T. McPherson. Cambridge, MA: The MIT Press.

Lowood, Henry. 2008. Found technology: Players as innovators in the making of machinima. In Youth, identity, and digital media. 165-196. Cambridge, MA: The MIT Press.

Mackey, Margaret. 2006. Digital games and the narrative gap. In Digital generations: Children, young people, and new media, ed. D. Buckingham and R. Willett. Mahwah, NJ: Lawrence Erlbaum.

McKibben, Bill. 1992. The age of missing information. New York: Plume.

McRobbie, Angela. 1994. Postmodernism and popular culture. London: Routledge.

Meyrowitz, Joshua. 1985. No sense of place. New York: Oxford University Press.

Mitchell, Claudia, and Jacqueline Reid-Walsh. 2002. Researching children's popular culture: The cultural spaces of childhood. London: Routledge.

Morley, David. 1992. Television, audiences, and cultural studies. London: Routledge.

Morse, Margaret. 1998. Virtualities: Television, media art, and cyberculture. Bloomington, IN: Indiana University Press.

Newkirk, Thomas. 1997. The performance of self in student writing. Portsmouth, NH: Boynton/Cook Publishers: Heinemann.

———. 2002a. Misreading masculinity: Boys, literacy, and popular culture. Portsmouth, NH: Heinemann.

———. 2002b. Sentimenal journeys: Anti-romanticism and academic identities. In

Writing with elbow, ed. P. Belanoff, M. Dickson, S. I. Fontaine and C. Moran. Logan, UT: Utah State University Press.

Paine, Charles. 1999. The resistant writer: Rhetoric as immunity, 1850 to the present. Albany, NY: State University of New York Press.

Pandey, Iswari. 2006. Imagined nations, re-imagined roles: Literacy practices of South Asian immigrants. University of Louisville, Louisville, KY.

Pflieger, Pat. 2008. Too good to be true: 150 years of Mary Sue. http://interalia.org/filestore/single_pages/MARYSUE.HTM (Accessed May 10, 2008).

Postman, Neil. 1985. Amusing ourselves to death: Public discourse in the age of show business. New York: Penguin.

Prensky, Marc. 2001. Digital natives, digital immigrants. On the Horizon 9 (5):1–6.

Rocha, Mark. 1988. The unsurprising case against television literacy. Freshman English News 17 (1):27–29.

Rutledge, Kay Ellen. 1994. Analyzing visual persuasion: The art of duck hunting. In Images in language media and mind, ed. R. Fox. Urbana, IL: NCTE.

Schloss, Joseph G. 2004. Making beats: The art of sample-based hip hop. Middletown, CT: Wesleyan.

Scodari, Christine. 2003. Resistance re-examined: Gender, fan practices, and science fiction television. Popular Communication 1 (2):111.

———. 2007. Yoko in cyberspace with Beatles fans: Gender and the re-creation of popular mythology. In Fandom: Identities and communities in a mediated world, ed. J. Gray, C. Sandvoss and C. L. Harrington. New York: New York University Press.

Scodari, Christine, and Jenna L. Felder. 2000. Creating a pocket universe: 'Shippers,' fan fiction, and the X-Files online. Communication Studies 51 (3):238.

Seiter, Ellen. 2008. Practicing at home: Computers, pianos, and cultural capital. In Digital youth, innovation, and the unexpected, ed. T. McPherson. Cambridge, MA: The MIT Press.

Seitz, David. 2007. Mocking discourse in rhetoric: Fake issue ads and critical identity. Paper Presented at the Conference on College Composition and Communication. New York. March 21-24.

Selfe, Cynthia L. 1999. Technology and literacy in the twenty-first century: The importance of paying attention, studies in writing and rhetoric. Carbondale, IL: Southern Illinois University Press.

Selfe, Cynthia L. and Gail E. Hawisher. 2004. Literate lives in the information age: Narratives of literacy from the United States. Mahwah, NJ: Lawrence Erlbaum.

Selfe, Cynthia L, and Richard J. Selfe. 1994. The politics of the interface: Power and its exercise in electronic contact zones. College Composition and Communication 45 (4):480–504.

Slatin, John M. 1990. Reading hypertext: Order and coherence in a new medium. College English 52 (8):870–883.

Smith, Matthew J. 1999. Strands in the web: Community-building strategies in online fanzines. Journal of Popular Culture 33 (2):87–99.

Smith, Michael W., and Jeffrey D. Wilhelm. 2002. "Reading don't fix no Chevys": Literacy in the lives of young men. Portsmouth, NH: Heinemann.

Steiner, Peter. 1993. On the internet, nobody knows you're a dog. The New Yorker, July 5, 1993, 61.

Stephens, Mitchell. 1998. The rise of the image, the fall of the word. Oxford: Oxford University Press.

Stern, Susannah. 2008. Producing sites, exploring identities: Youth online authorship. In Youth, identity, and digital media, ed. D. Buckingham. Cambridge, MA: The MIT Press.

Storey, John. 2003. Inventing popular culture. Oxford: Blackwell.

Street, Brian V. 1995. Social literacies: Critical approaches to literacy in development, ethnography, and education. London: Longman.

———. 2001. Introduction. In Literacy and development, edited by B. V. Street. London: Routledge.

Stroupe, Craig. 2004. The rhetoric of irritation: Inappropriateness as visual/literate practice. In Defining visual rhetorics, ed. C. A. Hill and M. Helmers. Mahwah, NJ: Lawrence Erlbaum.

Television Without Pity. 2008 [cited May 1, 2008.] Available from http://www. Televisionwithoutpity.com/index.php. (accessed January 26, 2009).

Thomas, Angela. 2007. Youth online: Identity and literacy in the digital age. New York: Peter Lang.

Thompson, Clive. 2007. Sex, drugs, and updating your blog. The New York Times, May 13, 2007.

Tobin, Joseph. 2000. "Good guys don't wear hats": Children's talk about the media. New York: Teachers College Press.

Vasudevan, Lalitha. 2008. Reimagining multimodality as lived, performed, and embodied. In International Conference on Multimodality and Learning. Institute of Education, University of London.

Weber, Sandra, and Claudia Mitchell. 2008. Imaging, keyboarding, and posting identities: Young people and new media technologies. In Youth, identity, and digital media, ed. D. Buckingham. Cambridge, MA: The MIT Press.

Welch, Kathleen. 1999. Electric rhetoric: Classical rhetoric, oralism, and a new literacy. Cambridge, MA: The MIT Press.

Welsh, James M. 2000. Action films: The serious, the ironic, the postmodern. In Film genre 2000: New Critical Essays, edited by W. W. Dixson. Albany, NY: SUNY Press.

Willett, Rebekah. 2008. Consumer citizens online: Structure, agency, and gender in online participation. In Youth, identity, and digital media. 49–69. Cambridge, MA: The MIT Press.

Williams, Bronwyn T. 2001. Reflections on a shimmering screen: Television's relationship to writing pedagogies. The Writing Instructor 2.0.

———. 2002. Tuned in: Television and the teaching of writing. Portsmouth, NH: Boynton/Cook.

———. 2003. What they see is what we get: Television and middle school writers.

The Journal of Adolescent & Adult Literacies 46 (7):546–554.

— — —. 2004. Television, authorship, and student writers. Academic Exchange Quarterly 8 (1):129–133.

— — —. 2008. "What South Park character are you?": Popular culture, literacy, and online performances of identity. Computers and Composition 25 (1):24–39.

Williams, Bronwyn T., and Amy A. Zenger. 2007. Popular culture and representations of literacy. London: Routledge.

Wright, Susan. 2008. The discourse of fan fiction. University of Louisville. Louisville, KY.

Yancey, Kathleen Blake. 2004. Made not only in words: Composition in a new key College Composition and Communication 56:297–328.

Author Index

Subject Index

Colin Lankshear, Michele Knobel, & Michael Peters
*General Editor*s

New literacies and new knowledges are being invented "in the streets" as people from all walks of life wrestle with new technologies, shifting values, changing institutions, and new structures of personality and temperament emerging in a global informational age. These new literacies and ways of knowing remain absent from classrooms. Many education administrators, teachers, teacher educators, and academics seem largely unaware of them. Others actively oppose them. Yet, they increasingly shape the engagements and worlds of young people in societies like our own. The *New Literacies and Digital Epistemologies* series will explore this terrain with a view to informing educational theory and practice in constructively critical ways.

For further information about the series and submitting manuscripts, please contact:

Michele Knobel & Colin Lankshear
Montclair State University
Dept. of Education and Human Services
3173 University Hall
Montclair, NJ 07043
michele@coatepec.net

To order other books in this series, please contact our Customer Service Department at:

(800) 770-LANG (within the U.S.)
(212) 647-7706 (outside the U.S.)
(212) 647-7707 FAX

Or browse online by series at:

www.peterlang.com